DarkLore

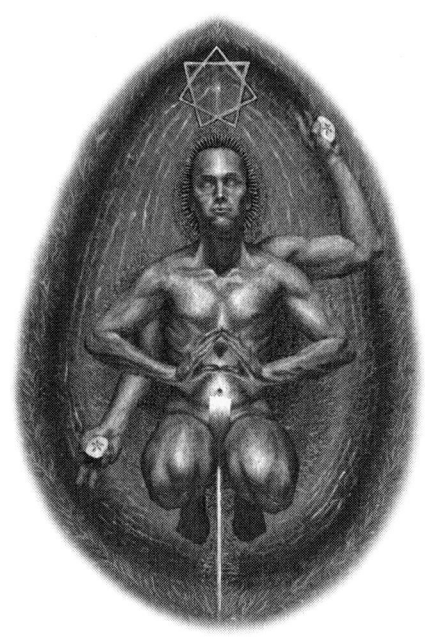

Daily Grail Publishing

Darklore Volume 9
Copyright © 2016 by Greg Taylor (Editor)

Contributing authors retain ownership and all rights to their individual pieces.

Cover art by Adam Scott Miller (www.adamscottmiller.com).
Cover design by Mark Foster of Artifice Design (www.artifice-design.co.uk).

All rights reserved. No part of this book may be reproduced, stored, or transmitted in any form without permission in writing from the publisher, except by a reviewer who may quote brief passages for review purposes.

ISBN: 978-0-9946176-0-6

Daily Grail Publishing
Brisbane, Australia
userhelp@dailygrail.com
www.dailygrail.com

Contents

Introduction	7
Secrets of the Club des Hachischins • *Mike Jay*	9
The Most Important Man on the Planet • *Adam Gorightly*	23
Opening Grimoires • *Blair MacKenzie Blake*	51
Rocks in Your Head • *Greg Taylor*	73
The History and Practice of English Magic • *John Reppion*	97
The Lycanthropes • *Robert M. Schoch*	141
Tribal Tripping in the Americas • *Paul Devereux*	163
The New Gods • *Ian 'Cat' Vincent*	201
Fossil Angels • *Alan Moore*	233
Endnotes and Sources	273

"Real magic can never be made by offering someone else's liver. You must tear out your own, and not expect to get it back."

- Peter S. Beagle

If you would like to be notified of future releases of *Darklore*, please send an email to darklore@dailygrail.com. Please be assured your contact details will not be used for any other purpose.

Editor's Introduction

Magic. A loaded term if ever there was one. For some, it is the world of Harry Potter, to others it's David Copperfield. To a science fiction aficionado it might signify the advanced technology of the future, as outlined by Arthur C. Clarke's famous third 'law'. Artists might view the act of creation as a magical work of the highest order. And for others, magic might best be defined as the exploration and control of our various states of consciousness.

Any readers who believe that only one of the above definitions (or some other) is the correct one may well find this latest release of *Darklore* a challenging read. Within the pages of Volume 9 we have Blair MacKenzie Blake surveying and reinterpreting the infamous grimoires of centuries past; Alan Moore asking if magic is in any way relevant to the modern world, advocating a scorched earth approach and new beginnings; John Reppion using a fictional work to illustrate the origins and practice of various magical traditions; and Cat Vincent looking at the origins and practice of various magical traditions and showing how many of them come from fictional works.

No *Darklore* release focuses on just one topic though. And so, along with the magical core of Volume 9, we have a number of fascinating articles on other topics of interest: Mike Jay reviews the 'hidden history' of the 19th century Club des Hachischins; Adam Gorightly looks at the amazing, controversial life of Kerry Thornley, co-creator of Discordianism and one-time JFK assassination suspect; Robert Schoch takes us beyond the Hollywood version of the werewolf to better understand the origins of this archetypal monster; Paul Devereux introduces us to the shamanic plants of the Americas; and Greg Taylor finds that the history of research into meteorites offers a valuable lesson to science on the value of listening to eye-witness reports. Enjoy!

Secrets of the Club des Hachischins

What was the 'Green Jam' that connected the ancient order of assassins with the scientists and artists of 19th century France?

by *Mike Jay*

In a pivotal scene of Alexandre Dumas' *The Count of Monte Cristo,* the young adventurer Franz d'Epinay visits the apparently deserted island of Monte Cristo on a hunting expedition. There he stumbles upon a band of smugglers who lead him, blindfolded, to a secret cave where their leader lives in Oriental splendor under the nom de guerre of 'Sinbad the Sailor'. Sinbad – whom we may already suspect is the Count of Monte Cristo in disguise – serves him a sumptuous feast, followed by a small bowl of pungent greenish paste. "What is this precious sweetmeat?", asks Franz. In reply, Sinbad tells him the story of Hassan-i-Sabbah, the Old Man of the Mountain, the leader of the Assassin sect during the Crusades, who recruited his followers by feeding them a drug that "would take them into Paradise", after which they would "obey his orders like those of God".

His guest recognizes the story. "In that case", he exclaims, "it's hashish".

It is, Sinbad confirms, "the best and finest hashish from Alexandria". "Nature wrestles with this divine substance", he continues, "because our nature is not made for joy but clings to pain. Nature must be defeated in this struggle, reality must follow dreams; and then the dream will rule, will become the master, the dream will become life and life will become a dream…Try some hashish, my friend! Try it!"

Dumas' scenario reflects his childhood immersion in *The Arabian Nights,* in which hashish-eating beggars are prone to imagine their hovels transformed into palaces; but it was also drawn from a more direct source. In February 1846, just as *The Count of Monte Cristo* reached the climax of its epic serial publication, the literary journal *Revue des Deux Mondes* published an article by Théophile Gautier entitled *Le Club des Hachischins*. Though archly fictionalised in mock-gothic style, it records a genuine literary salon. In 1845 the painter Fernand Broissard wrote mysteriously to Gautier inviting him to a private gathering in the lavishly-furnished upper rooms of the Hotel Pimodan on the Île de St. Louis, where Broissard lived. "Hashish will be taken", he announced, "under the auspices of Moreau and Aubert-Roche" (of whom more later). "Arrive between 5 and 6 at the latest. You will have your share of a light dinner and await the hallucination".

Gautier narrates from the perspective of a trembling neophyte making his way through the foggy winter night to the "half-worn, gilded name of the old hotel, the gathering-place for the initiates". He raps the carved knocker, the rusty bolt turns and an old porter points the way upstairs with a skinny finger. The first figure he encounters is a mysterious master of ceremonies, 'Doctor X', who spoons a morsel of green jam onto an elegant Japanese saucer and profers it to the novice with the blessing: "This will be deducted from your share in Paradise". The 'jam' – an Egyptian preparation known as *dawamesc,* hashish mixed with dried fruit and candied nuts to offset its bitterness – is washed down with Turkish coffee

Facade of the Hôtel Pimodan, Île de St. Louis – meeting place of the Club des Hachischins

and a feast begins: a beggar's banquet served in Venetian goblets, Flemish jugs, porcelain and flowered English crockery, no two pieces alike. The other guests are a flamboyant bohemian crew, complete with beards, medieval poignards and Oriental daggers. Gautier notices the drug's derangement of his senses beginning with taste: "the water I drank seemed the most exquisite wine; the meat, once in my mouth, became strawberries, the strawberries meat". His companions become distorted creatures with pupils "big as a screech owl's" and proboscis-like noses. Once dinner is over, the cry goes up, "To the salon!".

The salon is – as the upstairs suite of the Hotel Pimodan remains today – "an enormous room of carved and gilded panelling, a painted ceiling whose friezes depicted satyrs chasing nymphs through the grasses…here one inhaled the luxurious airs of times gone by". Slowly it fills with fantastical figures "such are found only in the etchings of Callot or the aquatints of Goya", a "bizarre throng" that plunges Gautier into a series of visions, hilarious and grotesque, interrupted by a piano recital that sends him into raptures, at first ecstatically soulful and then nightmarish, with demonic forms taunting him as he tries to escape but finds his movement slowed to a snail's pace by an unseen force. The narrative reaches a climax with gigantic courtyards, classical monsters and the Funeral of Time before the clock indicates eleven, normal time is reborn and normal consciousness resumed, and the stunned initiate finds his carriage waiting for him in the street below.

Origins of the Assassins

On publication of Gautier's reportage, the Club des Hachischins became a public sensation: the fantastic embodiment of a myth that had enthralled the European public. Since the first appearance of the Abbé Barrueil's *Memoirs of Jacobinism* in 1797, through half a century of popular insurrections and royal restorations, many had believed that secret societies such as the Freemasons and Illuminati were fomenting the nationalist movements that would erupt into mass revolt in 1848. The early Freemasons had looked to history for precedents to their transnational and elite enterprise, and some had retrospectively incorporated the Crusader orders of the Templars and the Teutonic Knights into their lineage. But where had the Templars' ritual secrecy and hierarchical structure come from? According to many, the Assassins were the original secret society, Hassan-i-Sabbah's system of initiation was the fount of all conspiracy – and the source of his mysterious and evil influence was hashish.

This was a connection that had received confirmation in 1809 from the great Orientalist Silvestre de Sacy, who had traced the lineage of the legendary Assassins and shown that their name derived from their alleged use of the drug for brainwashing and murder. Since that point, hashish had been regularly pressed into service to explain the ruthless fanaticism of revolutionaries through the ages. The most recent scholarly intervention was the *History of the Assassins* published in 1835 by Chevalier Joseph von Hammer-Purgstall, a respected Orientalist but also a reactionary monarchist who claimed that the sect of the Assassins was the ultimate source of all revolution, libertinism and atheism: an "empire of conspirators" with a "doctrine of irreligion and immorality" and, in hashish, a blasphemous substance that makes its subject "able to undertake anything or everything".

The Club des Hachischins was an outrageous satire on such beliefs, both appropriating and subverting them. "Hashish is replacing champagne", Gautier claimed provocatively; "we believe we have conquered Algeria, but Algeria has conquered us". Yet in the manner of a genuine secret society it succeeded in launching an enduring myth while leaving many of its mundane historical details in doubt. According to some contemporary accounts, it was elaborately styled as an Order of Assassins, with novitiates, initiates and a Sheikh or Prince who directed the ceremonies and rituals. In some versions it met once a month; others, perhaps more credible, suggest that there were only a handful of meetings and its active life was over by 1849; at least, the Hotel Pimodan seems to have been used only for a short period, the salons subsequently convening in smaller private rooms. The scenario of ritual gatherings and legions of initiates may perhaps be understood as part of the set-dressing, the ceremonial ambience it projected as a parody of the profane mysteries of the Assassin Order.

Gautier's reportage, though set within an exoticised and fantastical frame, announces the arrival of a recognizably modern drug subculture, with the enduring motifs of long hair, outlandish dress, radical politics, all-night partying, sexual libertinism, heavy drinking and, of course, a voracious curiosity about abnormal states of consciousness. It was also the opening salvo of a substantial body of 'drug literature' exploring the properties of hashish. In addition to Gautier's anticipation of gonzo journalism and Dumas' incorporation of the drug's reality-distorting effects into the most popular adventure of its day, Gustave Flaubert was obtaining his own supply of hashish from his chemist and embarking on a projected novel entitled *La Spirale,* whose protagonist was to be a hashish-taking painter on a journey to sublime madness. In 1851 Gerard de Nerval would incorporate a hallucinatory hashish tale into his *Voyage en Orient,* and Charles Baudelaire would publish his essay *Du Vin et du Haschisch,* which would in 1860 be revised and incorporated into *Les Paradises Artificiels.* The familiar roll-call of the Club's members includes further luminaries such as Honoré de Balzac, Victor Hugo and Eugène Delacroix, though all such claims dissolve into rumour, and are presumably subject to inflation in the same manner as the club's secret structures. It seems unlikely that many of the alleged members would have wished to undergo the experience very often: swallowing several grams of bittersweet paste and submitting to a prolonged derangement of the senses is a demanding ordeal, and some were doubtless glad to see their names added to the list of rumoured initiates without having to undergo it.

The 'Sheikh of the Assassins'

The salon is remembered for its artistic luminaries, but Fernand Broissard's letter to Gautier reminds us that the convenors of this famous literary scene were primarily scientists. The prime mover was a psychiatrist named Jacques-Joseph Moreau de Tours, who seems the likely candidate for master of ceremonies as self-styled Sheikh of the Order: there is a surviving sketch by Gautier of him playing the piano in Turkish ceremonial dress. Moreau's earliest partner in the project seems to have been his fellow doctor and hashish enthusiast Louis Aubert-Roche, whom he had met in Egypt and who in 1840 had published a paper on the use of the drug as a possible remedy for plague and typhoid.

Moreau's own engagement with hashish had begun in 1837 at the convergence of two sources: his career in psychiatry and an extended residence in Egypt. After completing his medical degree in 1826 he had studied at the Charenton Hospital under Jean-Etienne Dominique Esquirol, a central figure in the reform of hospitals and the emergence of a clinical psychiatry. Esquirol proposed the diagnosis of 'monomania' for cases where a patient became focused on a particular obsession, and it was on this disorder that the young Moreau wrote his thesis. This new clinical language aimed to release mental illness from moral and religious judgement. In the predominantly Catholic world of

Jacques-Joseph Moreau de Tours

French medicine, traditional presumptions about madness drew heavily on Christian doctrine: reason, or sanity, were viewed as God-given, and insanity as a recapitulation of the Fall and the descent into original sin. But Moreau believed that monomania, like many other mental disorders, was present to some degree in most sane people, not least psychiatrists; the insane were not lost souls, but merely those in whom these manias were magnified to an uncontrollable and debilitating degree. Reason and madness were not black and white, but a grey scale with an infinite number of gradations between them.

One of Esquirol's treatments for monomania was the 'rest cure', sending patients off to an unfamiliar place where their compulsive routines and fixations could be broken and they could have a chance to rebuild their lives. In cases involving wealthy patients, this often took the form of an extended tour of foreign parts, accompanied by one of his assistants. Thus it was that Moreau was assigned to accompany patients first to Switzerland and Italy, and then, in 1836, on a three-year trip to Egypt.

Exploring Cairo and sailing up the Nile, Moreau was struck by the uncanny mental world of the Arab people he encountered, who communed with supernatural *djinn* on a daily basis and took their nightly dreams to be omens or glimpses of the future. At the same time he noted the relative paucity of mental illness in their society compared to that of Europe. He decided to examine one of many conspicuous cultural differences: the absence of alcohol, and the prevalence of hashish. He began investigating the drug: reading de Sacy and all the available literature; studying samples of the local preparation, *dawamesc*; interviewing hashish users and adopting local dress and customs to infiltrate himself into the world of the Cairo *hashishin*. It was here that he made contact with Louis Aubert-Roche, an epidemiologist who had noticed that hashish-using Egyptians appeared less susceptible to certain diseases and was investigating it as a possible remedy for typhus. He experimented with various doses of *dawamesc* and on his return he brought some back to Paris where, under the supervision of two companions, he swallowed a large spoonful "at least the size of a walnut, about 30g" and recorded the results.

Moreau's primary observation was that all the sinister legends and stereotypes that had accreted around hashish up to this point had lacked a crucial piece of evidence: self-experiment. In his treatise of 1845, *Du Hachisch et l'Alienation Mentale* (*Hashish and Mental Illness*), he pronounced that "at the outset I must make this point, the verity of which is unquestionable: personal experience is the criterion of truth here". To observe a sprawled and supine hashish-eater and to assume that the drug simply produces sedation is to be misled by superficial symptoms. If people intoxicated by hashish are disconnected from the outside world, it is not because less is going on inside their heads than usual but far more, rendering them too introspectively engaged to move or speak. It is not normal practice for psychiatrists to subject themselves to foreign poisons, but, Moreau maintained, "there is essentially only one valid approach to the study…observation, in such cases, when not focused on the observer himself, touches only on appearances and can lead to grossly fallacious conclusions".

Moreau's self-experiment with hashish, of which he offered the fullest account thus far published by a European, dramatically illustrates the potency of the traditional dose and the limitations of previous suppositions about brainwashed assassins. He swallows the strange-tasting paste with difficulty, and notices its effects while eating oysters, suddenly finding the procedure irresistibly hilarious. Recovering from fits of laughter, he realises his companions are convinced there is a lion's head on the plate in front of them. When he finds himself grabbing a spoon and preparing to duel with a bowl of candied fruit, he decides it is time to leave the table, and is seized with an urge to hear music. He sits at the piano and prepares to play an air from the comic opera Black Domino, but is interrupted after a few bars by a vision of his brother standing on top of the piano, brandishing a forked, flashing and multi-coloured tail. The sense descends on him that this is some kind of theatrical performance, and he begins imitating the voices of various actors, then picking up a stove and dancing the polka with it. Now he is back at dinner,

DU HACHISCH

ET DE

L'ALIÉNATION MENTALE

ÉTUDES PSYCHOLOGIQUES

PAR

J. MOREAU
(DE TOURS),

Médecin de l'hospice de Bicêtre, Membre de la Société
orientale de Paris.

PARIS.
LIBRAIRIE DE FORTIN, MASSON ET Cie,
PLACE DE L'ÉCOLE-DE-MÉDECINE, 1,
Même maison, chez Léopold Michelsen, à Leipzig.

1845.

but this time five years in the past, with an old friend, 'General H.', serving a fish surrounded with flowers. Suddenly his spirits soar to intense delight, and he sees his young son sailing around in the sky with pink-trimmed white wings. "Surely there was never a nicer intoxication", he purrs, "an ecstasy that only the heart of a parent can understand". However, he has been crying and singing and has, in real life, woken his child; this brings him immediately back to his senses, and he hugs the infant "as if I were in my natural state". He goes out to a cafe and orders an ice, but finds the people out in the street stupid-looking and disturbing, and returns home, still rapt in "a thousand fantastic ideas".

For Moreau this was more than a bizarre flight of fancy: he saw in it a radical possibility for the advancement of psychiatry. Its greatest benefit, he suggested, would not be for patients but for doctors, allowing them direct access to the abnormal mental states they spend their professional lives attempting to treat. "We see only the surfaces of things", he argued; "can we be certain we are in a condition to understand these sick people when they tell us of their observations?...To understand an ordinary depression, it is necessary to have experienced one; to comprehend the ravings of a madman, it is necessary to have raved oneself, but without having lost the awareness of one's madness".

But Moreau was interested in the effects of hashish not only on the sick and those who treated them, but on the exceptional: artists, poets, men of genius. For this group, the exotic drug was known thus far in Paris by reputation alone, much as it was to Franz in *The Count of Monte Cristo*. In 1843 Gautier had written, as an aside in a theatre review in *La Presse,* that "hashish has been familiar to us only by name. Some Oriental friends had promised several times to let us taste it, but whether for difficulties in procuring the precious stuff or from some other reason, the plan has not yet been realised". Thus Moreau, together with Aubert-Roche, undertook to provide a forum for experiment.

Behind the mystique and ceremonial trappings of the Club des Hashischins, then, we can discern the hand of Moreau and his scientific method. If he wished to study how the drug affected literary and artistic minds, he needed an appropriate setting. A clinical or laboratory ambience would be likely to make subjects self-conscious and inhibited, or provoke anxiety about their physical or mental symptoms and turn the experience from dream to nightmare. As 'Sheikh of the Assassins' in his Turkish robes, Moreau was able to dispense the drug at the correct dose and supervise proceedings without explicitly taking on the physician's role, discreetly encouraging his subjects to embrace the experience in all its exuberant strangeness. The Club would live in history through the literary effusions of its members; but this literature was ultimately, for its instigator, a by-product of a primarily scientific intent: to guide the most gifted and audacious minds of Paris along the spectrum between sanity and madness, to witness them exploring their temporary derangement and, with due respect to his Hippocratic oath, to preside over their safe return to reason.

Mike Jay is the author of *Emperors of Dreams: Drugs in the Nineteenth Century*. His most recent book, *The Influencing Machine*, is now available in the US under the title *A Visionary Madness*.

THE MOST IMPORTANT MAN ON THE PLANET

Discordianism, Paganism, and JFK Conspiracy Theories:
The troubled yet fascinating life of Kerry Thornley

by *Adam Gorightly*

Kerry Thornley was born on April 17th, 1938 in Whittier, California, the very same conservative bastion of Orange County blandness that bestowed upon us the honorable Richard M. Nixon, who some consider the physical embodiment of the Curse of Greyface.[1]

In 1958 – as an apparent counterbalance to Nixon's ascension into the office of Vice President – Thornley and his teenaged pal Greg Hill (while sipping coffee in a Whittier bowling alley) inadvertently invoked Eris, the Greek goddess of chaos and discord. In the aftermath of their caffeine-induced vision, Hill and Thornley founded the so-called spoof religion Discordianism, as well as its disorganizational branch, The Discordian Society.

Initially an in-joke between Hill and Thornley, by the late 1960s the Discordian Society began to attract a loose knit group of writers, artists and free spirits who often adopted comical Pope names. Thornley embraced the Discordian persona of Lord Omar Khayyam Ravenhurst while Greg Hill became known as Malaclypse the Younger.

Other Discordian Popes included Playboy editors Robert Anton Wilson (Mordecai the Foul) and Robert Shea (Josh the Dill), who in tandem co-authored the counterculture classic, *The Illuminatus Trilogy*, with the first book in the series dedicated to none other than Hill and Thornley. Throughout *Illuminatus* are numerous references to Discordian memes such as The Law of Fives, The Sacred Chao, and the John Dillinger Died For You Society.

Many Discordian activities concerned pranks designed to not only poke fun at organized religion and uptight people, but also as a means of illumination through the use of surreal and irreverent humor. In recent years, the Discordian Society has grown into a worldwide underground phenomenon, although the only thing that its Popes and Momes can generally agree upon is that tried and true Discordian maxim: "We Discordians must stick apart!" For further information/confusion refer to *Principia Discordia or How I Found Goddess And What I Did To Her When I Found Her*.

During Thornley's junior year of high school in the spring of 1956, he enlisted in the Marine Corps Reserves, attending boot camp that summer, then returned to high school in the fall of 1957 for his senior year. The following year he attended the University of Southern California as a journalism major, but quickly lost interest in pursuing the academic life.

A budding writer intent on traveling the world, Thornley figured the most immediate way to do so was by fulfilling his two-year active duty in the Marines. Kerry enlisted in the spring of 1959, and his first stop was El Toro Marine Base, located near Irvine, California. It was here that his life was forever altered when his path crossed that of Lee Harvey Oswald.

The Prankster and the Assassin

"At the moment I have every reason to believe I may get 20 years in a Louisiana prison for: 1) having gone to USC at the same time as Gordon Novel did; 2) having written a novel based on Oswald which re-inforced his apparent Marxist cover; 3) having been from that point out the victim of either the most fantastic chain of incriminating coincidences or the most satanically evil plot in history...

I was never very interested in the Kennedy assassination until lately. But goddamn and sweet Jesus do I want to see those bastards brought to justice now! Not out of revenge, but just simple self-preservation.

As I've been telling people, I'm up to my ass in a cheap spy novel. And right now that means I am in over my head."

– Letter from Kerry Thornley to Greg Hill, dated February 17th, 1968

Kerry Thornley and Lee Harvey Oswald were stationed at El Toro over a three month period, and much of their interactions occurred either during off duty hours at the rec hall, or in between drills and field exercises when the two engaged in spirited discussions about Marxism, Atheism, George Orwell's *1984* and other subjects that were a bit on the taboo side for most of the other God-fearing jarheads in their squadron.

At El Toro, Oswald exuded an aura of rebellion and discontent, suffering the stigma of demotion. Formerly a radar operator with a security clearance, he'd now been relegated to janitorial duties, having lost his clearance due to repeated run-ins with the brass while serving at Atsugi Air Base in Japan. Thornley later described Oswald as "the outfit eight ball," earning this dubious distinction by subscribing to *Pravda*, cracking jokes with an exaggerated Russian accent and referring to his fellow Marines as "comrades." It was common knowledge that Oswald was studying Russian, and because of this, had acquired the nickname "Oswaldskovitch."

One curious thing about Oswald was that he was one of the few Marines to return stateside with the rank of private, which was unusual given the fact that most enlisted men, with as much service time, had been promoted to at least the rank of corporal. Apparently, Oswald's lowly status was due to an incident when he got drunk one night and poured a beer over a Staff Officer's head, permanently damaging any promotion potential.

In June 1959, Thornley was transferred to Atsugi Air Base in Japan where Oswald had previously been stationed. During this period, Atsugi was among the CIA's most critical installations from which the U-2 spy plane flights originated, and it was there that Thornley performed the same job as had Oswald, that of radar technician. According to researchers A.J. Weberman and Michael Canfield, Atsugi was devoted to grooming intelligence agents, one of whom they contended was Oswald, and it was at Atsugi that Oswald was taught Russian language as part of his intelligence training.[2]

Marine Kerry Thornley

During Oswald's stint at Atsugi, he spent many off-duty hours fraternizing with bar girls at a Tokyo nightclub, The Queen Bee, and there became acquainted with a mysterious Eurasian woman who helped him with his Russian-language studies, as well as sharing her many charms. It was later conjectured that Oswald's Queen Bee girlfriend was actually a Soviet spy who had ensnared the naive lad into a web of international intrigue, later setting the stage for his defection.[3] This theory of Oswald-as-Spy was seconded by another former Marine, David Bucknell. According to Bucknell, the Queen Bee bargirls were trying to pump Oswald for information, and when he reported this to the brass, he was encouraged to bed down the girls and feed them disinformation. This may explain a citation discovered in Oswald's Marine medical records – as published in the Warren

Report – that indicated he was treated for gonorrhea contracted "in line of duty, not due to own misconduct."

Thornley later speculated that Oswald may have been working for military intelligence to identify potential security risks at El Toro, such as those sympathetic to Marxism and other radical politics, using his supposed interest in Communism as a cover to gain the trust of those individuals targeted – one of whom, Kerry speculated, might have been himself. If this was true, that might explain why Oswald cultivated a relationship with Kerry, who was probably viewed by his superiors as somewhat of a free-thinking loose-cannon type.

On his trip to Japan in June 1959 aboard the U.S.S. Breckenridge (enroute to Atsugi), Thornley started work on *The Idle Warriors,* a novel about a young Marine's disillusionment during the Cold War era. The protagonist of this work-in-progress, Johnny Shellburn, was a composite character based on Thornley and other Marines he had known during this period, one of whom was Oswald.

In October 1959, Thornley was mind-blown when he read in the *Stars and Stripes* that Oswald had defected to the Soviet Union, a revelation that caused an immediate shift in focus to *The Idle Warriors,* and from that point forward the lead character, Johnny Shellburn, became based primarily on Oswald. The fact that Thornley was writing a novel based on Oswald (three years before the JFK assassination!) would raise the curious eyebrows of many JFK assassination researchers, who later came to suspect that Thornley's association with Oswald was much more than mere coincidence.

WEIRD SCENES IN NEW ORLEANS

Thornley was discharged from the Marines in October 1960, and in February 1961 he and Greg Hill moved to the New Orleans French Quarter. Besides partying and chasing skirts, Kerry's main motivation for making the New Orleans move was to gather material for future books he aspired to write, and to associate with the denizens of the French Quarter. Shortly after arriving, Kerry made the acquaintance of a couple of colorful characters – who were shady as all get out – named Slim Brooks and Gary Kirstein (aka "Brother-in-law".) Brooks and Kirstein were apparently involved in the New Orleans underworld and also claimed connections within the intelligence community embedded in New Orleans.

In the fall of 1962, Brooks and Kirstein engaged Kerry in a theoretical discussion about how to kill a President – and, in particular, JFK. Kerry suggested the use of a poison dart to blow the President's stomach apart, as well as another scenario involving a remote control airplane carrying a bomb. After Kerry finished with his ideas, Kirstein added, "And next we'll get Martin Luther King." At the time, these conversations on how to kill a President seemed nothing more to Kerry than a morbid intellectual exercise. Later, these conversations would come back to haunt him.

On the fateful day of November 22, 1963, Thornley was waiting tables at Arnaud's Restaurant in the French Quarter when news broke of JFK's assassination. As there were no TVs or radios in the restaurant, Kerry and the rest of the staff got their news from a waiter who'd been outside taking a break. According to the waiter, news outlets were reporting that the Dallas police had picked up a suspect identified as a former Marine. Although the waiter couldn't remember the suspect's name, it was reported that he'd defected to Russia for a couple of years before returning to the U.S. When Kerry correctly guessed the suspect's name as 'Lee Oswald' all hell broke loose among the serving staff. Someone even went so far as to ask Kerry if he'd had a hand in the assassination. "One cretinous individual," Kerry remembered, "even began gossiping, behind my back, that I was in fact Lee Harvey Oswald's brother."

Unlike many of his friends and fellow workers, Thornley was not the least bit heart-broken over Kennedy's death. In fact, Kerry had previously held JFK in contempt for his support of the NATO-

The Most Important Man on the Planet

Nightclub owner Jack Ruby shooting Lee Harvey Oswald two days after the JFK assassination

sanctioned conflict in Katanga (Congo Republic) that had led to the massacre of many innocent victims. On the basis of this, Kerry felt that JFK deserved to be shot – and was not bashful in sharing his opinions at the French Quarter bars and coffee houses he frequented. Kerry – it should be noted – reveled in playing the role of agitator and yanking people's chains, which is not to suggest that he wasn't sincere in his disdain for the slain President. Granted, Kerry's comments about shooting JFK were mere hyperbole delivered by a 23-year-old wet-behind-the-ears rabble rouser.

After finishing work at Arnaud's that afternoon, Kerry and his pal Carlos Castillo wound up at the Bourbon House restaurant where they made tongue-in-cheek toasts to the Marine Corps drill instructor who had taught Oswald to fire his rifle. Although in bad taste, this was an example of Kerry's irreverent sense of humor.

Not long after the assassination, Kerry was questioned by both the FBI and the Secret Service, who were most likely tipped off by someone at Arnaud's that had overheard Kerry drop Oswald's name – not to mention anyone who had witnessed the antics of he and his pal Carlos Castillo at the Bourbon House. Although the Feds seemed satisfied that he was innocent of any nefarious associations with Oswald, Kerry grew to suspect that – in the days following the assassination – he was being tailed around the French Quarter by men in dark suits.

Kerry later regretted his behavior following JFK's assassination, which alienated him from many of his French Quarter friends who took offence at his provocative antics. This, along with a messy split up with his then girlfriend, Jeanne Hack, precipitated his move not long afterwards to Arlington, Virginia. The Arlington move was also motivated by its close proximity to Washington, D.C and a possible appearance before the Warren Commission which had convened in late November. To this end, Kerry figured that if he could wangle an appearance before the commission it might provide good pre-publicity for his novel-in-the-works, *The Idle Warriors*. This gambit eventually paid off for Kerry when he was called in to testify before the Commission in the spring of 1964.

In 1965, Thornley returned to Southern California where he was editing a libertarian newsletter called *The Innovator*. In April of that year, New Classics Books released Thornley's first published work, *Oswald*, which presented how an individual involved in radical politics could evolve into a political assassin, a theory that deeply offended many Warren Report critics, one of whom was David Lifton. As it so happened, Lifton – who would go on to author the best-selling *Best Evidence: Disguise and Deception in the Assassination of John F. Kennedy* – lived nearby and arranged a meeting at Kerry's apartment in Culver City. For this meeting, Lifton brought along the entire twenty-six volumes of the Warren Report, which he proceeded to spread out over Kerry's floor like mixed up puzzle pieces, using them to present his case for Oswald's innocence.

Over the course of the evening, Lifton presented enough evidence to cause Kerry to do a 180-degree turn, coming to believe that Oswald was innocent and that there'd been a conspiracy behind the assassination. Afterwards, Kerry became a vocal Warren Commission critic and began speaking out against the Warren Report. These public denunciations appeared in a *Fact* magazine interview in December, and in an article Kerry wrote for *The Innovator* entitled "Oswald Revisited." In addition, Kerry gave lectures at the Henry George Schools in San Diego and Los Angeles, as well as an interview on public radio in Los Angeles.

The Summer of Love and Garrison

In late 1966, *The Innovator* published an article entitled "Postman Against the State" dealing with non-governmental postal systems throughout history that had functioned more effectively than government-operated systems. As the "Playboy Forum" was then

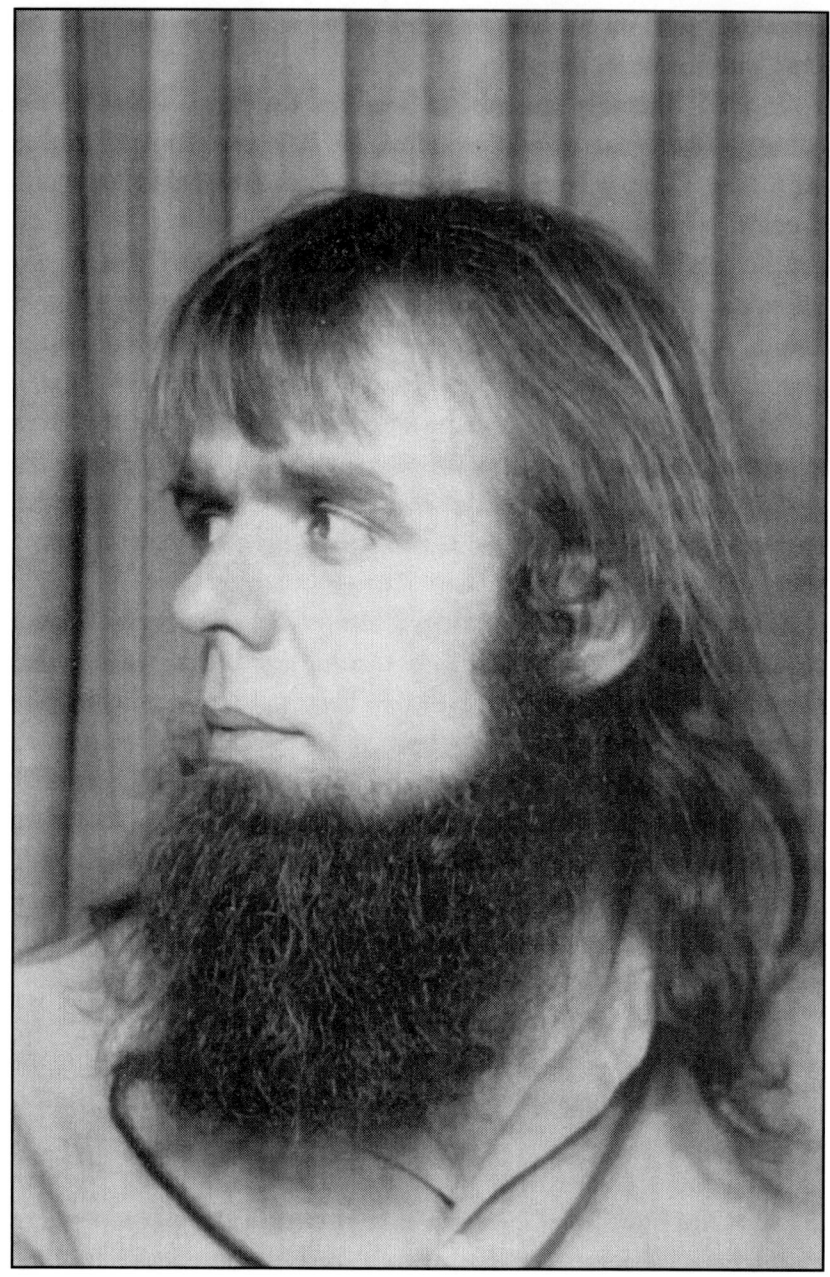

'Summer of Love'-era Kerry Thornley

receiving complaints from readers about snooping on the part of the U.S. Postal Service, Kerry sent a copy of the "Postman Against the State" issue to *Playboy*. Robert Anton Wilson – an associate editor at *Playboy* – received this issue and in turn responded to Kerry, which initiated a longstanding correspondence. As Wilson later described in *Cosmic Trigger*:

> We began writing long letters to each other…astonished at how totally our political philosophies agreed – we were both opposed to every form of violence or coercion against individuals, whether practiced by governments or by people who claimed to be revolutionaries. We were equally disenchanted with the organized Right and the organized Left while still remaining Utopians, without a visible Utopia to believe in.

As the 1960s progressed, Thornley immersed himself in the burgeoning counterculture, along the way experimenting with psychedelics, helping to organize the Griffith Park Human Be-Ins and formulating his own philosophy called Zenarchy.

As part of Kerry's interest in sexual liberation, he joined "a sexually swinging psychedelic tribe" into mate-swapping known as Kerista. Kerry – calling himself "Young Omar" – wrote several articles for the *Kerista Swinger,* the official newsletter of the group, of which the following is an excerpt:

> Kerista is a religion and the mood of Kerista is one of holiness. Do not, however, look for a profusion of rituals, dogmas, doctrines and scriptures. Kerista is too sacred for that. It is more akin to the religions of the East and, also, the so-called pagan religions of the pre-Christian West. Its fount of being is the religious experience and that action or word or thought which is not infused with ecstasy is not Kerista. And Kerista, like those religions of olden times, is life-affirming.

In *Drawing Down The Moon,* Margot Adler observed that Thornley's writings on Kerista signaled the true beginnings of the Neo-Pagan movement in contemporary culture, which since the mid-60s has expressed itself in myriad forms such as free love communes, Wicca practitioners, the back-to-nature movement, psychedelic experimenters and other groups dedicated to spiritual discovery. Adler cited Thornley as the first person to actually use the word *Pagan* to describe past and present nature religions.

At the same time that Thornley was embracing the 60s counterculture, New Orleans District Attorney Jim Garrison launched his now-famous investigation, which contended that a cabal of rogue intelligence agents had masterminded the JFK assassination, and that its base of operations was the Guy Banister Detective Agency in New Orleans. However, before Garrison was able to bring his case to trial, both Banister and David Ferrie – another suspect in the case – mysteriously died. At that point the key suspect in the case became Clay Shaw, director of the New Orleans Trade Mart and a former CIA asset.

In the spring of 1963, Lee Harvey Oswald had moved from Texas to New Orleans, and during this period became involved with different communist organizations, including the New Orleans branch of the Fair Play for Cuba Committee. Garrison claimed that Oswald had been directed in these activities by the Banister operation, working as an infiltrator to gather information on subversive organizations in New Orleans. Garrison further theorized that Banister and his crew set up Oswald as a fall guy by creating the cover story that he was a radicalized communist with an itchy trigger finger.

On February 21st, 1968, Garrison issued a press release stating that Kerry Thornley was a CIA agent who had participated in this assassination conspiracy with the likes of Banister, Ferrie and Shaw. Also listed among Garrison's suspects was Gordon Novel, who had attended USC with Kerry a decade earlier.

The principal witness against Thornley was a self-proclaimed "witch" and French Quarter scene maker named Barbara Reid, who claimed she had seen Oswald and Thornley together at the Bourbon House restaurant in September 1963. Thornley denied this allegation, insisting the last time he'd been in contact with Oswald was when the two served together in the Marines. Garrison charged Thornley with perjury, claiming he'd lied about this purported meeting with Oswald in New Orleans. Oddly enough, Barbara Reid was a friend of Thornley's, and also a member of the New Orleans branch of the Discordian Society. In fact, Reid even claimed, at one point, to be the incarnation of Eris.

> **Writer Blames 'Witch' in Probe**
>
> A free lance magazine writer from Tampa who served in the Marine Corps with Lee Harvey Oswald believes a New Orleans woman who practices witchcraft caused him to be subpoenaed by District Attorney James Garrison.
> "It came from Barbara Reed who believes she saw me with Oswald in the Bourbon House in New Orleans," Kerry W. Thornley said following Garrison's action.

Garrison further asserted that Thornley was part of the crew enlisted to set up Oswald prior to the assassination, and that his Warren Commission testimony – as well as his book, *Oswald* – were concocted to portray Oswald as a commie-influenced lone nutter. Garrison also suspected that Thornley had been intimate with Marina Oswald – all part of Thornley's supposed role as one of the notorious Oswald doubles running around New Orleans and Dallas (prior to the assassination) as part of a plot to paint Oswald commie red. It didn't help things that during his residence in New Orleans, Thornley had brief encounters with a number of Garrison's alleged conspirators, including Ferrie, Banister and Shaw. Thornley described these as brief and uneventful meetings, although Garrison suspected something far more sinister.

Oswald, as the theory goes, was set up as an assassination fall guy by Banister's operation. Kerry later suspected that he, as well, may have been set up in a similar manner – as a secondary patsy – had the Oswald set up gone awry. So, taking this one step further, it could be conjectured that Kerry's apparent chance meetings with the likes of Shaw, Banister and Ferrie were actually orchestrated to be later used against him. To Kerry, this seemed the only way to reconcile all the alarming coincidences that placed him in the company of Garrison's rogue gallery of suspects, as well as in proximity to Oswald's movements (or the movements of Oswald doubles) during August and September of 1963.

Operation Mindfuck and the Bavarian Illuminati

Among Jim Garrison's more colorful unofficial investigators (known as "The Dealey Plaza Irregulars") was one Allan Chapman, who subscribed to the theory that JFK's assassination had been orchestrated by the Bavarian Illuminati, that infamous secret society much ballyhooed in the annals of conspiracy lore. Chapman also claimed that the major television networks were controlled by the Illuminati.

After catching wind of Chapman's goofy Illuminati theory, Thornley – with the support of some of his fellow Discordian Society pranksters – initiated what became known as Operation Mindfuck (OM), a campaign designed to screw with Garrison's head by sending out spurious announcements suggesting that he (Kerry) was indeed an agent of the Ancient Illuminated Seers of Bavaria (AISB).

Under the auspices of "The Bavarian Illuminati", Kerry invented a Do-It-Yourself Conspiracy Kit, which included stationery containing dubious letterheads. Among the culprits who helped perpetrate OM was none other than Robert Anton Wilson. As Kerry later noted:

> Wilson and I founded the Anarchist Bavarian Illuminati to give Jim Garrison a hard time, one of whose supporters believed that the Illuminati owned all the major TV networks, the Conspiring Bavarian Seers (CBS), the Ancient Bavarian Conspiracy (ABC) and the Nefarious Bavarian Conspirators (NBC).[4]

ADVERTISEMENT

'Bavarian Illuminati' advertisement

These OM communiqués led Garrison to suspect that the Discordian Society had operated as a CIA front organization involved in the JFK assassination. As Wilson observed in *Cosmic Trigger*:

> Try to picture a jury keeping a straight face when examining a conspiracy that worshipped the Goddess of Confusion, honored Emperor Norton as a saint, had a Holy Book called "How I Found Goddess and What I Did to Her After I Found Her," and featured personnel who called themselves Malaclypse the Younger, Ho Chi Zen, Mordecai the Foul, Lady L, F.A.B., Fang the Unwashed, Harold Lord Randomfactor, Onrak the Backwards, et al…

Amazingly, the first edition of *The Principia Discordia* – of which only five copies were produced – is said to have been printed using a mimeograph machine in, of all people, Jim Garrison's office…two years before the Kennedy assassination took place! The clandestine

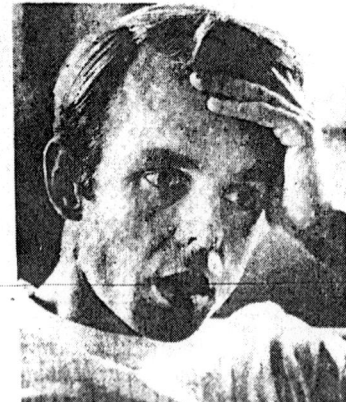

after-hours copying operation was allegedly perpetrated by a typist in Garrison's office named Lane Caplinger, who was friends with Thornley and Hill.

While it's a given that Thornley and Hill were both in possession of this first edition of *The Principia Discordia,* what is not commonly known is that Slim Brooks – another member of the New Orleans Discordian Society – also received a copy of this rare first edition. It can also be assumed that other recipients of *The Principia Discordia* first edition included Barbara Reid and Roger Lovin, both New Orleans Discordian Society members. Lovin – known in the Discordian Society as "Fang the Unwashed" – was identified by Garrison witness Bernard Goldsmith as being connected to Oswald in New Orleans.

Thornley later wrote that "Slim Brooks was an active participant in exchanging Discordian declarations and documents and Gary Kirstein would therefore have known about this network and may have used it as cover at some point or other. In 1968 Roger Lovin told me that Jim Garrison was investigating the possibility that the Discordian Society was some kind of CIA front – which, at that time, I thought was very funny and completely absurd of Garrison. Roger Lovin was another active Discordian in New Orleans…Roger was also a close friend of Slim Brooks and in 1968 when he fell under suspicion with Garrison's office much as I did…I believe it is very possible that Roger was unwittingly or somehow semi-wittingly involved in the assassination."

Garrison Throws in the Towel

In early 1970, Jim Garrison undertook a legal maneuver to try Kerry Thornley's case. At the time, this came as a surprise to Kerry who had assumed that the perjury charges against him had been dropped following Clay Shaw's acquittal in 1969.

Garrison came after me one last time in 1970 just for harassment purposes because I had put an advertisement in a Libertarian magazine that said, 'Good looking, young District Attorney will do anything for, or to, anyone for a chance to jack off to the John Kennedy autopsy photos.' (Laughs) This was just to prove I wasn't afraid of him…It was just my way of saying, 'Look, you fucker, you're not going to push me around…'[5]

Anyhow, the lawyer I wound up with in this anti-climactic episode, who happened also to be Garrison's brother-in-law, told me in no uncertain terms to stop writing things about Jim. So I stopped, and never heard from the lawyer again, much less from Garrison…[6]

The Ghosts of New Orleans

In the early 70s, new JFK assassination revelations appeared in the book *Coup d'Etat in America,* an acronym for the CIA's alleged complicity in the assassination. The authors, A.J. Weberman and Michael Canfield, presented the theory that the three mystery tramps picked up by police in Dealey Plaza (and released shortly after) were actually "spies in disguise" acting as an assassination hit team.

Weberman and Canfield presented photographic evidence indicating that one of the tramps, known as the "old man tramp," was actually E. Howard Hunt, a renowned CIA agent who had been involved in a number of covert capers including the Watergate burglary and the failed Bay of Pigs invasion. When Thornley came across this evidence, he immediately recognized Hunt as the shadowy character he'd met in New Orleans over a decade earlier named Gary Kirstein, a.k.a. "Brother-in-law." It should be noted that Hunt – during the course of a checkered covert career – was a renowned master of disguise who used a variety of aliases to conceal his activities.[7]

The 'three tramps' picked up by Dallas police in Dealey Plaza.

Thornley's "Brother-in-Law" revelations soon opened up a floodgate of associated memories as he began to suspect that he'd been set up as a substitute patsy in the assassination, and that Gary Kirstein (aka E. Howard Hunt) – or whoever he *actually* was – had been one of his "handlers."

One disturbing memory involved the theft of a typewriter from Kerry's French Quarter apartment following Memorial Day 1961. During this period, Kirstein commissioned Kerry to conduct research for a book project titled "Hitler Was a Good Guy." While working on the project at the New Orleans public library, Kerry had written "Hitler Was a Good Guy" on the top of each page – along with his own name – then turned the notes over to Kirstein.

Kerry suspected that these research notes – as well as the theft of his typewriter – had been orchestrated by Kirstein as a means to produce a manuscript, under Kerry's name, which could be used at a later date to trace him back to this typewriter and incriminate him in JFK's assassination.[8] A convoluted theory, yes, but not out of the realm of speculation, especially if Kirstein *was* E. Howard

Hunt, a man with a long history of falsifying documents. During the Vietnam War, Nixon aides enlisted Hunt to forge incriminating correspondence linking President Kennedy to the assassination of Vietnam Prime Minister Diem. Conspiracy theorists have also linked Hunt to the allegedly doctored diaries of Lee Oswald and Arthur Bremer, the fellow who attempted to assassinate Presidential candidate George Wallace in 1972. It's also of interest to note that Kirstein fancied himself an aspiring writer. E. Howard Hunt – it so happens – went on to author over 40 novels, many of these using a pseudonym.

So if Hunt was Kirstein, then who exactly was Slim Brooks? Kerry later suspected that the true identity of "Slim" was that of Jerry Milton Brooks, a former Guy Banister employee and member of the Minutemen, a far-right militia organization active during the 1960s. According to former Minutemen national spokesman, R.N. Taylor:

> The fellow mentioned as Slim Brooks, I think he was either Jerry Milton Brooks, or Jerry's brother…If it was Jerry, that was one the most bizarre individuals I have ever encountered. One of a kind. For better and worse. I know he spent some time down there with Banister and that crowd in the sixties. He was a walking card reference file of names, addresses, phone numbers, etc. Had a very photographic mind, quite amazing at times. Never knew really what side he was on. He will forever remain an enigma to me.[9]

According to Fred Turner in *The Garrison Commission*:

> Shortly after news of Garrison's investigation broke, I went to 531 Lafayette Place, an address given me by Minuteman defector Jerry Milton Brooks as the office of W. Guy Banister, a former FBI official who ran a detective agency.

According to Brooks, who had been a trusted Minuteman aide, Banister was a member of the Minutemen and head of the Anti-Communist League of the Caribbean, assertedly an intermediary between the CIA and Caribbean insurgency movements. Brooks said he had worked for Banister on 'anti-Communist' research in 1961-1962, and had known David Ferrie as a frequent visitor to Banister's office.[10]

American actress Grace Zabriskie – well-known for her role as Laura Palmer's mother in the cult television series *Twin Peaks* – was familiar with many of Kerry's French Quarter circle of friends, and had this to say about Slim Brooks:

> I met Slim several times, didn't really feel I knew him. All the things Kerry writes about Slim don't tally with anything I was privy to in him. All I ever saw was the laconic, sort of "country" affect he cultivated... I THINK I may have heard about Brother-in-Law back then, but it's possible I only heard about him later, in letters from Kerry. You know, though, it's also a fact that the mention of Brother-in-Law gives me a dark feeling, the kind it's hard to imagine I got without ever setting eyes on him. It's possible we were introduced at the Bourbon House, or somewhere around the Quarter.[11]

GERMAN BREEDING EXPERIMENTS AND MK-ULTRA

As the 70s progressed, Thornley became increasingly paranoid and began to suspect that everyone he'd ever known, even his closest friends and family, had some role in the ever-escalating conspiracy he perceived swirling around him, as demonstrated in correspondence from the period.

Robert Anton Wilson was the recipient of many of Thornley's rambling letters, which wove together a vast conspiratorial web featuring Kerry at center stage battling the very same shadowy spectres that had eliminated JFK, RFK and MLK.

At one point, Wilson received a letter from Thornley stating: "I am the most important man on the planet – I am the only one who knows all about the Kennedy assassination!" Due to this dangerous knowledge, Kerry insisted that his life was threatened by this sinister cabal who wanted him silenced. Wilson tried to rationalize the situation, reminding Kerry that there was a distinct difference between "theory" and "proof." Much to Wilson's shock, Kerry came to suspect him of being involved with an "assassination conspiracy team" and, furthermore, that Wilson was Kerry's CIA baby-sitter.

In one letter, Kerry related a particularly mind-blowing acid trip he'd taken where memories of his involvement in the assassination bubbled to the surface of his conscious mind, thus revealing his participation as an unwitting dupe – all part of a mind control experiment perpetrated by the Office of Naval Intelligence (ONI).

Kerry had previously suspected ONI of monitoring his activities during the time he was writing *The Idle Warriors,* and that both he and Oswald had been under surveillance. Later, Kerry filed a Freedom of Information request with ONI to get to the bottom of all this. When ONI finally responded, they claimed there were no references to either Thornley or Oswald in their files. In this regard, Kerry suspected that someone at ONI had either stolen or destroyed the files in question.

At one point, Thornley visited a hypnotherapist to help him uncover what had actually gone on during his service in the Marines, and if indeed ONI had brainwashed him to be some kind of sleeper agent. The hypnotist was unable to discover if there was any validity to this theory, which left Kerry only more uncertain. In 2002, Kerry's friend Robert Newport shared the following:

> There was a fella, and I don't remember his name – I think the only part of his name I ever heard was Gary – who came to see

Greg Hill in the early to mid 80s, and told Greg that he had been in ONI, and had known about the (LSD) experimentation on Kerry... That was provocative and intriguing, but I never did have the fella's last name – I didn't hear anything more. And Greg didn't seem to have much more than what I just told you, and he never had the ability or the interest – I don't know which – to follow that any more deeper.

A 1983 *Rolling Stone* exposé revealed that during the late 50s and early 60s the CIA conducted MK-ULTRA experiments at Atsugi Air Base, where both Oswald and Thornley had been stationed. Atsugi – it should be noted – was just one of two locations outside of the U.S. where the CIA stored LSD. The other storage facility was Manila, where – it so happens – Thornley was also stationed during his overseas duty. Curiously enough, E. Howard Hunt (according to his biography) was also stationed at Atsugi during the same time period as Oswald and Thornley.

By the mid 70s, Kerry suspected that he'd been implanted with a mind control device during his service in the Marines. Later, Kerry came to believe that this insidious mind zap had started much earlier, perhaps even before birth, and that he was a product of a "German breeding experiment" that presumably used both he and Oswald as human guinea pigs. Thornley even grew to suspect his own parents were Axis spies who had cut a deal with Nazi occultists conducting eugenics experiments, the ultimate purpose of which was to create Manchurian Candidates.

Some have suggested that Kerry pretended to be a victim of MK-ULTRA or mental illness as a means to conceal his true role in the JFK assassination. Jonathan Vankin wonders, in *Conspiracies, Coverups and Crimes*:

> Is Thornley's intricately conspiratorial autobiography an elaborate mind-game he plays with himself and anyone who'll join in? Or is

he really an intelligence agent, with a macabre cover story for his role in the John F. Kennedy conspiracy? Or ... is Kerry Thornley a helpless pawn in a game beyond anyone's comprehension, who somehow figured out what has been happening to him?[12]

Kerry in Little Five Points

During the last decade of his life, Thornley lived in the Little Five Points (L5P) district of Atlanta, Georgia, a bohemian enclave where he gained a reputation as a beloved and colorful character.

In December 1989, Frank Reiss opened A Capella Books in L5P and not long after encountered an "odd seeming character" – with intense eyes and a long beard – posting curious flyers around town concerning unfathomable conspiracies. As time went by – and Frank began to learn more about the L5P scene – he discovered that this fellow, Kerry Thornley, was a living legend around town, with a reputation as a "wild man." A couple years later – following the publication of *The Idle Warriors* and *Zenarchy* by IllumiNet Press – Frank approached Kerry and asked him if he'd be interested in doing a book signing. Much to Frank's surprise, he found this alleged madman to be "disarmingly charming." Without reservation, Kerry agreed to the book signing, and eventually Kerry ended up working at A Capella.

On his off time, Kerry could often be found selling his books and flowers at a stand in front of A Capella, where he spoke to passersby about his life following the Kennedy assassination, of being under CIA surveillance, and how the KGB had given him a disease after he'd been seduced by a comely Russian agent.

As Frank Reiss became more aware of the conspiratorial legends surrounding Kerry, he began to hear tales that everywhere Kerry had worked around L5P, mysterious strangers in dark suits would invariably show up. Frank never took any of these stories seriously until one Christmas when he treated all of the A Capella employees (including Kerry) to dinner at the Star Bar in L5P.

Sometime during the course of festivities, the bartender came over and passed around drinks to everyone, compliments of a gentleman seated at another table. In due course, Frank's wife, Cynthia, went over and thanked the fellow – a conservative-appearing middle-aged man – and invited him over to their table. After exchanging pleasantries, the fellow informed the group that he was a veterinarian, and spoke with – what Frank considered – an obviously phony Scottish accent.

As the evening wore on, the guy with the phony Scottish accent engaged Frank's table in conversation about one topic or another. However, after Kerry left, the conversation wound up being exclusively about him. As Frank recalled:

> It was so strange....clearly this guy wasn't who he said he was, and one way or another the conversation got around to Kerry and Oswald and all this other stuff...and that wasn't the only time...

> Within a couple of months of this incident, my wife and I were out for dinner in the neighborhood, and again – this has never happened before to us, and it has never happened since – we're sitting in a restaurant, and once again the waiter comes up and says, "This couple over here wants to buy ya'all a bottle of wine," and we accept and we invite them over to the table, and this time it's this young couple...And we start talking about everything in the world and before it's all over, we start talking about Kerry Thornley, and him working for me and what I knew about him... And those two incidents – whenever I end up talking to anybody about Kerry Thornley...there's something there...that stuff just wasn't out of the blue, and I told Kerry about it and it didn't faze him at all. He said, "Oh yeah, that stuff happens all the time – they're all over the place..."

(These incidents) fit the same description as what I had heard from other people who knew Kerry before me and would say: "Oh yeah, when (Kerry) used to work at The Pub there were always these men in dark suits."

In the early 90s, Kerry contracted a rare kidney disease called Wegner's granulomatosis, which in the coming years would cause a number of related maladies that ultimately led to his death on November 28, 1998. Up until the very end, he believed that this rare disease was the result of the very same conspiracy that bedeviled him for most of his troubled, yet fascinating life.

Adam Gorightly has been chronicling fringe culture and conspiracy politics in an illuminating manner for more than two decades. He has authored a number of books, including *Historia Discordia: The Origins of the Discordian Society*, *The Shadow Over Santa Susana: Black Magic, Mind Control and the Manson Family Mythos*, and *Happy Trails to High Weirdness: A Conspiracy Theorist's Tour Guide*. His most recent book is *Caught In The Crossfire: Kerry Thornley, Oswald and the Garrison Investigation*. You can visit his website at: www.adamgorightly.com.

The Most Important Man on the Planet

Opening Grimoires

Occult Physiology of Goetic Theurgy

by *Blair MacKenzie Blake*

> *"Ye shall be as Gods"*
> – The Serpent in the Garden of Eden

The very mention of the word "grimoire" tends to conjure up images of robed magicians hunched over vellum pages filled with ornate script, mysterious symbols, and woodblock engravings of motley devils. And if a layperson were to actually open one of the more notorious handbooks of magical instructions – if not regarding it as a mere literary curiosity of a bygone era – one would likely be both shocked and repulsed by the heights of human depravity contained therein. With lurid illustrations of nocturnal ceremonies carried out against medieval vistas, magic circles, arcane diagrams, and powerful incantations to raise malignant spirits for obtaining one's desires, little wonder such dark works were kept hidden away in sealed monastic libraries, museums of the macabre, and, according to legend, the secret archives of the Vatican. By including the forbidden rites of necromancy and abominable edicts of bloody sacrifices, the ancient practice of reducing the banned texts to ashes might appear to be justified. Of course, for most of us living in more rational times, such drastic measures are but occult clichés.

As for those books that survived the bonfires' crackling flames, when it comes to employing supernatural forces to unveil nature's most impenetrable secrets, or for the acquisition of wealth, or even to materialize things of a truly unbelievable nature, the modern consensus would be that the entire unsavory matter was merely a way of fleecing the gullible, with any positive results of the magical operations being deceptive illusions. For the most part, the present author is of like opinion, especially for those who used sorcery for baser motives, planning all along to bamboozle the Devil once their earnestly bargained for demands were granted. But that was all part of the books' grand design – the teasing ambiguity and lure of fabulous treasure, with the true masters being acutely aware of human impulses, utilizing the heretical symbolism and more frightening touches to ensure a continuous transmission.

But in today's world of digitized books, where the grimoires' perilous experiments appear at the touch of a keystroke, do they still have any relevance? Spells for repelling flies have been replaced with spray can insecticides, virtual assistants with synthetic voices offer an encyclopedia of knowledge, pixelated nudity requires no intoned enchantment, and easier get-rich-quick schemes arrive daily through electronic spam. So, what purpose does the grimoire serve, other than as a reminder of superstitious and heretical beliefs? The answer, as we shall see, might be something wholly unsuspected by even practitioners of the dark magical current, and the real reason for their mass suppression. Supposing that the dreadfully obscure text is even more heavily encoded (utilizing secret alphabets and/or 'invisible' layers of subtext to impart a completely different meaning) might we be surprised to learn that the ceremonial mechanics and black evocations of the grimoires have for centuries been terribly misunderstood?

This includes the diabolical pacts with the Chief Minister of Hell written in blood or phosphorous, the hideous appearance and nauseating smells of those (reluctant) spirits summoned into tangible manifestation, grisly relics of the blackest Arts such as the baneful "Hand of Glory", and why the tiresome operations are supposed to be performed directly upon the ground, whether in deserted cemeteries at midnight, or near the gaunt remains of ruinous churches.

With such fascinations in mind, let us dare to open these tomes bound in leather of questionable origin, seeking a possible alternate interpretation of their seemingly incomprehensible contents. At the very least we will be adding mystery to the already enigmatic, which, again, was surely the conscious intent of the ancient sages – so as to preserve their original message for the scholar-magicians of future generations.

Starting from 'Scratch'

To get a better understanding of the history of grimoires in the Western magical tradition, we should briefly attempt to trace their lineage as far back as modern academia allows. Although (to my knowledge) there are no accredited grimoireologists, social historians and occult scholars have chronicled their development. While the use of magic itself (here distinct from stage illusions à la Houdini and others) goes back to the emergence of human consciousness – as is evident from the imitative magic of Paleolithic cave art, ancient death cults, and the altered states of consciousness induced by shamans to perceive the spirit world – the earliest written accounts include the various rituals inscribed on the cuneiform tablets of Mesopotamia and the formulae of coffin texts and magical papyri rolls in ancient Egypt. There is also the inspiration of Jewish mysticism, Chaldean apotropaic sorcery, Babylonian astrological charts, and the Magi of Zoroastrianism. With regard to our study, it is in the fragments of the Graeco-Egyptian manuscripts of Hellenistic Egypt that we are able to identify similarities with the latter grimoires, being that they are not primarily concerned with remedies for diseases or protective spells (as those incised on amulets) but, rather, with the use of magical formulae to obtain advantages. Another early example would be the *Testament of Solomon,* one of numerous magical works ascribed to the Old Testament King, whom legend asserts summoned demons with the assistance of angels, a common theme of the medieval spirit catalogues. However, if we are looking for the true source of the venerable grimoires of Solomonic demonology, some might suggest that we need not look further than the apocryphal *Book of Enoch* with its account of the fallen angels called the Watchers. (More about the transgressions of these lofty teachers later.)

The Hidden Church and Worldly Gain

"Having their head in the highest heavens and their feet in the deepest hells"
- Michael Cecchetelli ("Crossed Keys")

The majority of oft-reprinted grimoires on bookshelves today are of false authorship and pretended origin. Legendary figures of antiquity known for their wisdom and authority figure prominently in the mix, along with other exotic pseudonyms.

This was both to further imbue the works with a numinous aura and to deceive the censors at a time when those involved with such heretical endeavors were subject to severe punishment. Even so, elements of Christianity run throughout most of the black books worthy of being kept in chained boxes, and it was the ecclesiastic courts that monopolized the possession and use of exorcism manuals and early grimoires. When ordained priests cast out demons, many were undoubtedly unable to resist the temptation of obliging the dark emissaries of Satan to reveal the location of valuable hoards or to impart earthly pleasures. For some who performed exorcisms, the financial rewards might have even been the underlying purpose of ensnaring the unruly spirits.

Such unorthodox ambitions and special benefits prompted some of the medieval peasant class to suspect that the priestly elite was keeping for themselves the true efficacy of the scriptures and non-canonical writings. However, with the advent of the printing press and subsequent rise in literacy, grimoires began to circulate among the populace, some of whom, in spite of the inherent danger, recited the lengthy benedictions and orisons in the hope of having the infernal manifestations do their bidding. And, when the demonologists published the torture chamber records of the Holy Inquisition, in their zealous campaign against trafficking with maleficent spirits, they unwittingly provided a wealth of magical information. Likewise with some of the more rational thinkers of the time, who were highly skeptical of the grimoires' dubious experiments and spurious attribution. Although the learned men dismissed the works as being utter nonsense, in their written critiques they made available a workable system for commanding demons.

And though it might seem like wild speculation, with regards to those clergymen who used inverted exorcisms to constrain demons for material gain, we shouldn't rule out the possibility that their occult pursuits served as a clever diversion of sorts that was either deliberately orchestrated (or tolerated) by an underground sodality within the Church of Rome. Members of the confraternity may have viewed any goetic chicanery as the lesser of two evils – a necessary (nay, essential) subterfuge to prevent at all costs the divulging of the far more consequential revelations encoded in the undiluted grimoires.

But the game was played on both sides. In the late 17th century, a book entitled *The Grimoire of Pope Honorius III* made the rounds. This contained similar content to the centuries earlier *Sworn Book of Honorius* which was purported to have been written by Honorius of Thebes, Egypt. In attributing a work of darkness – that contains, among other profanations, sacrifices of virgin kid and Solomonian precepts for binding demons – to a former crusading Pope (not exactly the same as those sorcerers' manuals ascribed to Biblical heroes as a means of elevating their potency), this may have been someone's way of seeking revenge on the Church for their continued persecution of heretics and fanatical suppression of grimoires. The imposter grimoire could also have been a signal that they were aware of the theological smokescreen. (Of further interest, perhaps, another diabolical grimoire was falsely attributed to St. Cyprian – a former Bishop, who, before his conversion to Christianity, had the reputation of being an accomplished black magician. Appropriately, parts of the text are written in reverse Latin.)

Though many grimoires were confiscated and destroyed by the Papal dragnet, others on the 1599 *Index of Prohibited Books* were

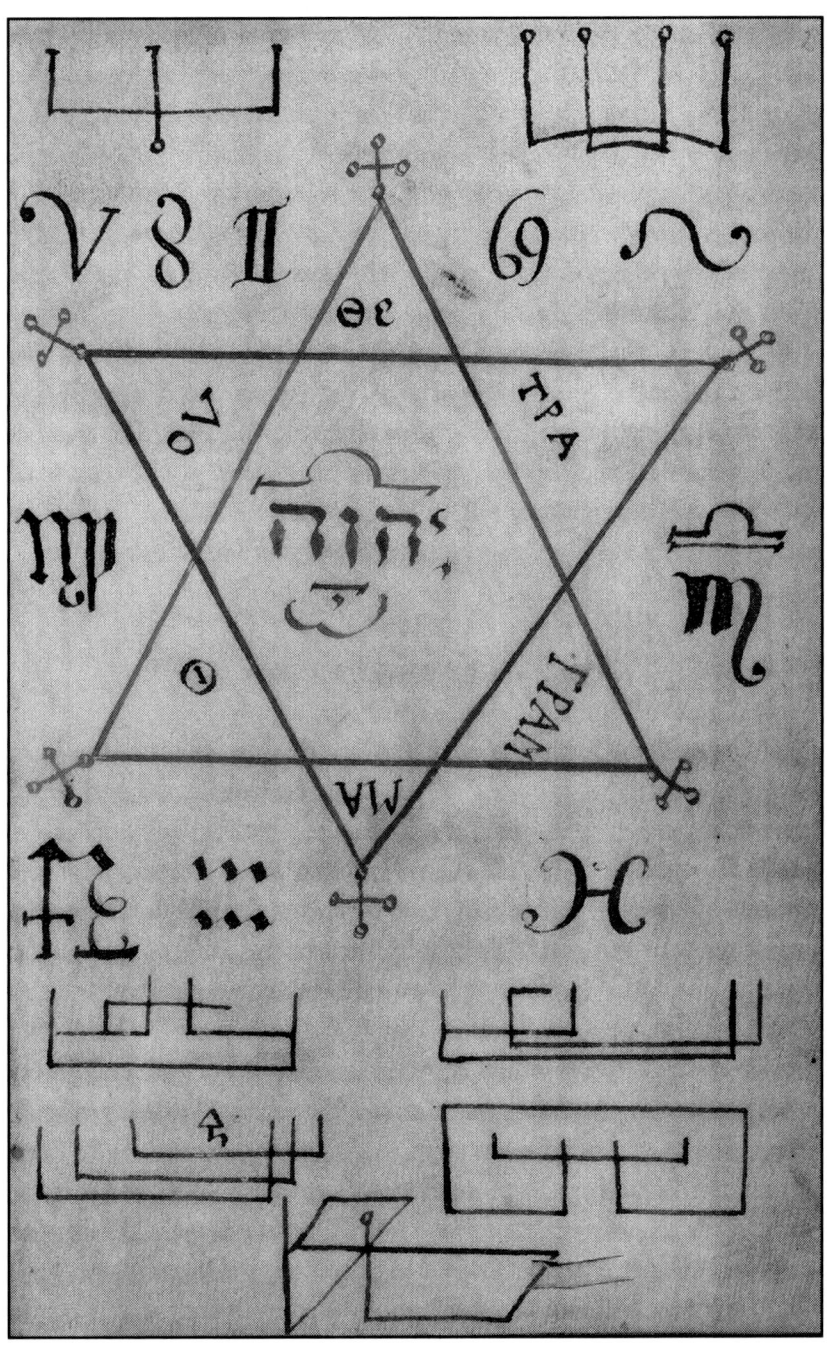

smuggled across borders where they gained an even wider audience. The Protestant Reform saw a further proliferation of these repositories of ancient wisdom, along with the resurgent interest in Hermeticism during the Renaissance and again in the late 1800s with the new academic discipline of Papyrology. As the treasure hunting obsession of the parish clergy reached a fever pitch in Europe, the first mass market grimoires appeared openly in the windows of Parisian bookshops. Most notable among them was *The Grand Grimoire/Le Dragon Rouge* – a derivative of the earlier Solomonic cycle of black notebooks that boasted the added greater risk of allowing an untrained layperson to make a ritualistic pact with Lucifuge Rofocale (Lucifer). The trend of making grammars of magic available to the general public continued with the pulp revolution, where budget versions of the dressed-up scarce originals became drugstore and bus station oddities.

Theory and Praxis

Having established that the once privileged access to grimoires is no longer the exclusive province of the Catholic priesthood and robed esotericists, our next concern might be the puzzling contents of the books themselves. With all their elaborate ritual preparations and rigorous operating procedures, can the process of high ceremonial evocation produce verifiable results, or are the technical formulas merely an exercise in futility? If we were to accept the former, as to whether or not the specific ends – the fulfillment earnestly bargained for – is of an objective or subjective nature, there are widely differing opinions among modern practitioners. One camp finds it perfectly acceptable to 'paint' the ritual in one's mind…say, while in one's apartment, including the protective devices and consecrated magical tools, while the other takes a much more literal approach, insisting on a strong adherence to the detailed instructions and stern injunctions, no matter how difficult or seemingly preposterous they might be. To these dyed-in-the-wool occultists, any short cuts or departure from the exact requirements as written down in the grimoires can only lead to complete failure with possibly a little tangential mischief.

Perhaps there is a valid reason for such admonitions, in that the strange requirements might disrupt brain mechanisms, as was suggested by the occultist Aleister Crowley when he wrote: "The peculiar mental excitement required may even be aroused by the perception of the absurdity of the process and the persistence of it." As for the "mumbo-jumbo" that critics of magic are quick to point out, the scarcely pronounceable barbarous Words of Power and/or sonorous evocations of mishmash Latin, when deeply intoned in a forceful, commanding manner, might also have a profound affect on the neurocognitive process, possibly creating vibrations of a specific resonance that deactivate a perceptual filter that otherwise blinds us from 'behind the scenery' realities. Concerning the lengthy orations, brain specialists will point out that infrasonic vibrations – such as those generated by pipe organs in churches – can cause one to experience not only heightened spirituality but also odd sensations associated with paranormal activity, including optical illusions such as ghostly apparitions.

In a like manner, those medical professionals who are skeptical will draw parallels with the perceived self-intoxicating rituals and neurological hallucinations such as autoscopic experiences, where those suffering from the disorder see an illusory second physical body near one's real form.

If not autoscopic phantoms, the demonic servitors visibly manifesting themselves in the energized portals – whether appearing as hideously bizarre or sublimely beautiful – will usually need a natural material basis to do so. With regards to these suffumigations (incense), the grimoires are also quite specific as to the ingredients required to compound them (as well as those for making special inks for spells and pacts). These include such vulgarities as the powdered brains of an eviscerated cat, earwax mixed with opium, the fat of a gibbeted criminal, and scrapings of coffin nails. According to the old-school Ceremonialists, the prescribed items are not meant to be allegorical or to serve as blinds. As to some of these obscure preparations, occultist Steven Flowers states "when one of the old spells called for the blood of a black ass; it was really no more a rare ingredient then, let's say, the crank case oil of a black Chevy pickup truck would be today." Be that as it may, such requisites may be just another example of those designed absurdities that mess with one's neural circuitry.

By now we should get the basic idea. Competent practitioners who can proficiently juggle certain magical axioms, including the concept of "subjective synthesis" – defined by physicist-magician Joseph C. Lisiewski as "a mental process which leads to an integrated belief system" in which acceptance is of paramount importance in the fusing together of unconscious beliefs and conscious expectations – are developing certain latent abilities or occult faculties by which the combined ceremonial elements are capable of producing results within the tangible grasp of the operator. In a similar manner, some recent-generation explorers of the human mindscape, with their intensely focused Will, are able to summon a multitude of psychic constructs – with the preference being those 'nightside' entities repressed or avoided by others – while at the same time hopefully being protected from any astral turbulence in their visualized impregnable circle. In both magical frameworks, where the parameters of consensus reality are blurred, arguments as to which is the correct method may be irrelevant, with no strict division between subjective versus objective (or invocations as opposed to evocations for that matter). This is especially true when we explore the omnijective territory of the grimoires, where the relationship between imaginary whims and concrete actualities are seamlessly interconnected, and our occult physiology facilitates a human interface with intersecting parallel realities. As for any dignified celestial seraphic forms or grotesque chthonic prince Belzebuths that materialize in the Triangle of Arte, to quote the occultist J.W. Brodie-Inns: "Whether they really exist is completely unimportant; the point is that the universe behaves as though they do." Now, we are getting closer to understanding the quantum potential of magic and, perhaps, something equally as mysterious.

15th Century Necromancer's Manual

For many years one of the most important manuscripts of the necromantic arts slumbered all but unnoticed in the State Library in Munich, Germany.

Almost completely intact, the miscellany is a true survivor of the Church's rabid attempts to eradicate genuine magical texts from the face of the earth. Thanks largely to the detailed analysis of its contents by Religious and History Professor Richard Kieckhefer in his book entitled *Forbidden Rites: A Necromancer's Manual of the Fifteenth Century*, the Munich manual is now considered to be one of the more curious works ever penned. Although it is an anonymous compilation, the handbook is thought to have been written by a member of the clergy, possibly a priest who shared a daring fascination with the Devil's arts in the same manner as those other members of the medieval clerical underworld that we touched upon earlier. Unlike some other grimoires, the material is long on demons and short on angels (yet, how is one to really know the difference?), and though its magic is described as being explicitly demonic, upon opening the sourcebook, one might not so quickly reach that conclusion.

The earlier experiments are of the illusionist types – a series of conjurations in the magician's repertoire for materializing illusory castles, extravagant banquets, and imaginary means of transportation such as flying thrones. These are then followed by testimonials boasting the magic's unparalleled efficacy. Although the rituals are highly complex and incorporate the usual ceremonial trappings, the results are but amusing spectacles (ostensibly) designed to captivate an audience. However, as part of the manual's capricious nature,

behind all the whimsical pageantry and fanciful adventures, the discerning reader is being initiated with privileged information that is unmistakably esoteric. The illusionist experiments – at first strictly for the amusement of all involved – suddenly take on added features, some of which are not for the squeamish, including auxiliary measures that call for a bloody sacrifice along with the formal conjurations.

These reveal the author's true motivation for the entertaining games and anecdotes concerning the uncertainties between fantasy and reality. How do I know this? Well, a little bird told me…

The emphasis in the Munich grimoire on the magical virtues of a hoopoe to necromancers, as well as the sacrificial offering of its heart's blood to malign spirits, points us in the direction of ancient Egypt, with links to the celebrated wisdom of King Solomon. (Magical techniques in the handbook that make a living person appear to be dead are another dead giveaway – a coded reference that is not merely paronomasic.) The fiery gold-crested hoopoe was sacred to the ancient Egyptians where it was strongly connected with death and the netherworld. As such, it was often depicted in variegated funerary scenes and in hieroglyphics on the flaming eye of royal scepters. With its dramatic solar helmet, the hoopoe was the fabled messenger of Solomon – that which had obtained knowledge of things that he had no previous knowledge of. As the legend goes, it overheard such incredible things during its habit of eavesdropping. According to medieval bestiaries, the hoopoe restored vision by licking the mist from the eyes of older birds. It also dwelt among burial places, taking pleasure in grief while feeding on dirt in hope of finding wondrous treasure. The rubbing of its blood on humans caused strange hallucinations and increased fantasies, even the appearance of the devil.

But, for all its magical virtues, the real reason that Solomon demanded the hoopoe was that it alone possessed the *shamir* – a miraculous worm of sorts known as "the opener" due to its uncanny penetrative power. Though minuscule in size, the supernatural organism had the ability to pierce hard surfaces with its glance

Engraving of a hoopoe in the tomb of Userkaf at Saqqara, Egypt.

alone (yet, another cryptogram). Could it be that the *shamir* legend conceals an endogenous mystification, such as a traversable micro-wormhole? Before entertaining any more possibilities, with regards to calling upon the assistance of malefic intelligences (as Solomon did to capture the hoopoe), let us now focus our attention on a demon-infested grimoire entitled the *Lemegeton, or The Lesser Key of Solomon*, in particular the first part which is called the *Goetia*.

Goetia, Watchers & Djinn

"The spirits of the Goetia are portions of the human brain." This statement made by Aleister Crowley in 'his' *The Book of the Goetia* really gets the goat of many old school ritual magicians, some of whom believe that it has hindered research on evocations for nearly a century. Whether this was meant to be tongue-in-cheek or not, Crowley's "rational explanation" of the Goetic system asserts that the operations stimulate regions and functions of the brain. To acquire specialized knowledge of something, the magician consults the spirit directory and activates the distinctive seal of the ruler whose particular attributes correspond to the neurological zones that are responsible for learning this or that. In desiring to have mastery over turning all metals into gold, prior to energizing the sigil (pictorial signature) of "Berith" (the 28th demon bound by Solomon), who "giveth true answers, Past, Present, and to Come", but also is "a Great Liar, and not to be trusted unto", the magician might reasonably question if this apparent inconsistency was intentional? Is it a trap for the undeserving, or just a careless mistake in translation? Or, to put a different twist on things is the "Great Liar" a signal that its seal is worthy of greater attention? Whichever is the case, in dealing with the intelligences of the *Goetia*, perhaps we should first call forth the 29th spirit, "Astaroth", who "will declare wittingly how the Spirits fell, if desired, and the reason of his own fall."

The Goetic spirit's revealing of "how the spirits fell" refers to the rebellious angels known in the Jewish apocalyptic literature as the Watchers. According to variants of the pseudepigraphic *Book of Enoch*, after swearing an oath, a number of the celestial hierarchy conspired against the Most High and descended to earth, where they illicitly instructed humanity in the arts and science, including the revealing of all of God's secrets. With their constantly changing nature the fallen Watchers so deeply embedded in the Enochian tradition start to appear more like human civilizers than starry messengers. As cultural exemplars, when the union of these 'sons of god' with the daughters of men produced a hybrid race of 'giants', the exceptional strain was violently eliminated in a drama that played out on biblical terrain. However, the 'evil' spirits of these mighty dead – those "heroes of old and men of renown" metaphorically transformed into disobedient angels – remain on the earth as "that which does not corrupt in the grave", and it is these disembodied terrestrial spirits that form the basis of the grimoire tradition.

With the origin of the Lucifer and fallen angels mythos being the curse on the king of Babylon – who is denied astral deification because of his pride and envy in wanting to raise his throne above the stars of God, but, instead, is cast down to the earth and covered with worms – we can now better recognize the sulphurous breath of those raised by necromantic rites as the ancient ancestral dead, rather than some errant resplendent angel of Judeo-Christian propaganda. As for stealing fire from heaven, it is the 'decayed-sciences' of our antediluvian benefactors that is the forbidden knowledge that should interest us the most.

While still amidst the howling sands of the Middle East, what are we to make of the infernal djinn that feature prominently in the Arabian storyworld? Rarely to be encountered in our perceptual sphere, these creatures made from smokeless fire in pre-Islamic lore share many similarities with the Goetic spirits, which is why the magically oriented King Solomon famously kept them imprisoned in a brass vessel. Of the true nature of this sealed spirit-trap, opinions differ among occultists, with some even speculating that the brazen receptacle was composed of some special alchemical metal. Being that the container remains unweighted, one could venture a guess as to the mercurial essence of that constrained within, as well as to the hazards of releasing such shape-shifting manifestations.

Akin to the fiery djinn are the ghouls who haunt burial grounds and gnaw on the dead. Although now the stuff of Hollywood B horror films, the unpalatable actions of the ghoul enshroud the secret of a necrophagus cult that nourished not on the putrefied flesh of corpses, but, rather, on a mysterious post-mortem residue preserved therein. In a process that is difficult to conceptualize, a penetrating worm-like organism (the shamir), made of smokeless and scorching fire, feasts (burns away) on the membrane or protective shell of an enigmatic organ in the deceased. This seeming desecration of the graves of the not so dearly departed for the solicitation of favors was consensual and evidently involved a contract that is now dimly

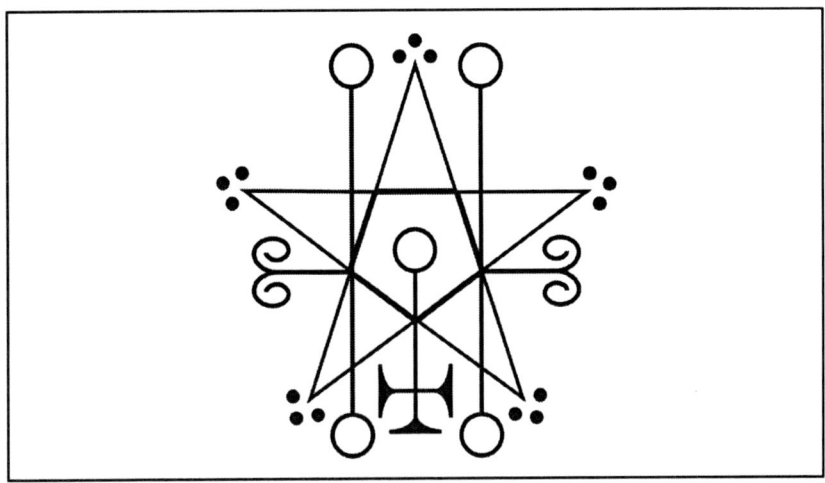

Seal of Asteroth

remembered in the annals of demonology as the *Pacta Conventa Daemoniorum* written in looking-glass Latin. Other distortions of the esoteric doctrines of the necromantic fraternity include tell-tale black beans placed in the mouth of a cadaver (the praised dead who are now truly dead), as one is instructed to do so for 'invisibility' in the *Grimorium Verum,* confections composed of brains in the Arabic sourcebook known as *Picatrix,* and a particular talisman in *The Black Pullet.* And then there is the frightful "Hand of Glory", described in *Petit Albert* as a pickled hand clenching a lighted candle that was displayed to prevent thieves from being detected, but whose eerie flame originally stupefied any spectators to keep them from knowing what was going on during the necromancer's bizarre process of raising the shades of the dead.

Through the Wormhole of Daath

When the famous occultist Eliphas Levi referred to sections of *The Grimoire of Honorius* as being "a tissue of repulsive absurdities", and "a veritable monument of human perversity" he was grasping at the shadow and losing the substance – a mistake made by many ceremonial magicians, who keep adding flesh to the bare bones of the rituals.

Grimoires are interspersed with many obstacles, and even with illuminated commentaries, it is the evocation technology that most often serves as a deathblow to the practitioner. Perhaps the occult window dressing that is so detestable in the popular mind – the grid of concentric circles, inscribed pentacles, inverted triangles, and of blessed chalk seals of the countless enumerations of deities, along with the perplexing devilry of magical implements gleaming in the flickering of burning lamps – was someone's ingenious way of keeping a precious secret both hidden and transmitted over time. Don't get me wrong. When Crowley spoke of the exhausting complexity of the grimoires' operations as disrupting brain mechanisms, he was correct in that the ever more complicated elaborations enabled the operator to undergo a radical personal transformation. However, as profound of an experience as "The Grand Dreaming of a Treasured Eye" might be to the participant, it is not of the same ontological magnitude as those who witness "The Dream of the Dreamless" – that which doesn't involve a trained imagination faculty.

Suppose for a minute that the dramatic ritual with its colorful smears of phantastical entities is merely an elaborate distraction. Does the casting of the magical circle act as a protective barrier for the magician, or for the authentic masters? As the links of a sympathetic chain, are the presiding spirits of the cardinal points, clockwork angels, astrological glyphs, and diagrams of a distinctive nature drawn with linear exactitude possibly a medieval corruption of the specific coordinates of an anatomical treasure map, with the X marks the spot of the arcane cartography having been mistaken for the starting point? If so, are the magicians moving further away, hurdle after hurdle, from the precise location of the death-borne substance – the worm-bitten black fruit of paradise that open one's eye(s) to our trans-human potential? Concerning this realm of hyper-consciousness, magical processes that enhance the faculty of inspection contained in the *Ars Notoria* ("The Notary Art of Solomon") might be of great value, especially those with eidetic memory capabilities.

As a final thought concerning this speculative physiological nexus hinted at by the necromantic masters of concealment, would it be 'Solomon wise' in the post-modern occult milieu to devise an updated ceremonial system? Not one that involves a conjoined manual of seemingly strange bedfellows, such as the recently published combined keys of *The Enchiridion of Pope Leo III* with *Le Veritable Dragon Noir*, but, rather, one with a newly established spirit-etiquette that does away with the curse of chains, blasting rods, offerings of burnt loaves, sacrificial doves' blood, prolonged contests of will, and the shackling of obstinate apparitions in a horrendous abyss. One in which the operator attempts to establish commerce in a less abusing and degrading way with the vivid intelligences that will assist us in exploring mindscapes beyond the matrix of the ordinary. Those who won't ask us to conjure a substitute because the one called upon has already been evoked by another magician with a fulminating hazel wand, or request us to adorn kid skin with garlands of verbena, or, in an even more ludicrous scenario, one with specters that won't arrive late into the Triangle of Arte due to a previous engagement, such as having attended an aerial gathering to celebrate the feast of the blessed Virgin!

Those magicians who still borrow liturgical formulae and inverted exorcisms that unleash terrifying shapes or pleasing forms in hopes of getting an eagerly awaited text message from a former lover, or an unexpected increase in their credit line – only to formally dismiss any distorted fulfillment of their clearly expressed charge with the License to Depart – might want to reconsider the surface content of these works of dubious lineage.

Whether the projections of personal conflicts lurking in the deepest recesses of the subconscious, or tricks of a tweaked perceptual apparatus in a lump of grey jelly, or the wondrous treasures on a plane of existence created solely by the fine matter of human thoughts, the mutating grimoires of the western magical tradition will continue to exert a fascination among the impressionable and undoubtedly will be misunderstood by the 'initiated.' For the sake of what might still be divulged by the textual ambiguities, acrostics, and idiosyncratic symbology, despite omissions, additions, and errors in the translation of the already mangled foreign tongues – these aren't exactly terrible things.

Blair MacKenzie Blake has been studying, practicing, and writing about the western esoteric tradition for over twenty years. He is the author of two books: *Ijynx* and *The Wickedest Books in the World: Confessions of an Aleister Crowley Bibliophile*. In his 'other life', he is the writer/content manager for www.toolband.com and www.dannycarey.com.

ROCKS IN YOUR HEAD

The history of meteor research is a lesson to science on the value of eyewitness reports

by *Greg Taylor*

On the 15th of February, 2013, a meteor tore through the sky above the southern Ural region of Russia at a speed of roughly 40,000 miles per hour. As it descended to an altitude of about 15 miles above the city of Chelyabinsk, the massive air pressure being exerted on the 7000 ton object caused a spectacular air-burst – since estimated as the equivalent of a 500 kiloton explosion – that blew in doors and shattered windows in the city below.

We all believe that this incident occurred as described – not so much on the basis of 'hearsay' testimony from witnesses, but instead mainly because of the high number of Russian vehicles that now carry dash-cams. Unlike the Tunguska blast of a century previous – which remains an event shrouded in mystery – the Chelyabinsk fireball was filmed from multiple angles for much of its short but violent life, from its initial appearance to the later shockwave which threw amateur videographers to the ground in fear. What's more, we also happily believe that a rock from space caused the incident, because through science we have come to understand and accept the fact that rocks from space, of various sizes and shapes, regularly bombard our planet.

It therefore comes almost as a shock to find out that the cosmic origin of meteors has only been an accepted fact in Western science for barely two centuries. Indeed, when Yale chemistry professor Benjamin Silliman proposed an extraterrestrial source for a meteor that exploded over the town of Weston in 1807, Thomas Jefferson is famously claimed to have retorted "I would more easily believe that [a] Yankee professor would lie than that stones would fall from heaven." As it turns out, the exact quote may be apocryphal – an embellishment by Silliman's son. But there is little doubt that, at that time, Jefferson was skeptical about the provenance of the Weston meteorite, writing that...

> ...a thousand phenomena present themselves daily which we cannot explain, but where facts are suggested, bearing no analogy with the laws of nature as yet known to us, their verity needs proofs proportioned to their difficulty. A cautious mind will weigh well the

The Chelyabinsk fireball

opposition of the phenomenon to everything hitherto observed, the strength of the testimony by which it is supported, and the errors and misconceptions to which even our senses are liable.[1]

At the time, while sightings of fireballs streaking across the sky were common enough that they were accepted by science as occurring, they were believed to be a still-mysterious atmospheric phenomenon similar to lightning, unconnected to tales of rocks falling from the sky (indeed, the word meteor comes from the Greek word for 'atmosphere', hence the naming of the profession of 'meteorologist'). One account attributed their appearance to "the fermentation of acid and alkaline bodies which float in the atmosphere...when the more subtle part of the effluvia are burnt away, the viscous and earthy parts become too heavy to be supported by the air, and then they fall." Another theory suggested that meteors were "a collection of nitro-sulphureous and fiery vapors, into a sort of a rolling globe, or whirlwind of fire."[2]

Jefferson's own leaning toward the 'atmospheric' assumption about meteors – and his skepticism that rocks could fall from the sky – is evident in a question he posed concerning the Weston meteorite: "is it easier to explain how it got into the clouds from whence it is supposed to have fallen?"

Jefferson's view, however, would soon be a relic of the past. Just thirteen years before the Weston meteorite fall the German physicist Ernst Chladni had published *On the Origin of Ironmasses*. In studying detailed reports of both fireballs and stone falls, Chladni noticed numerous similarities between the cases, and concluded that the phenomena were linked. He theorized that fireballs were falling stones that grew incandescent due to the heat energy generated via friction with Earth's atmosphere. Like Copernicus's 'heretical' heliocentric model, Chladni's intelligent work sparked interest from academic colleagues in private, but received little support in public.[3]

Just a year later, however, a stone three feet across plummeted from the sky in the United Kingdom, plunging into the earth not far from Wold Cottage, the home of magistrate Major Edward Topham, a well-known public figure. Major Topham gave an account of the incident in James Sowerby's *British Mineralogy*, published in 1804:

> When the stone fell, a shepherd of mine, who was returning from his sheep, was about 150 yards from the spot; George Sawden, a carpenter, was passing within 60 yards; and John Shipley, one of my farming servants, was so near the spot where it fell, that he was struck very forcibly by some of the mud and earth raised by the stone dashing into the earth, which it penetrated to the depth of twelve inches, and seven afterwards into the chalk rock – making in all a depth of nineteen inches from the surface.
>
> While the stone was passing through the air…numbers of persons distinguished a body passing through the clouds, though not able to ascertain what it was: and two sons of the clergy man of Wold Newton saw it pass so distinctly by them, that they ran up immediately to my house, to know if anything extraordinary had happened.
>
> …no circumstance of the kind had ever more concurrent testimonies; and the appearance of the stone itself, while it resembles in composition those which are supposed to have fallen in various other parts of the world, has no counterpart or resemblance in the natural stones of the country.

Topham was acutely aware of the controversial nature of such incidents, and thus "as a magistrate, I took [the witnesses] accounts upon oath", noting that he would have no truck with those who disbelieved the event had occurred as he had stated. "I mean not to enter into any literary warfare with those sceptics, who think it

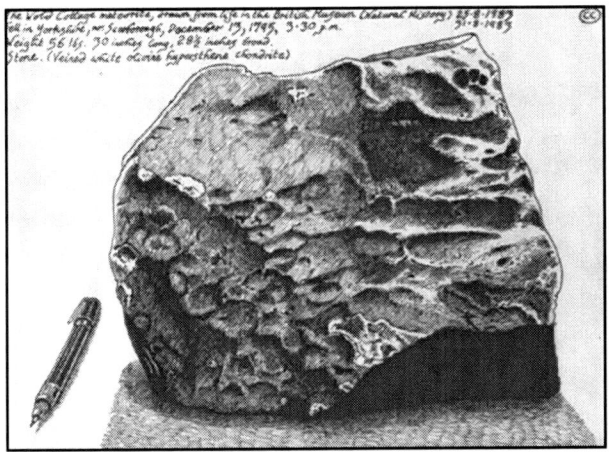

The Wold Cottage Meteorite

much easier to doubt every word of this account than to believe such an event could take place," he remarked. "There is no shorter way of disposing of any thing than to deny or disbelieve it". And he felt compelled to add a comment about one particular proposed explanation for falling stones, asking "what projectile force could throw a stone of 56 pounds in weight from any volcano upon earth to the spot near my house [in Yorkshire] where the stone fell?"

When Chladni's *On the Origin of Ironmasses* reached England in 1796, the Wold Cottage stone was on display in Piccadilly Circus, where the public were willingly paying a shilling each to view the curiosity.[4] Interest in the mystery was building, and Sir Joseph Banks, president of the Royal Society, commissioned a chemical analysis of stones that had been seen falling from the sky. The chemists involved identified common components, "including 'a coating of black oxide of iron' (fusion crust), 'curious globules' (silicate inclusions called chondrules) and a high nickel content in the iron, all of which distinguished their samples from terrestrial rocks."[5]

And yet, the Royal Society was still cautious enough about the research that they adjusted part of the title of the paper – "Observations on Certain Stony and Metalline Substances which Have Fallen at

Different Times on the Earth" (1802) – to "...Substances which *Are Said to Have* Fallen..." [my emphasis]

But the falling stones would not be denied. In the year immediately after this paper was published, the French village of L'Aigle, not far west of Paris, was pelted by thousands of rocks from the sky after a brilliant fireball had crossed the sky and exploded in three massive detonations. Upon hearing of the event, the French Academy of Sciences dispatched a young scientist by the name of Jean-Baptiste Biot to investigate. His meticulous investigation of "without a doubt the most astonishing phenomenon ever observed by man" included interviews with eye-witnesses, a mapping of the debris field, and comparisons of the rocks to the local mineralogy. It was enough to be a turning point in the debate over the origin of falling rocks, and subsequent meteorite falls – such as the one over Weston that sparked Jefferson's incredulous response – only helped to reinforce the veracity of eye-witness testimony that stones did indeed fall from the sky.

After the L'Aigle meteorite fall, the historian Eusebius Salverte criticized the way in which scientists had willingly refused to accept a conclusion that had been long been accepted by people of previous ages:

> The ancient historians all make frequent mention of the productions of stones [fallen from the atmosphere]. No doubt was maintained respecting them in the Middle Ages; but the difficulty of accounting for them induced us not only to suspend our belief until called forth by more regular observation, which was very prudent, but also, which was less reasonable, to carry with us in this research a predetermination to see nothing, or to deny what we had seen.

As the saying goes, science advances one funeral at a time, and despite these breakthroughs, it would not be until the 1850s that the extraterrestrial origin of meteorites would finally come to be accepted as an established scientific fact.

'Pure Fantasy'

It says something about the resistance of scientists to anomalistic eyewitness reports then, that two hundred years after this controversy erupted, another mystery concerning meteors continues to linger and be debated: that eyewitnesses have sometimes reported 'hearing' fireballs at the same time as they are seen, despite it being an 'impossibility'.

For example, a number of witnesses who watched an impressive fireball tear through the sky over England on the 19th of March, 1719 reported hearing it make a hissing sound as it passed overhead:

> I discern'd in the sky a large ball of fire, at about 20 or 25° height from the horizon, and bearing about W. and by N. or W.N.W. when I first saw it: It seem'd to be as large as the Moon at Full, with a pale blewish Light, and to have little motion; but in a moment it was thrown into the shape of a common meteor, the head diminishing 'till it was all turn'd into a long stream of light, which…made so strong a light while it was in its greatest extent, that for a moment the Moon, which was above a day past the first quarter, and all the stars, seem'd to disappear by the superiority of this new light; and at that moment one might have read the smallest print by it. *While it was throwing itself into this beautiful stream, I thought I heard a noise of hissing,* like what is made by the flying of a large rocket in the air, but I heard no other noise.[6] [my emphasis]

The famous and influential astronomer Edmund Halley (whom Halley's Comet is named after) was quick to dismiss these claims as "pure fantasy". Halley's reasoning was based in hard science: from various ground observations of the bolide's flight, he had been able to triangulate the height of the fireball. At more than 60 miles distant, Halley noted that it would have been impossible for anybody to hear the fireball at the same time as seeing it: as sound travels at 'only' around a fifth of a mile per second, it would have taken some five minutes to hear anything related to the event.[7]

In 1784 former army surgeon (and Secretary of the Royal Society) Thomas Blagdon gathered a number of similar reports in connection with a spectacular bolide that had been seen over Scotland, England and Europe a year previously. Blagdon too was baffled by these alleged hissing sounds heard coincident with the sighting of the fireball, and suggested that they might best be explained psychologically, as being the result of "an affrighted imagination". He was, however, respectful enough of the testimony of the witnesses to not reject it outright, admitting that he would rather "leave it as a point to be cleared up by future observers."

A half century later, during the great Leonid meteor shower of November 13th 1833, many people again reported anomalistic sounds accompanying the largest fireballs: hissing noises "like the rushing of a sky rocket" and slight explosions. But in this case, a scientist went against the established 'truth' of the matter. Denison Olmsted, Professor of Mathematics and Natural Philosophy at Yale, found himself at odds with Halley's and Blagdon's conclusions, noting that the descriptions of the sounds occurred "too uniformly, and in too many instances, to permit us to suppose that they were either imaginary or derived from extraneous sources."

But Olmsted's opinion continued to be in the minority within scientific circles. One reason for this was the capricious nature of the phenomenon: of two people standing beside each other, often only one might report hearing the sounds, lending credence to the idea that it was a psychological effect. Additionally, the accepted science of the time contained no mechanism that would allow for this 'instantaneous sound' phenomenon to be possible in the first place.

Nevertheless, there were aspects of the testimony that should have given pause to any serious scientist. Perhaps the most persuasive of these was that many witnesses reported that *it was the sound itself that caused them to look up* and observe the fireball. For instance, one witness wrote that "while walking in my garden my attention was attracted by a distant hissing sound, and on looking up I saw the meteor". In some cases this even extended to people within buildings hearing the sound, causing them to move to a window or outside to look for the source of the noise.

But it was an advance in science that would provide the real key to opening scientists' minds.

Ethereal Sound

For the likes of Edmund Halley, witness accounts of 'instantaneous' sound propagation from meteors could be dismissed out of hand, as the science of his time could supply no mechanism that would make this possible. However, between 1886 and 1889 Heinrich Hertz conducted a series of experiments that would prove the reality of 'electromagnetic waves' (which had been theorized by James Clerk Maxwell during the 1860s and 1870s).

This discovery would lead to some of the first real attempts by scientists at explaining – and accepting – meteoric sounds. After a spectacular fireball over Texas in 1917 elicited more eyewitness accounts of simultaneous sounds, Professor J.A. Udden of the University of Texas suggested that electromagnetic waves might provide the solution:

> Several parties who saw the bright body at a distance of about 200 miles (320 km) or less, report hearing a swishing or buzzing sound, which seems to have been simultaneous with the appearance of the light.
>
> If these observations are not subjective, the cause of the sounds may perhaps be sought in either waves that, on meeting the earth, or objects attached to the earth, such as plants or artificial structures, are in part dissipated by being transformed into waves of sound in the air.

Udden was still swimming against the tide of mainstream scientific opinion though. Even after the turn of the 20th century – with Hertz's electromagnetic wave theory now an intrinsic part of physics – the famous astronomer W.F. Denning would note that...

> ...hissing and similar noises...may be dismissed as imaginary... [an] observational illusion... They are either imaginative or due to causes not directly connected with the phenomena observed.

Even later, in an article in *Popular Astronomy* in 1932, C.C. Wylie, Professor of Mathematics and Astronomy at the University of Iowa, illustrated once again the dangers of using the words "without doubt" when he wrote that "the explanation [for meteoric sounds] is without doubt psychological."

Such negative opinions by acknowledged meteor experts "led many meteor scientists to shun the subject". One exception was prominent meteor scientist Harvey Harlow Nininger, who in 1939 wrote that perhaps the mystery was "a problem in physics rather than psychology". He was persuaded by the many cases on record "where the informants insist that the sound attracted them from behind or within buildings, and, in some instances of daylight meteors, the sound was commented upon before any light was seen or known about."

Nininger put forward a possible solution to the mystery, telling of how one "Mr. Elmer R. Weaver of the U.S. Bureau of Standards suggested to me in conversation that possibly ether waves are transformed into sound waves upon striking objects in the environment of the observer." He pointed out that it was common knowledge among radio engineers that powerful radio transmissions were sometimes reproduced by objects in the environment that acted as receivers – perhaps that was what was happening here?

Nininger also attempted to give a name to the phenomenon, suggesting that it be called "ethereal sound". However, the term that

would stick was proposed in the following year by Professor Peter Dravert of Omsk University: "electrophonic fireballs".

The problem remained, however, that at this stage there was still no actual evidence that bolides emitted radio signals. British astronomer Gerald Hawkins – perhaps best known for his influential research on astronomical alignments for ancient sites such as Stonehenge – was curious enough to dedicate some time to researching the idea in 1958, conducting a search for radio emissions from meteors at several specific frequencies, but he found nothing.

At this point, however, there was now enough ongoing interest in the mystery that a unique research group became involved: the U.S. Department of Defense, who awarded a contract to the Rand Corporation to study the phenomenon further. Though, it seems likely that they were motivated more by the Cold War and the threat of Soviet nuclear missiles, rather than any particular interest in the mysteries of meteors, expressing the hope that a better understanding of the topic might lead to "new techniques for determining the size, nature and path of any large body entering the earth's atmosphere". Enough said!

Despite presenting 88 references and a catalog of 41 observations in a 65 page report, the Rand Corporation study could reach no firm conclusion on the mechanism for the production of these sounds from meteors, except for attributing them to an "electromagnetic disturbance" and recommending that "the properties of the plasma sheath and ionized wake [of the meteor] should be the subject of further research".

But still, many meteor scientists – perhaps unconvinced by the Rand report's inability to propose a solid mechanism to explain the phenomenon – continued to stick with the psychological explanation for witness reports of electrophonic sounds from fireballs.

Keay to the Mystery

As with the L'Aigle meteorite fall – a momentous event which provoked the interest of a meticulous scientist and led to scientific acceptance of the idea that stones fell from the sky – one particular fireball event led to the involvement of another meticulous, open-minded scientist who would bring widespread acceptance to the study of the electrophonic meteor phenomenon.

About an hour and a half before sunrise on the morning of April 7th 1978, night suddenly turned to day near the city of Sydney, Australia, as a massive fireball crossed the sky, reaching a maximum brightness of at least -15 magnitude – so bright that some observers were temporarily blinded by it. In 1958 Soviet scientist Professor I.S. Astapovich had noted after studying witness reports that "only bolides brighter than -9 absolute visual magnitude produce sustained electrophonic sounds", so it is of little surprise that many witnesses on the ground in Sydney reported hearing strange noises while viewing this meteor overhead (the lower the number, the greater the visual magnitude).

Professor Colin Keay of the University of Newcastle (Australia) was intrigued when he read this flood of reports, though he admits that, like many others, he at first "rather fashionably dismissed these as a psychological effect". However, he was "persuaded otherwise" by a number of witness reports which clearly noted that the sound was heard before the fireball was seen.

> At Rose Bay, Sydney, 20km from the ground track of the bolide, S. McGrath "Heard a bang before seeing the light. It was like a person in the next apartment slamming a door like a screen door: rather rattley but not loud." This witness had time to get to a window and watch the bolide recede and disappear.
>
> At Edgecliff, Sydney, 20km from the ground track, A. Hayes "Heard a noise like an express train or bus travelling at high speed. Next an electrical crackling sound, then our backyard was as light as day."
>
> At Vales Point, 40km from the ground track, J. Ireland "Heard a sound like an approaching vehicle and saw a flash of light (from behind his right shoulder) as everything was lit up like daylight."
>
> At Kotara, Newcastle, 40km from the ground track, N. Jones heard a noise like a "phut" when the bolide flared, but "It was not loud enough to wake anyone." However a friend standing by the door on the other side of their car heard nothing.
>
> Other impressions of the sound simultaneous with the sighting were "a loud swishing noise"; "a humming sound like a transformer or distant siren"; "like steam hissing out of a railway engine for a count of about ten"; "a swishing sound like the onset of an unexpected high wind"; and "a low moaning, whooshing transcribable on a tape recorder."[8]

To Keay, it was obvious from the witness reports that "the psychological explanation was not realistic and a physical explanation had to be sought." It began a quest that became a life-long obsession for Keay, right up until his passing in August 2015, and which helped bring electrophonic meteor sounds into the bounds of accepted science.

Keay's research found that for about ten percent of those who witness a very luminous meteor fireball, "the mental impression is heightened by strange swishing, hissing and popping noises coincident with its passage across the sky".[9] He theorized that the answer to this mystery was in VLF (very low frequency) electromagnetic waves, suggesting that they were emitted by bright fireballs, and – following other researchers such as Udden, Weaver and Nininger – that this energy, traveling at the speed of light, not sound, was then "transduced by mundane objects such as frizzy hair or grass or pine needles" in the vicinity of the observer, thus producing the anomalous 'instantaneous' sounds.

Putting forward a theory is easy, but providing actual evidence is a little more difficult – meteors are unpredictable, and our environment is awash in electromagnetic radiation. But in 2014 – more than three decades after Keay first published his thoughts – scientists might have accidentally unearthed some. Researchers at the University of New Mexico were searching for mysterious events called radio bursts in 11,000 hours of data recorded by an observatory in New Mexico. These radio bursts manifest as points of radiation in images, but during their analysis the researchers also found ten 'smudges' right across the sky, similar to that of a fireball path, at low frequencies. Intrigued, they consulted a NASA telescope survey that records meteors, and found that these smudges did indeed correlate with known fireballs.[10]

And Keay himself has demonstrated that his transduction hypothesis works: in a laboratory, he created rustling sounds in objects including hair, wires, pine needles, and aluminium foil simply by exposing them to VLF radiation.

More difficult to figure out though is the mechanism that might be *producing* these low-frequency waves. As one paper on the topic put it: "the question of the generation mechanism of low-frequency electromagnetic radiation from meteors is nontrivial":

The most accepted theory of meteor ELF/VLF emission was introduced by Keay [1980a] and theoretically refined by Bronshten [1983]. The EM waves are produced by trapping and tangling of the Earth's magnetic field in the turbulent plasma wake of an ablating meteoroid. The main prerequisite of the theory is that the meteor plasma should enter the turbulent flow regime. This means that the theory is applicable only for slow and luminous bolides (absolute magnitude brighter than 12m), which are penetrating deep into the atmosphere (below heights of 20 km), i.e., type 1 electrophones.

In order to explain type 2 electrophones, Keay [1992b] suggested a refinement to his theory in which the VLF radio burst is produced by explosive disintegration of a fireball. According to this theory, even the meteors dimmer then 6m are capable of producing electrophones.

Recently, an alternative theory to explain type 2 electrophones was suggested by Beech and Foschini [1999]. The theory proposes that the charge separation takes place during the airburst of the meteoroid due to propagating shock wave through ionized meteor plasma. Rapid and strong electric fields are produced by the charge separation and they produce low-frequency EM radiation.[11]

Another more recent suggestion is that fireballs trigger unidentified, powerful atmospheric phenomenon at the boundaries of the ionosphere's layers. The idea that electromagnetic bursts might be produced by meteors interacting with the ionosphere has some support by observations of 'sprites' that appear to have been triggered by the entry of meteors into the atmosphere. The basic idea behind this theory might be supported by the fact that another atmospheric phenomenon – the aurorae – have also been found to produce anomalous sounds similar to electrophonic meteors.

Still, at the time of writing none of these theories has been proven, and so the mechanism that produces the VLF waves during the passage of fireballs across the sky remains a mystery.

Et tu, Spacecraft?

It's interesting to compare the history of reports of, and research into, electrophonic meteors with that of the UFO phenomenon. Witness reports of electrophonic meteors were dismissed by scientists as nonsense, just as UFO sightings still are. Electrophonic meteors were said to exhibit impossible behaviour (instantaneous sounds), as do UFOs (physically impossible manoeuvres). Both occur suddenly, without notice, usually to witnesses alone or in small groups in remote (dark) areas and/or in the middle of the night who provided 'anecdotes' rather than 'evidence'. Both are also capricious, in the manner in which multiple witnesses in the same group can report different things. And the mechanism or cause behind each phenomenon remain mysteries as well.

It's rather ironic, then, that Colin Keay, alongside his research into electrophonic meteors, was also involved with organized skepticism – which, given the similarities between UFOs and electrophonic meteors noted above – can only have led to occasional moments of cognitive dissonance. In a podcast interview[12] with noted Australian skeptic Richard Saunders about electrophonic meteors, Keay was moved to make a comment that is a staple in many UFO debates/arguments. "Some very notable people have reported them…so many people can't be wrong you might say," Keay noted. Saunders responded with a common skeptical retort to that claim, saying "well usually in the sceptical field we say it doesn't matter, because a lot of people can be wrong." Keay then defended his statement by replying, "Yes but when a lot of people with observational experience report it, you can't discount it."

Keay is not the only skeptic to have 'taken the side' of the anomaly in this case. Respected science journalist and UFO skeptic Jim Oberg assisted Colin Keay in investigating another "remarkable fact" related to electrophonic meteors: that witnesses have also reported these sounds being emitted by space shuttles during re-entry into Earth's atmosphere.

> The spectacular reentry of the Space Shuttle Discovery was observed by many Texans in the pre-dawn skies. Among these were Ben and Jeannette Killingsworth. As they observed the Space Shuttle streak across the sky, *"they both heard an unmistakable 'swishing noise' as it passed* south of their rural Galveston County home. The sonic boom came several minutes later – *but the swishing sound occurred simultaneously with the visual apparition*... Ben graphically described the sounds as 'like a skier coming down a slope,' but with a rapid fluctuation in loudness, 'about two or three hertz.' Jeannette compared the faint sound to the noise made by a fast boat as it slaps across waves on a choppy lake. 'But there was no motor noise,' she added, 'just a sound like repeated puffs of air through your mouth'."[13]

In the comments to an article on the popular UFO/conspiracy site AboveTopSecret.com, Oberg noted that electrophonic sounds are "a wonderful mystery of nature with a lot to teach serious ufologists", demonstrating that genuine mysteries rejected by orthodox scientists can be solved, if approached in the right manner:

> I think the primary lesson of this recently-validated phenomenon is that the eyewitnesses were right and the know-it-all scientists were wrong in proclaiming they could NOT have experienced what they described because it was contrary to science. Sound familiar?
>
> I don't doubt that Bill Nye would have lectured any witness severely for being over excitable and unscientific in even THINKING that sound could come from a distant fireball. Idiots all, these hicks. But the witnesses were NOT the idiots in this matter.
>
> The second lesson is the value that amateur observers and heretical researchers brought to the subject.
>
> The third lesson is that such "fringe phenomena" CAN succumb to research even over the objections of the scientific establishment, if reliable records and catalogs are compiled and distributed.
>
> Do the field work and do the raw report documentation – and the validation to weed out any unreliable or questionable reports.[14]

Beyond the larger similarities between the areas of research though, it's perhaps worth returning to the detail of these 'impossible' sounds being emitted by spacecraft entering Earth's atmosphere – because, strangely enough, there are numerous similarities with noises reported during UFO sightings. In both cases, a variety of the same sounds have been reported, including humming, hissing, buzzing, swishing and 'rushing wind' noises.

Some of the detailed reports of these sounds illustrate the similarities quite clearly. For example, just as the space shuttle was said to make a "swishing" sound by witnesses Ben and Jeannette Killingsworth (in the account mentioned earlier), and just as a witness to the 2001 Leonids reported seeing "a bright meteor pass by in the SE…It made a kind of swish noise as it passed by", so too do we find UFO reports – such as the following sighting report of Charles Early – that mention this same sound:

> Early was raking leaves at his home in Greenfield Massachusetts, under a clear sky, when *he heard a "swishing noise" as if a wind storm was coming.* He looked up and saw two rings parallel to each other, one on top of the other separated by a distance of about 4 feet. He estimated the diameter to be about 30 feet and described them as "bright, like polished chrome" and tubular.

Compare the italicised part of the report above to a description of the electrophonic sound emitted by the 1978 Sydney fireball (collected by Colin Keay): "a swishing sound like the onset of an unexpected high wind". And beyond the strikingly similar phrasing of the sound made, we also see that – just as with many electrophonic meteor reports – it was this sound that caused Early to look up and witness the object.

So too with another electrophonic meteor account, but this time of a different sound, made by the Murchison meteorite as it flew over Victoria, Australia in 1969:

> [A] lady … while spending the morning tending her garden, was startled by a hissing noise that reminded her rather strongly *of car tyres being driven over a wet road.* The noise seemed to emanate from a southerly direction and, there being neither cars nor roads nor excessive moisture in that immediate vicinity, she deemed it sufficiently odd to glance up from her gardening and investigate what could be making such a sound.

Compare the italicised portion of the above account to the famous 'close encounter' of Joe Simonton, which began with what the 60-year-old chicken farmer described as the noise of "tyres on a wet pavement", before spotting a silvery object like "two wash bowls turned face to face" hovering just above the ground.

I'm obviously not suggesting that UFO reports are all mistaken meteor sightings. Instead, the question is this: does this suggest that there is a VLF component to some of these unidentified object sightings in which similar noises are heard. And if so, does this suggest a validity to the UFO reports with this component?

Is there any other evidence to support a connection between the phenomena of electrophonic meteors and UFOs? This Australian meteor report contains something interesting:

> The Wiluna Meteorite was observed to fall on September 2, 1967 at 22:46 hrs. Along with sonic phenomena, a fireball was seen. An estimated 1,000 stones fell over an arid sheep grazing area approximately five miles east of the Wiluna Township, Western Australia. Almost the entire town (including people from surrounding stations [ranches]) was gathered in the outdoor movie house when the fireball came over. *They heard electrophonic sounds* – crackling and hissing while the fireball was visible and incandescent. *The diesel generator which powers the town cut out, and when the policeman went to jump in his Landcruiser and investigate, it would not start until well after the fireball was over.*[15]

Engines stopping as an object flies overhead – anybody that has read through UFO literature, or at least watched *Close Encounters of the Third Kind*, will be familiar with this famous aspect.[16] In one well-known case, the 1957 Levelland sightings, there were seven separate reports of "car disablement and subsequent rapid, automatic recovery after the passage of the strange illuminated craft".[17] And in a number of 'engine stoppage' encounters, we find a confluence of both engine- or electronics-related problems, and anomalous sounds. For example:

> About five kilometres out of town his surroundings were illuminated by an orange hue. *Suddenly the engine stopped and the lights went out. The ignition light on the dashboard failed to come on, and despite efforts the engine could not be restarted.* He steered the car to the side of the road and braked to a halt. Getting out he saw, at fifty metres altitude, an oval shape with three to four "windows". It was stationary, almost directly above the car. It remained motionless for two to three minutes *with a continuous buzzing sound being audible.*[18,19]

Interestingly, during Colin Keay's research into the possible mechanism behind electrophonic meteor sounds, he noted that soldiers in bunkers sited in the vicinity of nuclear tests sometimes reported a "click" sound as the blast occurred, at the same time as "an intense burst of radio emission...of sufficient intensity to burn out electronic equipment".[20]

In fact, once you start reading through scientific papers on electrophonic meteors you find yourself stumbling across all sorts of interesting 'additional' aspects that are bound to make Forteans sit up and take notice:

> Appearance of smell simultaneously with a bright meteor has a similar history. There is one...report mentioning a smell of sulphur, one of ozone, and one of "lightning" (probably also ozone)... The smell of sulphur and onion was reported during the 1833 Leonids. More recently, a "foul metallic, chemical or sulphurous odor" was reported to accompany the flight of the Tagish Lake meteorite in 2000.

> Another interesting unusual phenomenon related to an electrophonic fireball: a warm "puff of wind ... towards the end

of the duration of the sound". Similar tactile phenomena like "oscillations and shaking of the air" or "oppression of air" have been reported since the beginning of the history of electrophonic phenomenon.

[A witness reported that he] woke up and went to a window for no reason, probably because of a "stimulus of some sort".[21]

This is a whole other rabbit hole to go down, so I won't linger on it long in this essay. But those that have read my previous article on sounds heard during paranormal and Fortean encounters ("Her Sweet Murmur: Exploring the Aural Phenomenology of Border Experiences", in *Darklore Volume 1*) will notice that many of the anomalous sounds of electrophonic meteors – buzzing, hissing, swishing, 'rush of wind' – are strangely similar to those reported during 'Fortean' events of all kinds. The addition of the other elements mentioned above reinforces that perception even further. But why would there be any transducing of VLF sounds in Fortean events such as, say, a near-death experience? It seems to suggest we are looking at completely different 'sounds' that just happen to be similar in description. However, if we dig deeper, there is the remote possibility of a common thread.

Neuroscientist Michael Persinger has put forward the (admittedly controversial) theory that electric and electromagnetic fields "can create unstable conditions in the brain, especially the deep portions of the temporal lobes." Persinger suggests that this instability "can lead to hallucinatory experiences which people interpret in terms of their cultural and learning history as well as their private beliefs, so they are interpreted and then seen as spirits, the Virgin Mary, angels, alien spacecraft or ghosts."[22]

In "Her Sweet Murmur" I mentioned the similarities of 'paranormal' sounds to those reported by sufferers of temporal lobe epilepsy – so perhaps there could indeed be some relationship. Is it possible that electrophonic meteors point the way to a new approach to understanding paranormal experiences, framing them in terms of temporal lobe stimulation? It seems unlikely, but if there's anything that the history of research into meteors should teach us, it's that we shouldn't dismiss anomalies, but instead pay attention to eyewitness reports, look for patterns, think critically, all the while having an open mind to all the possibilities.

Greg Taylor is the owner and editor of the online alternative news portal, *The Daily Grail* (www.dailygrail.com), and is also the editor of *Darklore*. He is widely read in topics that challenge the orthodox worldview, from alternative history to the mysteries of human consciousness. Greg currently resides in Brisbane, Australia. His most recent book *Stop Worrying! There Probably is an Afterlife* is an exploration of the evidence for the survival of consciousness after death.

The History and Practice of English Magic

Folklore and fairies, magic and madness, as seen through the mirror of Susanna Clarke's acclaimed fantasy novel, *Jonathan Strange and Mr Norrell*

by *John Reppion*

In March 2006 my wife, Leah, and I flew over to Dublin, Ireland for the first time in either of our lives as guests at the third annual Phoenix Convention (or P-Con, as most people knew it). The guest of honour that year was Susanna Clarke – author of *Jonathan Strange & Mr. Norrell* which had, at that point, already been out for eighteen months and won a Hugo Award. I, a chronically slow reader at the best of times, had not yet started reading the 800ish page novel, and I think that Leah was only part of the way through it. Nevertheless, we found that we got on well with Susanna and her partner, sci-fi writer Colin Greenland – who were both lovely, charming and funny – and the brief time we spent together over the course of the con was very enjoyable. It was perhaps two years later that I finally finished reading *Jonathan Strange & Mr. Norrell*. I have on only a couple of occasions in my life finished a book and at once turned to the front to begin reading it again. I thought about doing that with *Strange & Norrell* but I am, as I have said, a very slow reader. Instead I immediately downloaded the thirty-two-hour-long audio-book version, which to date I have listened to perhaps three or four times.

In a piece entitled "Why I Love Jonathan Strange and Mr. Norrell" published on the Guardian website in May 2015, Neil Gaiman recalled writing to the book's editor to say that it was, in his opinion, "the finest work of English fantasy written in the past seventy years".[1] I am not so widely read as Mr. Gaiman and I don't pretend to be an expert in such matters, but what I can say with certainty is that I, like Neil, love *Strange & Norrell*. The blend of alt. history and fantasy, the handling of Englishness and of English Magic, of otherness and madness, the subtlety, the comedy, the eeriness, the epicness – in every sense; all these factors combine to make *Jonathan Strange & Mr. Norrell* a work which does not so much stand apart as it does occupy a space that seems no other work could ever fill. It is as though a *Strange & Norrell*-sized gap waited hungrily on some shelf in the realm of forms up until a decade or so ago.

In November 2012, the BBC announced that an adaptation of *Jonathan Strange & Mr Norrell* had been commissioned for BBC One. The production was officially greenlit as a seven hour miniseries in April 2013, with a projected 2014 premiere date.[2] As it was, the series (adapted by British playwright and screenwriter Peter Harness) actually premiered in May 2015. Clarke's wonderful world of magicians – theoretical, practical, and street – beamed into living-rooms across this scepter'd isle, and soon after, thanks to BBC America, beyond. The series introduced a whole new audience to Messrs. Strange and Norrell, and rekindled the interest of many who had enjoyed the book previously. This renewed interest in *Strange & Norrell* provided me with an opportunity to pluck out some of the more easily disentangled fragments of folklore, magic, and the like from Clarke's incredibly rich text and inspect them more closely in a series of articles originally published on The Daily Grail (www.dailygrail.com), now collected, polished, and presented here for your consideration.

The Language of Birds

We are, at the opening of *Strange & Norrell,* introduced to the Learned Society of York Magicians, all of whom are theoretical magicians. As their president Dr. Foxcastle explains it:

> [Theoretical] magicians study magic. The history of magic. We do not perform it. We don't expect an astronomer to create stars, or a Botanist to invent new flowers.

The York Magicians are gentlemen historians, antiquarians who would never dream of casting a spell of their own, yet they have studied, discussed, and written upon the subject. The precious few texts the York Society have to examine are chiefly those deemed unworthy to reside within the prodigious library at Hurtfew Abbey belonging to Mr. Gilbert Norrell.

Susanna Clarke provides extensive footnotes (near two-hundred in total) throughout her book, outlining an entire fictional history and corpus of magical scholarship. She divides what we may think of as Magic Books into two broad categories: Books of Magic and Books on Magic. The former were largely written pre-17th century during the era of the potent Golden Age magicians. The latter mostly date post-17th century, written by the less accomplished (sometimes wholly powerless) Silver Age magicians and those who followed them. Books of Magic are of the greatest interest to the practical magician, leaving only Books on Magic (and precious few even of them) for theoretical magicians to study.

More than thirty Magic Books (and papers) are mentioned in *Strange & Norrell.* Several, such as *How to putte Questions to the*

Dark and understand its Answeres, and *Gatekeeper of Apollo,* are mere titles but we do get considerably more detail about a handful of others. One of the most intriguing of these is *Treatise concerning the Language of Birds* by Thomas Lanchester, upon whose possible contents and origins it might be fun to speculate a little here.

> There is nothing else in magic but the wild thought of the bird as it casts itself into the void. There is no creature upon the earth with such potential for magic. Even the least of them may fly straight out of this world and come by chance to the Other Lands. Where does the wind come from that blows upon your face, that fans the pages of your book? Where the harum-scarum magic of small wild creatures meets the magic of Man, where the language of the wind and the rain and the trees can be understood, there we will find the Raven King.
>
> – from *Treatise concerning the Language of Birds by Thomas Lanchester*

In Kabbalah, Renaissance Magic, and Alchemy, the language of the birds was considered a secret divine language and the key to perfect knowledge. In this context the language of birds was also sometimes also referred to as the *langue verte,* or Green Language.

In Norse mythology a taste of dragon's blood could grant the consumer the gift of understanding the birds as, according to the *Poetic Edda* and the *Völsunga Saga,* it did for the hero Sigurd. Sigurd's story is also depicted in the eleventh century Ramsund carving in Sweden.

In the old folk tales of Wales, Germany, Greece, and beyond there is a long tradition of protagonists being granted the gift of understanding the birds by some magical means. The birds then invariably go on to inform or warn the hero about some danger or hidden treasure following the same patten as the stories of Sigurd (the Russian folk tale "The Language of the Birds" is another example).

The Sigurd Stone located at Gök in Sweden (Sö 327)

In writings by and upon the ancient Greeks the ability to understand birds is often attributed (though perhaps metaphorically) to real people such as the philosophers Democritus, Anaximander, and Apollonius of Tyana, as well as to mythical figures like the soothsayer Melampus.

> Most wonderful is that kind of Auguring of theirs, who hear, & understand the speeches of Animals, in which as amongst the Ancients, Melampus, and Tiresias, and Thales, and Apollonius the Tyanean [Apollonius of Tyana], who as we read, excelled, and whom they report had excellent skill in the language of birds: of whom Philostratus, and Porphyrius [Porphyry] speak, saying, that of old when Apollonius sate in company amongst his friends, seeing Sparrows sitting upon a tree, and one Sparrow coming from elsewhere unto them, making a great chattering and noise, and then flying away, all the rest following him, he said to his companions, that that Sparrow told the rest that an Asse being burdened with wheat fell down in a hole neer the City, and that the wheat was scattered upon the ground: many being much moved with these

words, went to see, and so it was, as Apollonius said, at which they much wondered.

– from *De Occulta Philosophia Libri III* by Heinrich Cornelius Agrippa von Nettesheim, 1533[3]

Tiresias was one of the most celebrated soothsayers of the early ages of Greece. He lived in the times of Oedipus, and the war of the seven chiefs against Thebes. He was afflicted by the Gods with blindness, in consequence of some displeasure they conceived against him; but in compensation they endowed him beyond all other mortals with the gift of prophecy. He is said to have understood the language of birds. He possessed the art of divining future events from the various indications that manifest themselves in fire, in smoke, and in other ways but to have set the highest value upon the communications of the dead, whom by spells and incantations he constrained to appear and answer his inquiries and he is represented as pouring out tremendous menaces against them, when they showed themselves tardy to attend upon his commands.

– from *Lives of the Necromancers: or, An account of the most eminent persons in successive ages, who have claimed for themselves, or to whom has been imputed by others, the exercise of magical power* by William Godwin, 1834[4]

The belief that the vocalisations and behaviours of birds are indicators of things yet to come runs deep. In England we have the tradition that if the Tower of London ravens (once-wild birds attracted by ready supply of carrion supplied by executions, now tame corvids with clipped wings) leave, the Crown will fall and Britain with it. The 18th century *One for Sorrow* rhyme is another example, still recited by many upon sighting a gathering of magpies (which is, after all, called a tiding). Birds do speak, of course, and there are still those who understand them.

A study conducted in Yellowstone National Park in 2002 recorded ravens socializing with wolves even when there was no potential prey or carrion present. The ravens were seen swooping down to pull wolves' tails, interacting with wolf pups at den sites and engaging in playful chasing. Bernd Heinrich, author of *Mind of the Raven, Investigations and Adventures with Wolf-Birds,* and advisor on the study, also frequently observed ravens hunting with wolves. This relationship between the two species was deemed especially interesting considering that wolves were absent from Yellowstone National Park for nearly seventy years, until their reintroduction in the mid-1990s.[5] Our own bond with the ancestors of today's domestic dogs began during the Stone Age, when humans were hunter gatherers working with the canines to secure food for the two species, just as the ravens and wolves still do. Tales of hunting interaction involving wolves, ravens, and humans figure in the storytelling of Tlingit and Inuit Native American tribes of the Pacific Northwest and Alaska. Some of these stories describe the birds tipping in flight, effectively pointing with their wings, to direct hunters to caribou.

Today there are fifteen species of honeybird in Africa and, as you might deduce from their name, they're quite interested in bees and their nests. In truth it is not so much the honey the birds are after as the larvae and wax contained within the hive. Breaking into a nest to get at the honey comb is a nigh on impossible task for these relatively small birds, which is why they talk to humans. First formally studied in the 1980s, the nomadic Boran people of Kenya have a long-standing agreement with the honeybirds of that region.

> Each partner knows how to get the other's attention. To attract the birds, the Borans call them with a penetrating whistle (known in the Boran language as Fuulido) that can be heard over distances greater than a kilometer and that is made by blowing air into clasped fists, modified snail shells, or hollowed-out palm nuts. Comparably, hungry honeyguides flag down humans by flying

up close, moving restlessly from perch to perch, and emitting a double-noted, persistent "tirr-tirr-tirr-tirr" call.[6]

The bird flies along before perching on a branch, waiting for the human to catch up, then flies on again, leading the would be honey gatherer on toward the nearest hive. The behaviour and calls of the honeybird (or honeyguide as they are also known) also indicate other factors like the distance of the hive from the current location. Arriving at the nest (which is still often unseen by the person following) the honeyguide gives a new call and once again modifies its behaviour.

> This call differs from the previous guiding call in that it has a softer tone, with longer intervals between successive notes. There is also a diminished response, if any at all, to whistling and shouting by humans. After a few indication calls, the bird remains silent. When approached by the searching gatherer, it flies to another perch close by, sometimes after circling around the nest. The resulting flight path finally reveals the location of the colony to the gatherer. [...] After using smoky fires to reduce the bees' aggression, the Boran honey gatherers use tools or their hands to remove the honey comb, and then break off pieces to be shared with their honeyguide partners.[7]

In so many of the old stories the idea is that, through the power of flight (in itself seemingly magical and unobtainable), birds could travel vast distances, see things no human eye could, and report back to one who spoke their language. One could argue that, in the 21st century, drones are beginning to practically fill the role of Odin's legendary Hugin and Munin. Yet drones are mindless, soulless things, alien invaders in any natural landscape, whereas birds have been here far, far longer than we humans. No longer, as in my youth, do we describe the dinosaurs as having died out – not completely, at least – because birds are now classified as modern theropod dinosaurs. In a paper published in August 2015, scientists reported a new fossilised specimen of a previously undiscovered feathered bird species, *Archaeornithura meemannae,* which lived roughly 130.7 million years ago in northeastern China.[8] That is 128 million years older than the oldest human remains which were discovered in Ethiopia recently.[9] Their ancestors were the closest things to dragons that ever lived, soaring high above everything while our shrew-like furry forebears squeaked and scurried for cover. They must have looked up into the sky in fear at first but over time, generation after generation after generation after generation, that fear turned to awe. How did they move through the air? Forces and powers they could not comprehend, things outside of their own nature and experience. Magic. What did they see? What did they know? If only, thought the hominid, we could speak the language of the birds.

On Fairies and Witchcraft

The word fairy derives from Middle English *faierie* (also *fayerye, feirie, fairie*), a direct borrowing from Old French *faerie* (Modern French *féerie*) meaning the land, realm, or characteristic activity (i.e. enchantment) of the legendary people of folklore and romance called (in Old French) *faie* or *fee* (Modern French *fée*). In *Jonathan Strange & Mr. Norrell* Faerie (or the Other Lands as some magicians call them), the home of the fairies, is an Otherworld realm connected to England by magical means. Clarke's Faerie is a large land with many kingdoms and territories. There is Lost-Hope, the home (or *brugh*) of the fairy known only as 'The Gentleman With The Thistle-Down Hair', which at times borders or intersects with real world locations such as Sir Walter Pole's Harley-street home. The Gentleman's other kingdoms include The City of Iron Angels, and a place called Blue Castles. There is Pity-Me ("a miserable little place" according to The Gentleman) which, oddly enough, has the name of a real village in Durham, England; "a whimsical name bestowed in the 19th century on a place considered desolate, exposed or difficult to cultivate" according to the Oxford

Dictionary of British Place Names. There is also Untold Blessings ("a fine place, with dark, impenetrable forests, lonely mountains and uncrossable seas"). John Uskglass – the almighty 12th century magician known as the Raven King – is held to have possessed three kingdoms: one in England, one in Faerie (the name of which is not given) and "a strange country on the far side of Hell" sometimes called the Bitter Lands. Indeed, relations between Faerie and Hell are well established, not least in Scottish folk tradition where "the *teind*" (tithe) must be paid by the former to the latter every seven years. Mortals who have strayed into the Other Lands are sometimes taken as payment, as hinted at in the 16th century ballad of Tam Lin and the 15th century romance of Thomas the Rhymer (itself later condensed into a ballad). Though the teind itself is not mentioned in Susanna Clarke's book, it is briefly referred to in the third episode of the television series.

It may surprise you to learn that, in Britain, consorting with fairies was once a capital offence. Midwife Bessie Dunlop, a resident of Dalry, Scotland was burned at the stake in 1576 after admitting to receiving magical tuition from a fae Queen of the "Court of Elphyne" (elfland or fairyland).[10] Allison Peirson (or Pearson) of Fife, Scotland was likewise punished for the same offence seven years later. In a 1583 ballad written about the then Bishop of St. Andrews, Patrick Adamson, the Scottish balladeer Robert Semphill makes reference to the scandal surrounding the trial of Allison Pearson when it was discovered that Adamson had sought advice from the magician (or witch as the court called her). In Semphill's ballad he has Pearson taking part in the 'Fairy Rade' described in Thomas Keighley's 1870 work *The Fairy Mythology* thusly:

> The Fairy Rade, or procession, was a matter of great importance. It took place on the coming in of summer, awl the peasantry, by using the precaution of placing a branch of rowan over their door, might safely gaze on the cavalcade, as with music sounding, bridles ringing, and voices mingling, it pursued its way from place to place.[11]

Semphill's version of the trooping of the fae seems to have been mixed up with the witches Sabbath, the event even taking place on Halloween rather than the eve of the Summer. The 16th and 17th centuries – while at the tail end of the Golden Age of Magic in *Strange & Norrell* – were not a good period to be a practitioner of magic in Britain. In England, Scotland and Ireland, a series of Witchcraft Acts enshrined into law the punishment (usually death, sometimes incarceration) of individuals practising, or claiming to practise magic. Many books were written upon the subject of magic and the detection of those who practised it at the time and among them was King James VI of Scotland (later also James I of England)'s *Daemonologie, In Forme of a Dialogie* (written as a conversation between two characters named Philomathes and Epistemon). Published in 1599 the work was divided into three parts, the last of which is entitled *The Description Of All These Kindes Of Spirites That Troubles Men Or Women*. In the fifth chapter of this book, *The Description Of The Fourth Kinde Of Spirites Called The Phairie: What Is Possible Therein, And What Is But Illusiones,* Epistemon makes it clear that he (and therefore King James) believes that fairies and the

From *The History of Witches and Wizards,* 1720

Other Lands are mere illusions created by the Devil to trick humans. The old beliefs, stories, and practices are dismissed in one fell swoop: anything non-Christian is automatically anti-Christian and therefore the work of the Arch Fiend itself. Faerie and Hell no longer near neighbours but, in the eyes of the King and his loyal subjects, the self-same place. So it was that for centuries there was no magic in Britain, only Witchcraft. No magicians, only witches.

Witches (as opposed to magicians) are mentioned as such only two or three times in *Strange & Norrell,* the practical magician Mr. Gilbert Norrell describing them as "those half-fairy, half-human women to whom malicious people were used to apply when they wished to harm their neighbours". Clearly they are, or were, not respectable in Norrell's estimation – but then he is a man who disapproves of almost all magic that is not done by himself. Are, or were, there then any female magicians? The story of *"The Master of Nottingham's daughter",* an adventure concerning a magical ring and a wicked sorceress named Margaret Ford, appears in one of Susanna Clarke's ample footnotes for Chapter Twenty-five. It is quite a long story, very much in the Fairy Tale tradition but, at its conclusion, we are given the following information:

> There is another version of this story which contains no magic ring, no eternally-burning wood, no phoenix – no miracles at all, in fact. According to this version Margaret Ford and the Master of Nottingham's daughter (whose name was Donata Torel) were not enemies at all, but the leaders of a fellowship of female magicians that flourished in Nottinghamshire in the twelfth century. Hugh Torel, the Master of Nottingham, opposed the fellowship and took great pains to destroy it (though his own daughter was a member). He very nearly succeeded, until the women left their homes and fathers and husbands and went to live in the woods under the protection of Thomas Godbless, a much greater magician than Hugh Torel. This less colourful version of the story has never been

as popular as the other but it is this version which Jonathan Strange said was the true and which he included in *The History and Practice of English Magic*.

The world of gentlemen magicians is an undeniably patriarchal one then, yet so too was the historical era in which *Strange & Norrell* is set. Even so, it is perhaps interesting to note that the enchanting Fairy Queen, ruler of Faerie of our own traditions, seems to have been replaced by Clarke with a host of male fairy Kings, Dukes, and so on. In *Strange & Norrell*'s alternative history the witch-trials never happened; magic instead being, if not celebrated, then feared and respected during the Raven King's reign over Northern England (the area between the rivers Tweed and Trent) which lasted from 1111 up until his disappearance in 1434. Even so, with magic in decline – both in employment generally and in potency when employed – in the centuries after the Raven King's departure, it seems people did find cause to speak and write against it. Published in 1698, skeptical magio-historian Valentine Munday's *The Blue Book: being an attempt to expose the most prevalent lies and common deceptions practised by English magicians upon the King's subjects and upon each other* denied the existence of the Other Lands entirely and stated that anyone who claimed to have visited them was, not in league with Satan as King James would have had them, but merely a liar. In the mannerly world of *Strange & Norrell* the ruining of his or her reputation seems to be very worst punishment that could be levelled against any magician then.

Away with the Fairies

In *Strange & Norrell* the practical magician Mr. Gilbert Norrell is very much anti-fairy and warns strongly against consulting with, or employing, them:

> A more poisonous race or one more inimical to England has never existed. There have been far too many magicians too idle or ignorant to pursue a proper course of study, who instead bent all their energies upon acquiring a fairy-servant and when they had got such a servant they depended upon him to complete all their business for them. English history is full of such men and some, I am glad to say, were punished for it as they deserved. Look at Bloodworth.

Simon Bloodworth's tale is given in one of Clarke's many wonderful footnotes (in chapter five of the book) and mentioned briefly in episode five of Harness' television adaptation. According to Clarke, Bloodworth was a none-too-impressive 14th century magician from Bradford on Avon who was one day unexpectedly offered the services of a fairy calling himself Buckler.

> As every English schoolchild nowadays can tell you, Bloodworth would have done better to have inquired further and to have probed a little deeper into who, precisely, Buckler was, and why, exactly, he had come out of Faerie with no other aim than to become the servant of a third-rate English magician.

Buckler did ever more and ever better magic upon Bloodworth's behalf, and as he did so he grew stronger. Soon the fairy took on a larger, more human, appearance ("his thin, piebald fox-face became a pale and handsome human one") which he claimed to be his true form, the former being merely an enchantment.

> On a fine May morning in 1310 when Bloodworth was away from home Mrs Bloodworth discovered a tall cupboard standing in the corner of her kitchen where no cupboard had ever been before. When she asked Buckler about it, he said immediately that it was a magical cupboard and that he had brought it there.

Buckler told Mrs. Bloodworth that it pained him to see her and her daughters slaving away washing and cleaning all day long. If she would but step into the cupboard, he said, she would be transported to a place where she might learn spells which "would make any work finished in an instant, make her appear beautiful in the eyes of all who beheld her, make large piles of gold appear whenever she wished it, make her husband obey her in all things" and so on and so on.

> Seventeen people entered Buckler's cupboard that morning and were never seen again in England; among them were Mrs Bloodworth, her two youngest daughters, her two maids and two manservants, Mrs Bloodworth's uncle and six neighbours.

Two hundred years later, author of *De Tractatu Magicarum Linguarum* (*On the Subject of Magical Languages*), the magician Dr. Martin Pale, entered Faerie and visited the brughs of fairies Cold Henry and John Hollyshoes. In the latter the doctor found an eight-year-old girl washing a great pile of dirty dishes. She said she had been told that when the things were clean she could go home to England. The girl thought she had been washing-up for two weeks or so and would be done in a day or two more. Pale recorded that the girl told him her name was Anne Bloodworth.

The danger of humans being lost, trapped, or even imprisoned in Faerie is a recurring theme throughout the old folk-tales of England, Ireland, Scotland, Wales, and beyond. In the 15th century romance of Thomas the Rhymer[12] the titular character meets and falls in love with the beautiful Queen of Elfland, travelling willingly with her upon a milk-white horse whose mane hung with bells. In his collection *Fairy and Folk Tales of the Irish Peasantry*, William Butler Yeats wrote the following, more detailed and much less pleasant sounding, description of what may be considered the same arrangement:

The Leanhaun Shee (fairy mistress), seeks the love of mortals. If they refuse, she must be their slave; if they consent, they are hers, and can only escape by finding another to take their place. The fairy lives on their life, and they waste away. Death is no escape from her. She is the Gaelic muse, for she gives inspiration to those she persecutes. The Gaelic poets die young, for she is restless, and will not let them remain long on earth – this malignant phantom.[13]

Others like Burd Ellen, sister of Rowland in the old English Fairy Tale *Childe Rowland,* stray into the Other Lands entirely by accident. Burd Ellen unintentionally ran around a church widdershins (anti-clockwise) and disappeared – taken to the Dark Tower by the King of Elfland. After seeking advice from the great magician Merlin, Rowland set out on a rather bloody quest to rescue his sister. One must never eat or drink in Faerie, as Merlin warns:

> Bite no bit, and drink no drop, however hungry or thirsty you are; drink a drop, or bite a bit, while in Elfland you be, and never will you see Middle Earth again.[14]

If fairy food is eaten then the devourer will be bound to remain in the Other Lands for an allotted time, just as Persephone daughter of Zeus and Demeter was doomed to remain half a year in Hades (the Greek Underworld which it may be noted shares characteristics with both Faerie and its near neighbour Hell) by the consumption of food there. This seems to have become a steadfast "fact" of fairy lore but, for my part, I cannot find reference earlier than *Childe Rowland* relating specifically to the fae.

Robert Kirk's 1691 book *The Secret Commonwealth of Elves, Fauns and Fairies* is regarded by many as one of the most important works on fairy lore ever committed to paper, yet it contains no reference to the perils of dining upon fairy foods. Kirk, it is said, paid a

heavy price for his involvement with the fairy folk, however. In his introduction to the 1893 edition the renowned folklorist Andrew Lang gave the following biographical account of the author and his strange demise.

> The Rev. Robert Kirk, the author of *The Secret Commonwealth*, was a student of theology at St. Andrews: his Master's degree, however, he took at Edinburgh. He was (and this is notable) the youngest and seventh son of Mr. James Kirk, minister of Aberfoyle, the place familiar to all readers of Rob Roy. As a seventh son, he was, no doubt, specially gifted, and in *The Secret Commonwealth* he lays some stress on […] By his first wife he had a son, Colin Kirk, W.S.; by his second wife, a son who was minister of Dornoch. He died (if he did die, which is disputed) in 1692, aged about fifty-one; his tomb was inscribed --
>
> ROBERTUS KIRK, A.M.
> *Linguæ Hiberniæ Lumen.*
>
> The tomb, in Scott's time, was to be seen in the east end of the churchyard of Aberfoyle; but the ashes of Mr. Kirk are not there. His successor, the Rev. Dr. Grahame, in his *Sketches of Picturesque Scenery*, informs us that, as Mr. Kirk was walking on a *dun-shi*, or fairy-hill, in his neighbourhood, he sunk down in a swoon, which was taken for death. "After the ceremony of a seeming funeral," writes Scott, "the form of the Rev. Robert Kirk appeared to a relation, and commanded him to go to Grahame of Duchray. 'Say to Duchray, who is my cousin as well as your own, that I am not dead, but a captive in Fairyland; and only one chance remains for my liberation. When the posthumous child, of which my wife has been delivered since my disappearance, shall be brought to baptism, I will appear in the room, when, if Duchray shall throw over my head the knife or dirk which he holds in his hand, I may

be restored to society; but if this is neglected, I am lost for ever.'" True to his tryst, Mr. Kirk did appear at the christening and "was visibly seen;" but Duchray was so astonished that he did not throw his dirk over the head of the appearance, and to society Mr. Kirk has not yet been restored. This is extremely to be regretted, as he could now add matter of much importance to his treatise. Neither history nor tradition has more to tell about Mr. Robert Kirk, who seems to have been a man of good family, a student, and, as his book shows, an innocent and learned person.[15]

The form that fell down as if in death upon Aberfoyle's Fairy Knowe was thought then to have been a "stock" or "fetch" or "waff": a mere magical facsimile of Kirk, created by the fairies to trick mortals into believing he had died while he was in fact in the Other Lands.[16]

Besides washing-up, what do these humans do while they're in Faerie? Well, many seem to spend an awful lot of time dancing.

It is, of course, to be noted that the modern Greek superstition of the Nereids, who carry off mortal girls to dance with them till they pine away, answers to some of our Fairy legends.[17]

Again, these are the words of Andrew Lang in his introductory notes to *The Secret Commonwealth*. *The Twelve Dancing Princesses* (or *The Worn-Out Dancing Shoes*, or *The Shoes that were Danced to Pieces*) is a German fairy tale originally published by the Brothers Grimm in 1812. In the story the princesses all sleep every night in the same locked room. Every morning, much to the confusion of the staff and their father the king, their dancing shoes are found to be worn through. This, it transpires is because every night the princesses sneak through a trapdoor in their bedroom floor down into the Fairy Realm where they travel to a fairy castle and dance with twelve fairy princes. Once discovered and proved this leads to the fae princes each being cursed for the same length of time they kept the young women dancing.

According to Mrs. Ella Mary Leather's 1913 collection *The Folklore and Witchcraft of Herefordshire,* girls were still dancing themselves (almost) to death in Faerie in the late 19th century. A seventy-five-year-old woman told Mrs. Leather that she remembered her mother telling of a first cousin of hers who was so passionately fond of dancing she who would visit any dance she heard of and could get to. One evening the young woman was walking home from such an occasion when she heard beautiful music coming from within a fairy ring (*elferingewort,* or "elf-ring" in Middle English; *ronds de sorciers,* or "sorcerers' rings" in French; and *Hexenringe* or "witches' rings" in German). Dancing into the ring, she immediately disappeared. Guessing what must have happened to her dance-crazed daughter, the mother knew that the only way to get her back was to wait outside the ring exactly one year after the vanishing. This she did and when her child reappeared suddenly within the ring the mother seized her in silence (so as not to bring herself to the attention of the fairies) and dragged her back into England. The young woman thought less than a day had elapsed – time in Faerie passing much slower than it does in our own realm. Mrs. Leather was told that the young woman went to work as a shop assistant in the market town of Kington, but was for the rest of her life prone to seeing fairies who would, apparently, steal from the shop. Though she warned the fairies they would be found out, the woman was careful not to say that she could see them in case, as in the tale of the *Fairy Ointment*, she was subsequently blinded by them.[18]

In *Strange & Norrell*, just as in tragic "true" tales such as those of Robertus Kirk and the dancing girl of Kington, fairy tale endings cannot be counted on it seems. In a letter to Mr. John Murray, on December 31st, 1816 (possibly unsent), the practical magician Jonathan Strange wrote:

> Stories of magicians freeing captives from Faerie are few and far between. I cannot now recall a single one. Somewhere in one of his books Martin Pale describes how fairies can grow tired of their human guests and expel them without warning from the brugh; the poor captives find themselves back home, but hundreds of years after they left it.

Whether little Anne Bloodworth ever made it back to England remains unrecorded.

Magic and Madness

"I am not at all surprised that you could not help His Majesty," said Mr Norrell. "I do not believe that even the Aureate magicians could cure madness. In fact I am not sure that they tried. They seem to have considered madness in quite a different light. They held madmen in a sort of reverence and thought they knew things sane men did not – things which might be useful to a magician. There are stories of both Ralph Stokesey and Catherine of Winchester consulting with madmen."

> "But it was not only magicians, surely?" said Strange. "Fairies too had a strong interest in madmen. I am sure I remember reading that somewhere."
>
> "Yes, indeed! Some of our most important writers have remarked upon the strong resemblance between madmen and fairies. Both are well known for talking without sense or connexion."

Talking without (seeming) sense or connection, in the world of *Strange & Norrell,* is one effect of what is referred to only as a "muffling spell": an enchantment signified by a phantom rose at the mouth of the subject (to those magically inclined enough to see it). The apparent nonsense spoken by those thus enchanted proves, in fact, to be old fairy and folk tales which, though unrelated to what the person is trying to say, are nevertheless coherently told. So it is that those who have had a muffling spell cast upon them may appear insane but not (necessarily) be so. Clearly, this can be read as a metaphor for depression, and any number of mental health conditions in which the sufferer feels unable to articulate their problems, or is unable to imagine them being understood (or taken seriously) if they do so.

Madness and otherness are themes that run throughout *Strange & Norrell*. In one footnote we are given a note on the thoughts of Richard Chaston (1620-95), an author who the practical magician Mr. Gilbert Norrell agrees with (on this matter, at least):

> Chaston wrote that men and Fairies both contain within them a faculty of reason and a faculty of magic. In men reason is strong and magic is weak. With fairies is the other way round: magic comes very naturally to them, but by human standards they are barely sane.

Here then, magic seems to be the very opposite of reason, but does that make it madness?

In Clarke's world fairies and Faerie may seem at first to be the opposite of Englishmen and England but, in fact, (as Chanston hints) they prove to be more like mirror images of the same; their characteristics merely inverted.

Strange & Norrell draws on various Romantic literary traditions and is set during the Romantic Era – an era when England was itself ruled over by "mad" King George III. The self-elected poster-boy of Romanticism Lord Byron was infamously described as "mad, bad, and dangerous to know" by Lady Caroline Lamb; a phrase which has become synonymous with hell-raising, raucous, rebellious behaviour ever since. Madness then, was and is an important part of the Romantic aesthetic.

> Poets cultivated the association among insanity, eccentricity, and genius in their life-styles and their work to distinguish themselves from the philistine public and from writers of lesser talent. [...] Two general reasons for the prevalence of genuine and feigned madness in this period were the increased acceptability of public displays of emotion and the cult of the genius poet.[19]

Yet while Byron's madness may have been something of an affectation, other poets such as William Blake, and Friedrich Hölderlin did unquestionably struggle with their mental health (the latter almost certainly being schizophrenic). Another was John Clare, the "Peasant Poet" from Northampton, who was in and out of asylums for much of his adult life.

> In 1837 he was admitted to Dr Allen's High Beech asylum near Epping and was reported as being "full of many strange delusions". He thought he was a prize fighter and that he had two wives, Patty and Mary [a girl Clare fell in love with as a boy but who, in reality, he seems to have never had any actual relationship with]. He started to claim he was Lord Byron. There

is an interesting letter that Dr Allen wrote about Clare to *The Times* in 1840:

'It is most singular that ever since he came... the moment he gets pen or pencil in hand he begins to write most poetical effusions. Yet he has never been able to obtain in conversation, nor even in writing prose, the appearance of sanity for two minutes or two lines together, and yet there is no indication of insanity in any of his poetry.'

An interesting picture of Clare during [his time at Northampton Asylum circa 1860] comes from the asylum superintendent, Dr Nesbitt, who wrote of his condition:

'It was characterised by visionary ideas and hallucinations. For instance he may be said to have lost his own personal identity as with the gravity of truth he would maintain that he had written the works of Byron, and Sir Walter Scott, that he was Nelson and Wellington, that he had fought and won the battle of Waterloo, that he had had his head shot off at this battle, whilst he was totally unable to explain the process by which it had been again affixed to his body.'[20]

Clare's own affliction apparently worked as the mirror opposite of the muffling spell of Clarke's world – him being able to speak with absolute clarity and mastery through one medium alone. The madman as genius in his single field of specialisation.

In a paper published in the *Journal of the Royal Society of Medicine* in 2001, Allan Beveridge wrote the following:

At the beginning of the nineteenth century, two major factors contributed to the awakening interest in the art of the insane—the Romantic movement, which identified madness as an exalted state allowing access to hidden realms; and the emergence of the asylum, which provided a location for the production of patient-art. Romanticism saw madness as a privileged condition: the madman, unrestrained by reason or by social convention, was perceived as having access to profound truths. The Romantics emphasized subjectivity and individualism, and hailed the madman as a hero, voyaging to new planes of reality. Although the equation of madness and genius originated with Plato, it was only in the nineteenth century that it became an important feature of cultural discourse. From the proposition that the genius was a kind of madman it was logical to ask whether the mad themselves create works of genius.[21]

The art of the insane, along with the art of children, and the "primitive" art of other cultures, were studied and admired by the likes of the Expressionists and the Surrealists. To them such art represented an absolute break from the conventions of western formalism – from the established etiquette and symbolism of art as it stood (just as the wild magic of fairies contrasts with Mr. Norrell's controlled, formalised English Magic). In the first *Surrealist Manifesto,* André Breton, the leading theorist of the movement, wrote:

> The confidences of madmen: I would spend my life in provoking them. They are people of a scrupulous honesty, and whose innocence is equalled only by mine.

A quotation worthy of Lord Byron himself in terms of its apparent pomposity.

One cannot write of magic, madness, fairies, and art and not include the tragic, talented Richard Dadd.

> Richard Dadd was born August 1, 1817 in Chatham, Kent, England. At age 13 the family moved to London, and in 1837, Dadd, age 20, was admitted to the Royal Academy of Art. Dadd showed talent at

the Academy and gathered a number of painterly friends, known collectively as 'The Clique'. He won several awards while at the Academy, and began exhibiting his work during his first year.

In 1841, he received a commission to do the woodblock illustrations for a book called the *Book of British Ballads,* as well as an oil painting called *Titania Sleeping,* which is perhaps the best example of his early work. Overall, his style was not particularly remarkable, no more so than any other moderately gifted painter in Victorian England during the stylistic phase now referred to as "The Fairy School".[22]

In 1842 Richard Dadd set out on the not-yet-quite-out-of-fashion Grand Tour (of Europe and the Middle East) with Sir Thomas Phillips, who had employed the artist to document his travels. All went well until the duo reached Egypt where Phillips and others believed that Dadd must have caught sunstroke. Dadd himself was under a rather different impression however, namely that he had been possessed by the ancient Egyptian God Osiris. Osiris is the God of the afterlife, of the dead, and, perhaps crucially, of the underworld (the connections between Hades, Hell, the classical underworld, and Faerie having already been discussed in part).

Upon his return to England Richard was clearly changed and troubled. He was taken by his family to rural Kent for a bit of rest, relaxation, and recuperation. There, in August 1843, Dadd took a knife and murdered his father, who he now believed was not his father at all but a supernatural double (a "fetch", or a "waff", as some might say). Richard fled the country but was arrested just outside Paris when he attempted a second murder, this time with a straight razor. Dadd confessed to killing his father and was returned to England, where he was committed to the criminal department of Bethlem psychiatric hospital, better known to many as Bedlam.

In Bedlam (and later in the equally infamous Broadmoor Hospital where he died in 1886) Richard Dadd was encouraged to continue with his painting. His artwork was, as is perhaps to be expected, somewhat changed ("possess[ing] a strange compelling quality absent from the work he completed when sane", according to Beveridge[23]) but it was no less wonderful. So wonderful in fact that in 1855 the then Head Steward at Bedlam, George Henry Haydon, asked Dadd if he would paint a picture for him. Dadd spent nine years on the painting – a canvas measuring a mere 54 x 39.5 cm (21 x 15.5 inches) – which, though it remained unfinished in his eyes, now hangs in London's world famous Tate Gallery. The painting is entitled *The Fairy Feller's Master Stroke* and is described on the Tate website thusly:

> With the exception of Shakespeare's Oberon and Titania, who appear in the top half of the picture, the figures are drawn entirely from the artist's imagination. The main focus of the painting is the Fairy Feller himself, who raises his axe in readiness to split a large chestnut which will be used to construct Queen Mab's new fairy carriage. In the centre of the picture the white-bearded patriarch raises his right hand, commanding the woodsman not to strike a blow until the signal is given. Meanwhile the rest of the fairy band looks on in anticipation, anxious to see whether the woodsman will succeed in splitting the nut with one stroke.
>
> The magician-like figure of the patriarch wears a triple crown, which seems to be a reference to the Pope. Dadd saw the Pope during a visit to Rome in 1843 and was apparently overcome by an urge to attack him. Although the patriarch may be interpreted as a father figure, the tiny apothecary, brandishing a mortar and pestle in the top right of the picture, is in fact a portrait of the artist's father, Robert Dadd.[24]

Yes, Dadd's father was depicted by the artist among the fairies.

In the very first issue of the Tate magazine, *Tate Etc*, published in May 2004 (four months before *Strange & Norrell*), the German Capitalist Realist painter and photographer Sigmar Polke (1941–2010)

Richard Dadd's *The Fairy Feller's Master Stroke* (1855-1864), with highlighted section showing his father Robert Dadd, who he murdered in 1843 after becoming convinced he was a supernatural double of his true father.

wrote a piece on Dadd's *Fairy Feller's Master Stroke* entitled "Private View". While I do not pretend to be familiar with Polke, either as a painter or a writer, there are nevertheless perhaps some insights to be gained from an artist's perspective on Dadd and his master-work. Here are a couple of choice quotations from the piece:

> I've known Richard Dadd's *The Fairy Feller's Master-Stroke* 1855–64 since the 1970s. When I look at it again today, it's as if I were looking into a tapestry and losing my way. Its composition is quite unlike any other Victorian fairy painting. The point of view is not clearly defined. Instead, the individual elements appear to be linked by almost invisible forces.
>
> At that time, the fantasy life of fairies – from Grimm to Shakespeare – enjoyed widespread popularity as an imaginary world fully integrated into reality. Dadd's appropriation of this world is, however, neither kitsch, nor facile, nor garrulous, because it does not obey the then current pictorial conventions. Nor does his vision echo the spirited confections of popular draughtsman J.J. Grandville's fantastic book *Un Autre Monde* 1844. Instead, one senses the extraordinary intensity of an enduring dialogue between the artist and the universe of figures that he created. Isolated from the outside world, he painted the picture for the director of the hospital. Did he perhaps want to present it as proof of his sanity?

A strange idea; attempting to prove one's sanity by creating a hyper-realistic representation of Faerie.

In the final paragraph Polke talks briefly about Dadd's madness but in place of a conclusion to the piece there is, instead, a rather curious quotation.

> One more curlicue, a whorl, my coda follows in the form of an ancient Celtic saying:

> A city lasts three years,
> A dog outlives three cities,
> A horse outlasts three dogs,
> A person outlives three horses,
> A donkey outlives three people,
> A wild goose outlives three donkeys,
> A crow outlives three wild geese,
> A hart outlives three crows,
> A raven outlives three harts,
> And the Phoenix outlives three ravens.[25]

I have not been able to find the source of the quotation and I'm left wondering exactly what Polke was trying to communicate, and whether he was freely able to do so…

In *Strange & Norrell* madness and magic may not be the same thing but they are bedfellows nonetheless; each having some bearing and effect upon the other. Even so…

> There were remarkably few spells for curing madness. Indeed he had found only one, and even then he was not sure that was what it was meant for. It was a prescription in Ormskirk's *Revelations of Thirty-Six Other Worlds*. Ormskirk said that it would dispel illusions and correct wrong ideas. Strange took out the book and read through the spell again. It was a peculiarly obscure piece of magic, consisting only of the following words:
>
> "Place the moon at his eyes and her whiteness shall devour the false sights the deceiver has placed there.
> Place a swarm of bees at his ears. Bees love truth and will destroy the deceiver's lies.
> Place salt in his mouth lest the deceiver attempt to delight him with the taste of honey or disgust him with the taste of ashes.
> Nail his hand with an iron nail so that he shall not raise it to do the deceiver's bidding.

Place his heart in a secret place so that all his desires shall be his own and the deceiver shall find no hold there.
Memorandum. The colour red may be found beneficial."

However, as Strange read it through, he was forced to admit that he had not the least idea what it meant.

THE RAVEN KING

Strange & Norrell (the novel) is divided into three volumes: the first is *Mr. Norrell*, the second *Jonathan Strange*, and the third is entitled *John Uskglass*. In the novel, *The History and Practice of English Magic* is a book written by Jonathan Strange and published in 1816 by John Murray. The third volume of *Strange & Norrell* opens with Strange's prologue to his book which is a summation of what is known of John Uskglass – the magician they called the Raven King.

> In the last months of 1110 a strange army appeared in Northern England. It was first heard of near a place called Penlaw some twenty or thirty miles north-west of Newcastle. No one could say where it had come from – it was generally supposed to be an invasion of Scots or Danes or perhaps even of French.
>
> By early December the army had taken Newcastle and Durham and was riding west. It came to Allendale, a small stone settlement that stands high among the hills of Northumbria, and camped one night on the edge of a moor outside the town.

The farming people of Allendale (a real and extant village in Northumberland, settled since prehistoric times – known today for its flaming tar barrel hurling New Year's celebrations), anxious to befriend the army, sent a party of young beautiful women ("a company of brave Judiths") to make contact, and peace, with the force. There on the moor the women found a host of curious looking soldiers, wrapped in black cloaks, lying on the ground looking like corpses, with ravens roosting on and around them. One soldier stood up and one brave Allendale woman stepped forward to kiss him. They kissed, and kissed, and then they danced, and danced.

> This went on for some time until she became heated with the dance and paused for a moment to take off her cloak. Then her companions saw that drops of blood, like beads of sweat, were forming on her arms, face and legs, and falling on to the snow. This sight terrified them and so they ran away. The strange army never entered Allendale. It rode on in the night towards Carlisle. The next day the townspeople went cautiously up to the fields where the army had camped. There they found the girl, her body entirely white and drained of blood while the snow around her was stained bright red.
>
> By these signs they recognized the Daoine Sidhe – the Fairy Host.

The fairy army fought many battles and won them all. By late December they held Newcastle, Durham, Carlisle, Lancaster (which was burnt to the ground), and were at York. In January the fae army met that of King Henry I at Newark on the banks of the River Trent. The King lost.

> The King and his counsellors waited for some chieftain or king to step forward.
>
> The ranks of the Daoine Sidhe parted and someone appeared. He was rather less than fifteen years old. Like the Daoine Sidhe he was dressed in ragged clothes of coarse black wool. Like them his dark hair was long and straight.

He was pale and handsome and solemn-faced, yet it was clear to everyone present that he was human, not fairy.

King Henry asked the boy his name.

The boy replied that he had none.*

King Henry asked him why he made war on England.

The boy said that he was the only surviving member of an aristocratic Norman family who had been granted lands in the north of England by King Henry's father, William the Conqueror. The men of the family had been deprived of their lands and their lives by a wicked enemy named Hubert de Cotentin. The boy said that some years before his father had appealed to William II (King Henry's brother and predecessor) for justice, but had received none. Shortly afterwards his father had been murdered. The boy said that he himself had been taken by Hubert's men while still a baby and abandoned in the forest. But the Daoine Sidhe had found him and taken him to live with them in Faerie. Now he had returned.

He had settled it in his own mind that the stretch of England which lay between the Tweed and the Trent was a just recompense for the failure of the Norman kings to avenge the murders of his family. For this reason and no other King Henry was suffered to retain the southern half of his kingdom.

---

* When he was a child in Faerie the Sidhe had called him a word in their own language which, we are told, meant "Starling", but he had already abandoned that name by the time he entered England. Later he took to calling himself by his father's name John d'Uskglass but in the early part of his reign he was known simply by one of the many titles his friends or enemies gave him: the King; the Raven King; the Black King; the King in the North. [this is Clarke's original footnote from *Strange & Norrell*]

That day he began his unbroken reign of more than 300 years.

In a 2004 interview with BBC Nottingham Susanna Clarke was asked whether her master magician, the Raven King, was based upon any historical figure.

> The Raven King had an odd genesis. Ursula Le Guin has a magician in the *Earthsea* trilogy who has no name: the Grey Mage of Plan, whose magic was so dubious, his name was forgotten. And there's a magician in *The Lord of the Rings,* right at the very end, who comes out of Mordor to do battle against our heroes, and no one knows his name because he himself has forgotten it. I thought this was rather cool, and when I was developing my magicians, I wanted one without a name. Unfortunately I hadn't quite understood what would happen if I had a major character without a name. The consequence has been that he has acquired more names than most people: the Raven King, John Uskglass, the Black King, the King of the North and a fairy name that no one can pronounce.[26]

While the initial seeds of Clarke's John Uskglass may have been literary, the Raven King's roots stretch deep into the fertile soil of English history and folklore.

Puck is a name we are most familiar with today from Shakespeare's *A Midsummer Night's Dream* – that "shrewd and knavish sprite", "that merry wanderer of the night", and entertainer of Oberon, the fairy king. Puck pre-dates the Bard by a long way however.

> Parallel words exist in many ancient languages – *puca* in Old English, *puki* in Old Norse, *puke* in Swedish, *puge* in Danish, *puks* in Low German, *pukis* in Latvia and Lithuania – mostly with the original meaning of a demon, devil or evil and malignant spirit.[27]

When not being applied generally to household sprites (the kind that helped with chores in exchange for an offering of food and/or drink which was left by the hearth for them), Puck is then the name of one particular fae who also uses the alias Robin/Robyn Goodfellow. This fairy was portrayed in a 1785 painting by William Blake in which he resembles the Greek God Pan, and an 1841 painting by Richard Dadd as a human-looking child.[28] Post his role in Shakespeare's play, Puck/Robyn found himself the subject of many 17th century ballads in which he was often portrayed as the son of Oberon and an English woman.[29] A creature of several names then, and neither wholly human nor fairy.

Writing as Strange upon Uskglass, Clarke gives us:

> The boy said that he was already a king in Faerie. He named the fairy king who was his overlord. No one understood.

Richard Dadd's 1841 painting of Puck

The accompanying footnote reads:

> The name of this Daoine Sidhe King was particularly long and difficult. Traditionally he has always been known as Oberon.

A connection to Oberon, as (foster) father hinted at, at least.

In chapter one of her 1933 work *The God of Witches,* entitled "The Horned God", Dr. Margaret Murray wrote the following:

> The most interesting of all the names for the god is Robin, which when given to Puck is Robin Goodfellow. It is so common a term for the "Devil" as to be almost a generic name for him "Some Robin the Divell, or I wot not what spirit of the Ayre". Dame Alice Kyteler called her god, Robin Artisson, and the Somerset witches cried out "Robin" when summoning their Grandmaster to a meeting, or even when about to make a private incantation.[30]

While Murray's writings are viewed by many as rather fanciful these days there is, nonetheless, value in her cataloguing of these matters and, I would also argue, in her interpretation of things (even if she did get a little carried away at times). She goes on:

> A fact, noted by many writers and still unexplained, is the connection between Robin Goodfellow and Robin Hood. Grimm remarks on it but gives no reason for his opinion, though the evidence shows that the connection is there. The cult of Robin Hood was widespread both geographically and in time, which suggests that he was more than a local hero in the places where his legend occurs. In Scotland as well as England Robin Hood was well known, and he belonged essentially to the people, not to the nobles.[31]

ROBIN Good-Fellovv,

His Mad Prankes, and merry Iests,

Full of honest Mirth, and is a fit Medicine for Melancholy.

LONDON,
Printed for F. *Grove* dwelling on Snow-hill
ouer against the Sarasens head. 1628.

In his 1895 essay *The Devil and His Imps: An Etymological Inquisition*, Charles P. G. Scot wrote briefly upon the connections and confusions between Hood and Goodfellow:

> Robin Hood seems to have been sometimes confused in kitchen tales with Robin Good-fellow, and so to have been regarded in the light of a fairy – or in the dark of a goblin. Reginald Scot, speaking of Hudgin, a German goblin, says:
>
> *There goe as manie tales upon this Hudgin, in some parts of Germanie, as there did in England of Robin Good-fellow. But this Hudgin was so called, bicauſe he alwaies ware a cap or a hood; and therefore I thinke it was Robin Hood.*
>
> – 1584 R. Scot, Discourse upon divels and spirits, ch. 21 (app. to Discoverie of witchcraft, repr. 1886, p. 438; ed. 1651, p. 374).

Keightly, no conclusive authority, mentions Robin Hood as another name for Puck or Robin Goodfellow:

> *Puck . . . his various appellations: these are Puck, Robin Goodfellow, Robin Hood, Hobgoblin.*
>
> – 1828 T. K[eightley], Fairy mythology, 2 : 118.[32]

The oldest surviving document mentioning Robin/Robyn/Robe Hood (also Hod, Hode, Whood, Wood, and so on) is a 14th century poem entitled *The Vision Concerning Piers Plowman* which alludes fleetingly to the "rhymes of Robin Hood" – therefore suggesting that the tales were already well-told and known. The real Robin Hood (if there ever was one) is long obscured by the hundreds, if not thousands, of tellings, re-tellings, and re-imaginings of his life and deeds which continue to entertain into the present day. There are at least three sites in England which claim to be the outlaw's final resting place and though Sherwood, Nottingham is the location most of us automatically associate with Robin, many historians now believe that Yorkshire was his (or his tale's) place of origin.

> Robin [Hood] has been presented as a personification of the Green Man (he was always dressed in Lincoln Green), a folk character with fairy origins, a political rebel, and even a Witch-Cult figure.[33]

Though a yeoman in the earliest ballads, the idea of Robin Hood being the rightful Earl of Huntingdon, robbed of his title by scheming family members who abandoned him as an infant, goes back to the late 16th century at least. Robin is supposed then to have been raised by Gilbert Whitehand (a now largely overlooked member of the Merry Men), and schooled by him in the ways of the bow and the staff. In later versions Robin is said to have quarrelled with the king (almost always King John by this point, though an unspecific Edward in the original tales) and was forced to flee north, taking refuge in Sherwood Forest.[34]

Compare this with Strange's account of John d'Uskglass' origins: the entitled noble, abandoned as a child, raised and schooled so well he bettered his master, living in the north while the true king remains in the south. (I could go on, bringing in other sources, but for the constraints of time and word-count).

I am not suggesting that Susanna Clarke meant in any way to deliberately base The Raven King upon Robin Hood or Robyn Goodfellow, merely that such figures – complex, elusive, many-named, trickster-ish, champions of "otherness" who live and operate outside the normal rules and constraints of society – are now and always have been part of the English psyche.

Robin Hood is a greatly sanitised version of the archetype, the Raven King a darker, more alien, and dangerous one. Lincoln Green and Raven Black.

There is, of course, also the shared avian nomenclature: the robin and the raven. The former having recently been voted the National Bird of Britain,[35] the latter not even making the top ten. The robin is a cheery, plucky bird that reminds us of Christmas and all the Victorian trappings and customs we carry with the season (consciously or not). The raven is a midnight-hued carrion eater with an IQ comparable to that of a primate, long associated with omens, magic and witchcraft. The raven represents the ancient, the untamed, the occult while the robin represents whimsy, nature at its back-garden level, and the familiar. England may try to maintain its Victorian composure, try to keep up appearances, but in the fields, and on the concrete roofs of blocks of flats, along the motorways, and even in the Tower of London, the ravens watch and wait.

> All of Man's works, all his cities, all his empires, all his monuments will one day crumble to dust. Even the houses of my own dear readers must – though it be for just one day, one hour be ruined and become houses where the stones are mortared with moonlight, windowed with starlight and furnished with

the dusty wind. It is said that in that day, in that hour, our houses become the possessions of the Raven King. Though we bewail the end of English magic and say it is long gone from us and inquire of each other how it was possible that we came to lose something so precious, let us not forget that it also waits for us at England's end and one day we will no more be able to escape the Raven King than, in this present Age, we can bring him back.

– *The History and Practice of English Magic* by Jonathan Strange, pub. John Murray, London, 1816.

Concluding Thoughts

Here I ask the reader to indulge me in a brief outro in an effort to bring my own tenuous acquaintance with Susanna Clarke up to date, and the piece to something approaching a conclusion. At the end of July 2015, following the *Strange & Norrell* television series and the publication of my articles online, I found myself composing a hasty email to someone by the name of Clark. As I typed the name into the To: field, Mozilla Thunderbird suggested "Susanna Clarke". I clicked on the name and, sure enough, there was Susanna's email address which I had completely forgotten we had. So, naturally, I sent Susanna a message wishing her and Colin all the best, saying how much Leah and I had enjoyed the television series, and even mentioning the articles I'd been writing. As I wrote at the beginning of this piece, I had not yet read *Strange & Norrell* when first we met, so I took the opportunity to thank Susanna for writing what has become one of my very favourite books of all time. And, the very next day, I received an email back. She was warm, friendly, chatty and full of praise for Peter Harness' work on the adaptation. She was also characteristically kind about my writing on *Strange & Norrell*: "I've had a read of your Daily Grail pieces – fascinating. There's masses there I didn't know. You are very learned. Thank you very much for giving the show (and book) such a boost."

As if the Friends of English Magic needed any help from me.

John Reppion is an English writer based in Liverpool. A lifelong fascination with folklore, forteana, weird and forgotten history runs through all of his work, from comics (co-authored with his wife, Leah Moore), to Weird Fiction, to his essays and articles. His website is moorereppion.com and he can be found on Twitter @johnreppion.

'The Wolfman', by Chris Butler

The Lycanthropes

Examining the legends, and reality, behind one of
the most enduring of all monster myths:
the Werewolf

by *Robert M. Schoch, Ph.D.*

In the Biblical book of Daniel[1] it is recounted that God humbled the mighty Babylonian king and conqueror of Jerusalem, Nebuchadnezzar (reigned circa 605–562 BCE), in the following manner. Nebuchadnezzar was "transformed" into a wild beast living in the fields for seven years, away from humanity, eating grass as cattle do. Was this a bout of insanity, the earliest recorded case of the clinical psychiatric delusion now commonly referred to as lycanthropy?[2]

The term lycanthropy, derived from the Greek *lykos* = wolf and *anthropos* = human, specifically refers to the supposed transformation of a human into a wolf – that is, a werewolf (also "werwolf", from the Old English *were* or *wer* = adult male human and *wulf* = wolf) or lycanthrope. In the modern psychiatric literature lycanthropy generically refers to the delusion that one can undergo metamorphosis into an animal, be it a wolf or some other beast (also referred to as therianthropy or zoanthropy). In the psychiatric literature various

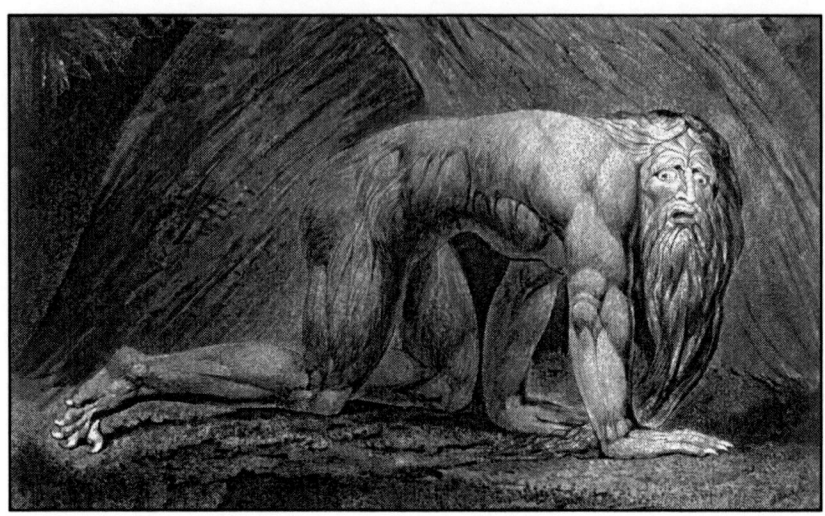

Nebuchadnezzar transformed into a wild beast; illustration by William Blake (1757–1827).

patients have thought themselves transformed not only into a wolf or werewolf, but also into a dog, cat, tiger, cow, horse, rabbit, gerbil, bird, frog, bee, and various unspecified animals.[3] In the classical, medieval, anthropological, and folkloric literature some of the animals most frequently encountered – depending on the geographic region – are wolves (around the world in the Northern Hemisphere), leopards (Africa and Asia), jackals (Africa and Asia), hyenas (Africa and Asia), tigers (Asia), bears (Americas, Europe, and Asia), cougars or pumas (Americas), and other large carnivores.[4]

Shape-Changers

As commonly construed, however, the concept of lycanthropy includes much more than a simple clinical condition of delusions and/or hallucinations. Traditionally, in folklore and mythology, some humans are said to have been physically transformed into animals. Certainly this strains modern credulity and is open to serious question. According to one version of an ancient Greek myth (for there are many contradictory versions), mentioned by Hesiod (circa 8th–7th century BCE) and retold by later writers, Lycaon (king of Arcadia) killed and cooked one of his own sons, serving the resulting dish to Zeus in order to test the god's true divinity.[5] As punishment for such impiety, and the horrific deed carried out, Zeus turned Lycaon into a wolf. Of course this is only a myth, and not to be taken literally, but many modern stories of lycanthropy from Africa have, at least by some, been taken quite seriously. Here is a typical example, which took place in Northern Nigeria in 1915.

> Lieutenant F. was camped near the village of an inferior tribe. Some hyenas had made depredations in the flocks, and the lieutenant sat on watch at a short distance from a goat tied up as bait. As soon as a hyena appeared, and before it could attack the goat, he fired twice and wounded the beast, which fled. Twenty-five minutes later

Zeus turns Lycaon into a wolf; engraving by Hendrik Goltzius (1558–1617).

drumming was heard in the village summoning the inhabitants to a funeral, as is usual with them in the event of a death.

With the first light of dawn the officer followed up on the tracks of the wounded beast, noticing that these pointed towards the village, up to a place where there was a zone of mould worked by black ants. There the print[s] of paws ceased and were replaced by human footsteps, which went towards the village as far as its entrance. A short time later the lieutenant was told of the death of one of the notables, who had died during the night of a large gunshot wound in the head. No one knew how it had been produced, but they would not allow the officer to see the body.[6]

Lieutenant F. recounted other similar cases, including examples where a hyena (or another beast) was wounded in a trap and fled, followed by drumming from the village announcing a death and funeral. Each time when he followed the tracks of the wounded animal they led to a black ant mound and there the tracks changed from paw prints to human footprints.

Another similar case (one of many) from the same time period, and also from Northern Nigeria, was relayed by a certain Captain H. H. Shott.

The captain...[shot]...a very large hyena, whose tracks were easy to trace. Severely wounded in the head, it fled across a field. The tracks were followed at once. They led to a place where the lower jaw of the animal was found lying near a large pool of blood. Immediately after the prints led to a path towards the village.

On the next day the inhabitants presented themselves to Captain Shott, to tell him, without any signs of regret, that he had killed their Nefada (junior chief), who had lost his lower jaw, carried off evidently by a gunshot... The Nefada had a bad reputation; everyone knew that he was a man-hyena and that he transformed himself into an enormous beast of this kind showing extraordinary astuteness.[7]

What do we make of such stories? The classic explanation is that these are not true lycanthropic transformations at all, but simply cases where perfectly normal humans dressed up as animals, including "shoes" and "gloves" made of animal paws, and then went prowling. It is reported that in Africa there were secret societies of men who promoted the belief in lycanthropy among the general populace, and they went on rampages dressed as various animals – leopards, hyenas, crocodiles, and so forth.[8] The members of these societies were reported to be cruel and sadistic, and often cannibalistic – in their beastly forms they not only attacked and ate raw wild animals, but also human victims. To disguise themselves and their activities, they deliberately left "animal tracks" on the ground.

But would experienced colonial military officers, such as Lieutenant F. and Captain Shott, have consistently mistaken, even at night, men dressed as animals for genuine wild beasts? Although this may seem unlikely, the alternative (that men could really transform into animals and then back into men) is even more difficult to accept.

Along the same lines as the secret societies of Africa, in Medieval and Renaissance Europe the concept of lycanthropes (werewolves) was associated with witchcraft (witches would meet together in secret) and with outright criminal activity. An infamous case of a supposed "werewolf" was that of Peter Stumpp (also known by numerous other names, including Peter Stübbe, Peter Stumpf, Abal Griswold, Abil Griswold, and Ubel Griswold).[9] A wealthy farmer from the area of Bedburg (North Rhine-Westphalia, Germany), in 1589 Stumpp was tried, convicted, tortured, and executed for being a werewolf. He confessed, under the threat of torture, to killing and cannibalizing fourteen children and two pregnant women whose fetuses he tore from their wombs, devouring the babies' hearts. Stumpp admitted

A Werewolf; print by Lucas Cranach the Elder (1472–1553).

to practicing black magic and claimed that he had a special belt, courtesy of the Devil, which when he wore it turned him into a ferocious wolf. Despite the overlay of magic and lycanthropy, from a modern perspective Stumpp can be viewed as a vicious serial killer. Furthermore, he may have suffered from some severe form of psychosis resulting in loss of mental and emotional contact with reality and delusional thinking.

All in the Mind?

By various modern medical analyses, lycanthropic symptoms and phenomena can be associated with a number of different types of mental disorders, including but not limited to various types of psychoses, psychotic depression, affective disorders (mood disorders), various types and levels of depression, dementia, hysteria (a rather classic nineteenth-century diagnosis), bipolar disorder, epilepsy, and schizophrenia.[10] As P. Garlipp and colleagues (of the Hanover Medical School, Germany) write,

> The symptomatology can be seen as a continuity spectrum of development and culture dependent normal behaviour via transitional... and partial forms to the whole picture of lycanthropy ... People who live in preindustrial societies and people living on isolated countrysides are predisposed. Other precipitating factors seem to be subconscious sexual conflicts.[11]

Lycanthropic impulses and tendencies may be induced by or exacerbated by the use of drugs. Hallucinations involving metamorphoses into various animals both real and mythological due to drug ingestion are well documented.[12] In the past lycanthropic psychoses, behaving like a wild animal and the sensation of growing fur or feathers, may have been brought on specifically by the use of belladonna (favored in some witchcraft circles) and similar drugs. In medieval times a condition known as versipellis, or a changing of the skin ("Turnskin",[13] and by extension, a changing of shape or form), which in modern terms was probably the condition known as paraesthesias (a tingling sensation caused by nerve damage), may have been caused by ointments and salves used by witches. Such versipellis, in turn, was interpreted as evidence of hair growing on the inside of the skin, which in turn was evidence that a person was transforming into a werewolf.[14]

The use of various drugs among indigenous peoples in the Americas was widespread. In this context, Caesar de Vesme names such substances as coca, tobacco, peyotl (peyote), mezcal, cohoba, huanto, and *yagé* (=*ayahuasca*).[15]

Working in Colombia among the tribes of the Caquetá region in the late nineteenth century, Dr. Rafael Zerda Bayon observed,

> The patient who has ingested the *yagé* sometimes thinks himself to be an animal, according to the greater or less interest which certain species inspire; it may be the puma, the tapir, the cobra, or some other wild animal. . . . He then runs to the forest, imitating the actions of the beast into which he thinks he has been changed, attacking and seeking to devour such individuals as he may meet.[16]

Although in modern times documented cases of fully developed lycanthropy and/or associated symptoms apparently induced by drug use are rare, perhaps because the general public no longer strongly "believes" in werewolves and like entities (that is, the form mental disorders take can be culturally bound or affected), lycanthropic symptoms associated with drug use are still occasionally documented. A case in point is an Iranian man who developed delusional symptoms and a variant form of lycanthropy after consuming the drug ecstasy, which he took as part of a program at an "unofficial opium cessation center".[17] Lycanthropic symptoms have also been associated with psychotropic substances such as cannabinoids, alcohol abuse, and various forms of drug abuse generally.[18]

Another mental condition that has been sometimes associated with lycanthropy is that of extreme suggestibility, often associated with forms of hysteria. Various forms of this phenomenon are known under diverse names around the globe; for instance, *latah* in Malaysia[19] and *miryachit*[20] or *olonism*[21] among the people of the Siberian region. The anthropologist J. H. Hutton provides a graphic description:

> Yet another pathological condition may contribute to cases of lycanthropy, and that is the condition of extreme suggestibility known to Malays as *latah*. It is a common game among Malay children to pick out a child subject to this affliction and if it be a male, make it think it is, say, a civet cat and behave accordingly, pouncing on chickens and devouring them raw and so forth. Similarly, small girls are caused to suppose themselves apes, when they perform feats of arboreal agility quite inconceivably impossible to them in a normal state. The subject is hypnotized by being made to go on all fours when he is covered with a sheet and patted and stroked by other children marching round and round repeating a rhymed formula which is changed when the hypnosis begins to take effect. The subject loses consciousness of his humanity and becomes as one possessed. In the belief that he is a polecat or a peacock or whatever animal is chosen (sometimes it is an elephant) he chases the others, climbs up trees, leaps from branch to branch and risks serious injury by venturing on boughs too frail to support him. In the end he is recalled to his senses and humanity by repeatedly addressing him by name. Parents naturally are much averse to hypnotic diversions of this kind being practised on their children. Suggestibility of this sort seems to be sometimes contagious. Oesterreich quotes a case of an hysterical nun who supposed herself a cat, and from whom the delusion spread to

the convent generally, the whole company of nuns running about and mewing like cats. Another case is quoted of hysteria in a girl who, when in the country, used to bark like a dog. Hysteria of this kind must no doubt share with spiteful responsibility for beliefs in demoniacal possession.[22]

External Physical Maladies

There were physical characteristics that in some cases were used to label "werewolves", such as eyebrows that met in the middle of the forehead. By the power of suggestion, someone who was marked by his or her culture and community as a potential lycanthrope might indeed take on the attributes, behavioral and psychological, ascribed to him or her. Then there are even more obvious, but also very rare, physical characteristics that might suggest the concept of a lycanthrope.

In terms of the hirsute, perhaps the extreme cases are hypertrichosis (Ambras or werewolf syndrome) and related medical conditions in which abnormal amounts of hair can grow on the face and body, giving the appearance of a werewolf. A famous early example of a person with this syndrome is Petrus Gonsalvus (Pedro Gonzalez),[23] who was born in Tenerife (Canary Islands) in 1537, was a member of the courts of France and the Spanish Netherlands, married and had seven children (four of them also had hypertrichosis), and died sometime after circa 1617. Gonsalvus was treated fairly well, as far as can be determined, although some contemporaries apparently viewed him as sub-human. In the 19th and early 20th centuries some such persons were relegated to freak shows and circuses – a famous example is Fedor Jeftichew (1868–1904),[24] known as Jo-Jo the Dog-Faced Boy/Man who appeared in Russian sideshows and was brought to the United States by P. T. Barnum for his circus. But in earlier times might cases of hypertrichosis have inspired tales of werewolves?

Portrait of Petrus Gonsalvus (1537–after circa 1617); artist unknown.

Portrait of Petrus Gonsalvus and his wife by Joris Hoefnagel
(Georg Hoefnagel; 1542–1600 or 1601).

Possibly, except that such medical cases are incredibly rare and tales of lycanthropes appear around the world among virtually all peoples and cultures.

Besides extreme hypertrichosis, there is another medical condition with oftentimes extreme and obvious physical symptoms that has been proposed as the historical basis for some lycanthropic beliefs: congenital porphyria.[25] Porphyria is a rare hereditary disease associated with abnormal metabolism of blood hemoglobin. Porphyrins, a group of natural organic compounds essential for the proper functioning of hemoglobin, build up in the body. This can cause many complications, including affecting the skin, internal organs, and the nervous system. Persons with the disease may have an extreme sensitivity to light, they may excrete dark-colored urine, and they may be mentally disturbed.

Cutaneous porphyrias, forms of the disease that include oversensitivity to sunlight, are characterized by such symptoms as: "Sensitivity to the sun and sometimes artificial light, causing burning pain", "Sudden painful skin redness (erythema) and swelling (edema)",

"Blisters that take weeks to heal", "Itching", "Fragile skin", "Scars or skin color changes from healing blisters", "Increased hair growth", and "Red or brown urine".[26] Acute porphyrias, forms of the disease affecting the nervous system, include the following types of symptoms: "Severe abdominal pain", "Swelling of the abdomen (abdominal distention)", "Pain in [the]…chest, legs or back", "Constipation or diarrhea", "Vomiting", "Insomnia", "Heartbeat…(palpitations)", "High blood pressure", "Anxiety or restlessness", "Seizures", "Mental changes, such as confusion, hallucinations, disorientation or paranoia", "Breathing problems", "Muscle pain, tingling, numbness, weakness or paralysis", and "Red or brown urine".[27]

In addition to the symptoms listed above, in porphyria, skin lesions (due to extreme photosensitivity) can ulcerate and the ulcers in turn can severely affect cartilage and bone.[28] Over the years various exposed body parts, such as the head, face, hands, arms, and legs (and any other body parts an individual may expose to sunlight) can become progressively scarred and mutilated. Additionally, hypertrichosis (although not of the same extent or nature as we discussed above relative to Petrus Gonsalvus and Fedor Jeftichew) and abnormal pigmentation may develop. The teeth may appear red or reddish-brown due to the porphyrins building up on dental surfaces. Individuals with the disease may also suffer from jaundice, giving a pale or yellowish discoloration to the skin, and they may have red eyes. Epilepsy has also been associated with the syndrome.

Classical and medieval Byzantine physicians (who carried on the classical traditions of late antiquity) describe lycanthropy not so much in terms of "hairiness", but in terms that arguably better fit porphyria. For instance, the seventh century Byzantine physician Paul of Aegina, summarizing earlier writings on the subject, had this to say:

> Those labouring under lycanthropy go out during the night imitating wolves in all things, and lingering about sepulchres until morning. You may recognize these persons by these marks; they

Photograph of Fedor Jeftichew (1868–1904), known as Jo-Jo the Dog-Faced Boy.

are pale, their vision feeble, their eyes dry, tongue very dry and the flow of the saliva stopped; but they are thirsty, and their legs have incurable ulcerations from frequent falls.[29]

Returning to the suggestion that porphyria may have inspired or underlain some forms of lycanthropy, L. Illis writes,

> [S]uch a person [suffering from the disease], because of photosensitivity and the resultant disfigurement, may choose only to wander about at night. The pale, yellowish, excoriated skin… together with hypertrichosis and pigmentation, fit well with the descriptions, in older literature, of werwolves [werewolves]. The unhappy person may be mentally disturbed, and show some type or degree of abnormal behaviour. In ancient times this would be accentuated by the physical and social treatment he received from the other villagers, whose instincts would be to explain the apparition in terms of witchcraft or Satanic possession.[30]

Psychic Links with Wild Beasts

There is another aspect of lycanthropy that particularly interests me, given my serious studies of psychic (parapsychological) phenomena.[31] Some lycanthropes do not claim to physically transform their human body into that of an animal, but rather they develop a telepathic rapport with a genuine wild animal or project their "astral body" into a wolf, jackal, hyena, leopard, or some other animal in the wild.[32] This concept of psychically linking with an animal has been popularized in George R. R. Martin's *A Song of Ice and Fire* book series and the television shows based upon it. In Martin's novels, a "skinchanger" is a person who can psychically enter and bond with an animal, seeing through the animal's eyes, and controlling the animal's actions; a "warg" is a skinchanger who can link with a dog or wolf. In the television series, the term "warging" is used as the equivalent of "skinchanging" and the term "warg" has been expanded to include individuals who may psychically link with animals other than wolves[33] (just as in "real life" the terms lycanthropy and lycanthrope have been generally applied to cases involving not only humans transforming into wolves, but into other animals as well).

Returning to the anthropological and psychical literature, of such projection into a wild animal Caesar de Vesme cited the comments of a Mr. André Nervin (reporting from Dakar, Senegal, in 1908) who stated:

> They showed me the 'empty' body [in some form of a trance state] of a sorcerer who had gone on one of these expeditions [projecting his "soul" or "astral body" into an animal].
>
> You can touch him, strike him, prick him, cut him, or sit down on him. Put your hand over his heart; you will feel no beating, for he takes his heart with him. His body is only an envelope which he leaves in the care of his wife, for other sorcerers might prevent his return. When they wander abroad sorcerers can take the most diverse forms and incarnate in the bodies of animals.[34]

Ostensibly such sorcerers, wizards, or shamans can enter the body of a wild animal and by such means travel to distant places, gaining information about things that would otherwise be unknown and unavailable to them. In a case from the 1890s in Lado (South Sudan – northwestern Uganda), a local *m'logo* (wizard or sorcerer) claimed to have traveled via a jackal to a location hundreds of kilometers away, observed steamboats and described an Englishman who, the wizard said, was headed for Lado and would arrive a month later. Indeed, the wizard's descriptions and prediction of the Englishman's arrival proved correct.[35] How could this be? The Europeans had initially been highly skeptical of the claims of the *m'logo*, but could not deny the veracity of his statements. It was apparently impossible (according to all accounts) that the *m'logo* could have received the information by any normal means (quick communication, such as a telegraph, between the two distant points did not exist), and furthermore even a jackal could not have covered the distance involved in only one night, as the *m'logo* claimed. A possible explanation is that the *m'logo* gained his information through clairvoyance and telepathy, although he may have imagined that he had "traveled" via a jackal.

At this point we can refer back to our discussion of drug-induced lycanthropic phenomena. In some cases, ingesting drugs induces trances, and during such trances telepathic abilities may be enhanced. An important point that de Vesme and other serious psychical researchers have made is that the drugs themselves do not bring about telepathic abilities, but only strengthen and bring to the fore such abilities as are already present in the person using the drug. Furthermore, I would point out that drug use is certainly not the only means, nor safest nor most efficacious means, to heighten latent telepathic rapport. Rituals, ceremonies, songs, chants, drumming, fasting, and other methods can be used to produce similar or more powerful results.

Considering *yagé* (=*ayahuasca*), Dr. Zerda Bayon observed,

> During the mental alienation produced by *yagé* the patient enters into an extremely curious psychological state, which may be explained telepathically. In delirium he sees and hears distant events, and these very clear visions are consistent with exact observation of things of which the patient neither has, nor could have, the least previous knowledge. This circumstance is highly important, for it excludes entirely the hypothesis of an awakening of subconscious memory.[36]

Dr. Zerda Bayon goes on to relate an experiment confirming such assertions.

Colonel Custodio Morales... expressed to me a lively desire to try the effect of *yagé* on himself in the cottage occupied by me on the shore of the Gacha. After long hesitation I consented, and I administered fifteen drops of a preparation of *yagé*. He took the mixture in the evening, in a glass of water. In the morning, on awaking, he told me that during the night he had had a vision; his father, who lived at Ibague, had died, and his younger sister, whom he greatly loved, was ill. No one who had arrived could have communicated this news to him; the postal and telegraph office nearest to us was fifteen days' distance from my habitation. About a month after this remarkable vision, a postal mail arrived, bringing letters informing the colonel of the death of his father and the cure of his sister from a severe illness which had stricken her.[37]

As we noted previously, there have been instances wherein users of *yagé* exhibit lycanthropic behavior. Could it be that this is due, at least in part, to a true telepathic rapport established with genuine wild beasts? Or might a person simply receive information telepathically from others (or from one's future self, which is one explanation of precognition as there is evidence that the future can influence the past and present to some extent[38]), but perceive in their own mind (or

A woodcut of a werewolf; Germany, circa 1722.

rationalize) that they are "seeing" and receiving information through the eyes of an animal?

In some situations a human identifies with a specific individual wild animal, which effectively becomes their "familiar". In Assam, India, and Northern Burma there were "tiger-men", each of whom identified himself with a particular individual tiger that lived in the vicinity.[39] If the tiger was injured, then the tiger-man would suffer the same injuries or symptoms. If the tiger died, then inevitably it seemed the tiger-man would die also. These phenomena have been attributed to the power of suggestion inducing psychosomatic illnesses and even death. Supporting this contention is the fact that in many documented cases the illness or death of the tiger-man did not ensue until after he had learned about the injury or death of his tiger familiar. But, I wonder, was this inevitably the case? Could there not have been some situations where the tiger-man (or other individual identifying with a particular animal) was in genuine telepathic rapport with the animal and thus would gain, via paranormal means, information from and about the animal? Although not the conventional point of view, I do not think this would be impossible. In fact, there are cases that in my opinion are very difficult to explain otherwise. Reporting on the "leopard-men" of the Naga Hills of India and Burma (Myanmar), J. H. Hutton described his own fieldwork:

> Another acquaintance of mine, Zhukiya of Kolhopu village, was in the habit of telling his fellow villagers in the morning where they could find the remains of pigs and dogs killed and only partially eaten by his leopard during the night, and these were collected by his fellow villagers. On one occasion he told them that they would find the body of a calf in a tree near the river six or seven miles [about 9.6 to 11.3 kilometers] away, which they duly retrieved. This was vouched for by the chief of the village. This same Zhukiya showed me fresh marks on his body which he said were two months old and caused by shot which had wounded his leopard familiar.[40]

If the accounts regarding the remains of pigs, dogs, and the calf in the tree are true (and there is no strong reason to doubt them, in my opinion, unless one simply dismisses all potential paranormal phenomena as impossible – the close-minded view of the arch-skeptic and debunker), then it seems impossible that Zhukiya could have consistently gained such knowledge via normal means. I suggest that we must be open to the possibility of true telepathic rapport between human and animal, and in this sense the lycanthrope may exist in reality.

Robert M. Schoch, Honorary Professor at the Nikola Vaptsarov Naval Academy and a full-time faculty member at Boston University, earned his Ph.D. in geology and geophysics at Yale University. His most recent book is *Forgotten Civilization: The Role of Solar Outbursts in Our Past and Future* (Inner Traditions, 2012). Dr. Schoch's personal website is www.robertschoch.com.

The Lycanthropes

HIGH TIMES IN THE NEW WORLD

by *Paul Devereux*

Perhaps the greatest mystery about ancient and traditional hallucinogen use in the Americas is simply that there is too much of it compared to the Old World. The recognised authority on New World hallucinogens, Richard Evans Schultes, originally made this observation back in 1963. Over forty years later, this imbalance is even more marked, as an increasing number of Native American hallucinogens have been discovered – many by Schultes himself through his heroic fieldwork. By the end of the 1970s, Schultes could write: "Of the probable half-million species in the world's flora, only about 150 are known to be employed for their hallucinatory properties… Nearly 130 species are known to be used in the Western Hemisphere, whereas in the Eastern Hemisphere, the number hardly reaches 20." Mexico, in particular, "represents without a doubt the world's richest area in diversity and use of hallucinogens in aboriginal societies."

Anthropologist Weston La Barre agreed with Schultes, and referred to a "New World narcotic complex" (using the term "narcotic" to cover substances whose prime action is hallucinogenic) which extends from a mid-United States latitude southward to include much of South America. La Barre was himself staggered at "the enormous number of psychotropic drugs that were used ritually – narcotic mushrooms, cacti, beans, seeds, leaves, barks and vines, and in Amazonia even a narcotic bamboo-grub." The Old World has a far greater landmass than the New, and its people have been present for far longer than those in the Americas and so had more time to discover the hallucinogenic properties of its equally rich flora. So why the disparity? Both Schultes and La Barre sought a cultural explanation, and that brings us to the question of the origin of the Native Americans.

Ancient Origins

Although there is growing evidence that over a huge span of time the Americas were subject to a variety of migrations (or more likely relatively short encounters) by people coming via the Pacific from South-East Asia, and even via the north Atlantic from Europe in remote prehistory (there is now both tentative genetic and archaeological evidence for this), most authorities currently agree that the ancestors of the present-day Native Americans came originally from Asia. Siberia and Alaska were once connected by a low-lying landmass known to geologists as "Beringia" – the famous "land bridge" between the Old and New Worlds. Around twenty-five thousand years ago a period of bitter cold ensued and the sea levels fell, providing the land bridge. This lasted until around fourteen thousand years ago, when the rapid post-glacial warming began, and the modern Siberian and Alaskan coastlines began to form. The people who crossed the land bridge from Siberia, following big game, may have gradually filtered their way down into the warmer reaches of what is today the United States and points south, along the Pacific coast or through corridors in the retreating glacial ice masses. There is still debate as to how exactly the migration proceeded southwards at the end of the Ice Age, and archaeologists admit that the actual timing when human beings set foot on the land bridge is "a complete mystery" – estimates for when people first began to migrate into North America range wildly. But come they did, and remains of early human activity scattered through the Americas have been archaeologically investigated. In some cases challengingly early dates have been claimed: radiocarbon dates reaching back nearly twenty thousand years were obtained at the Meadowcroft Rockshelter in Pennsylvania, for instance. But more certain chronology emerges with what archaeologists call the "Clovis culture" around twelve thousand years ago, when widespread and repeated evidence of human presence appears in the archaeological record – "a veritable explosion in the number of archaeological sites throughout North America, from the California deserts to the Eastern Woodlands" as anthropologist Brian Fagan puts it.

Archaeological evidence confirms the use of hallucinogens in the Americas from almost the Clovis time line. This is best indicated by the so-called Red Bean or Mescal Bean, in reality the seed of *Sophora secundiflora,* an evergreen shrub or small tree native to Texas and northern Mexico (not related to mescal, a distilled Mexican liquor, or to peyote). It causes nausea and convulsions, and can be fatal in high doses. It is not strictly hallucinogenic, and it is thought that its visionary effects are created by a kind of delirium. It was used by Indians of the American Southwest up until the nineteenth century. About a dozen or so finds of the seeds have been uncovered in association with evidence of human occupation in caves and rock shelters in Trans-Pecos Texas (the region west of the Pecos River and south of the New Mexico state line) and northern Mexico giving radiocarbon dates to 8440 B.C. At Fate Bell Shelter in the Amistad

Reservoir area of Trans-Pecos Texas, *Sophora secundiflora* seeds have been unearthed that date to 7000 B.C. These seeds were found in association with the seeds of another shrub, *Ugnadia speciosa*, known as Texas (or Mexican) Buckeye. These seeds are genuinely hallucinogenic and have been found in association with *Sophora secundiflora* seeds in other, similar archaeological contexts, and also with finds of peyote (*Lophophora williamsii*) dating to 5000 B.C. in one rock shelter. Peter Furst, an expert on Native American religion, has long noted that the area of the Fate Bell Shelter is rich in ancient shamanistic rock paintings, another telltale sign of hallucinogen usage. Other Native American hallucinogens also have a secure archaeological record, as we shall see.

Although religious historian Mircea Eliade referred to the use of hallucinogens as "a decadent form of shamanism," Furst reports that shortly before his death Eliade confided in him that these ancient American dates for hallucinogen usage were part of the evidence that made him change his mind on this issue, and that he had come to accept that there was no essential difference between ecstasy achieved by plant hallucinogens and that obtained by other archaic techniques.

The tradition of using plant hallucinogens in ritual context is well-established in the Americas, seemingly, for as long American Indians have been there. This gives strong support to the cultural explanation for the "New World narcotic complex" offered by La Barre. He observes that the Siberian-Asiatic origin for the American Indians is "overwhelming," and sees this indicated in many shared traits between Siberians and Native Americans, such as tone-languages, the use of bow-and-arrow, skin-covered tipis and bark-covered wigwams, the birchbark canoe, slit-eyed snow goggles, the practice of scalping, and so on. Most importantly, he suggests that shamanism is a key trait the Paleo-Indians brought with them out of north-east Asia. "Shamanism of a specifically Eurasiatic type is distributed from ancient Scandinavia to eastern Siberia, and continues from

Alaska eastward to Greenland and southward to Patagonia in the New World." Shamanism, he points out, is deeply-rooted in ecstatic, visionary experience, well manifested in the Native American vision quest, known also to the Paleo-Siberians, in which a young man goes out into the wilderness seeking a meaningful vision or dream. The goal of such a quest was the accumulation of supernatural power. La Barre argues that hallucinogens have a relationship to this primal motivation, and that "ecstatic-visionary shamanism is, so to speak, *culturally programmed for an interest in hallucinogens and other psychotropic drugs*" (La Barre's emphasis). The ritual use of hallucinogens therefore harks back to Palaeolithic and Mesolithic shamanism, which lingered in the form of shamanistic usage of the fly-agaric in various parts of Eurasia into the twentieth century. In this essay we will be seeing vestiges even of that specific mushroom tradition in the Americas. The plant hallucinogens themselves represented, manifested and conferred supernatural power – they fed the visionary hunger of the Paleo-peoples for otherworldly encounter. La Barre speaks of "the Sibero-American ur-culture" that underpinned this search for and exploitation of plant hallucinogens. Native American shamanism and vision-questing provided "a cultural preoccupation with finding plant hallucinogens…the Indian inhabitants of the New World have discovered more, both relatively and absolutely, of such hallucinogens." La Barre noted "the traditional high value placed on abnormal 'psychedelic' states" by Native Americans.

La Barre made the important point that the New World is "flatter, simpler in its time depth" than the Old World. Because the Americas have not been subjected to the same cultural time-scales, invasions, influences and overlays, the migrations, and all the myriad socio-cultural complexities of the Old World, they represent a kind of "Mesolithic fossil," culturally speaking. Through the study of the lifeways and practices of ancient American societies, "one can creep up on Eurasiatic history and protohistory so to speak from the flank, and along an immense time depth..." Native American shamanism provides us with an echo of the Eurasian spiritual impulse that has reverberated down untold corridors of time, and its remains are now clearer in the New World than in most of the Old.

The range of hallucinogens that have been ritually employed and exploited by ancient Native Americans is vast. We will briefly review the more important ones, mentioning just a few lesser-known hallucinogens to indicate the remarkable scope and effects of New World mind-altering substances (for detailed discussion of hallucinogen use right across the ancient world, see my book *The Long Trip: A Prehistory of Psychedelia*, which this essay is excerpted from).

The Great Mushroom Hunt

The use of "sacred" mushrooms is one of the strongest Native American hallucinogenic traditions. The antiquity of their ritual use is strongly hinted at by curious "mushroom stones," about three hundred of which have been found to date, from highland Guatemala, southern and western Mexico, Honduras and El Salvador. They integrate various mushroom shapes with a face or other figurative element, and occasionally with the indication of a metate or grinding stone – it is this detail that specifically indicates their association with mushroom preparation and practices. Most are between twelve and fifteen inches in height, and date from the first millennium B.C. until about the time when the Spanish arrived. The chronicle of the Spanish priest Bernardo Sahagún in the late sixteenth century tells of the sacred mushrooms of the Aztecs. They called them *teonanacatl*, "flesh of the gods."

Despite such early documentation, the likely significance of the mushroom stones was not fully recognized until the 1950s. The major American botanist, William A. Safford, was certain that there was no such thing as a native mushroom cult. He held that *teonanacatl* referred to by Sahagún was the peyote cactus. Ethnobotanist Blas Pablo Reko was working in Mexico and was aware that there was indeed a surviving mushroom cult, but was unable to make his academic peers listen. In 1936, ethnologist R. J. Weitlaner actually collected some samples from Mazatec Indians in Oaxaca, Mexico, but by the time they arrived at the Botanical Museum of Harvard University they were too badly deteriorated to be identified. In 1938, Weitlaner, Jean Bassett Johnson and colleagues were the first outsiders since the Spanish conquerors to witness an Indian all-night curing ritual. It took place at the remote village of Huautla de Jiménez, in Oaxaca, and involved the eating of psychoactive mushrooms by a Mazatec shaman.

Writing about this unique experience in 1939, Johnson pointed out that several kinds of hallucinogenic mushrooms were known to the Indians. Only a month after this session, Reko and Schultes

A mushroom stone depicting a girl or goddess emerging from the stipe, holding a metate or grinding stone *(Author's drawing)*

started research in the same region, and secured samples of the mushrooms used ritually in Huautla de Jiménez, one of which was later identified as *Stropharia cubensis*. In 1939, Schultes's paper on the sacred mushrooms of Oaxaca was published.

But the credit for bringing an extended knowledge of the ancient Native American usage of mind-altering mushrooms to the world at large went to retired banker and amateur mycologist Gordon Wasson and his wife, Valentina. "In the fall of 1952," Gordon Wasson recalled, "we learned that the 16th century writers…had recorded that certain mushrooms played a divinatory role in the religion of the natives. Simultaneously we learned that certain pre-Columbian stone artifacts resembling mushrooms…had been turning up, usually in the highlands of Guatemala, in increasing numbers… Like the child in the Emperor's New Clothes, we spoke up, declaring that the so-called 'mushroom stones' really represented mushrooms, and that they were the symbol of a religion." The Wassons set off to find what kinds of mushrooms had been worshipped in Central America, and why. They learned of the work of Reko, Weitlaner, Schultes and the others, and all needles pointed to Oaxaca, so they went there in 1953. Two years later, having established sufficient trust with their Indian hosts, especially and crucially with Maria Sabina, an important *curandera* in Huautla de Jiménez, Gordon Wasson and his "friend and photographer" Alan Richardson were allowed to be the first white outsiders to actually take part in a Mazatec mushroom vigil or *velada*. The two men were offered portions of mushrooms to eat, and Maria Sabina sang "not loud, but with authority…infinitely tender and sweet" as Wasson described it. Her voice hovered around the hut, even sounding at times as if it were passing beneath them. She struck various parts of her body at the same time, producing differing percussive beats. Wasson and Richardson lay on their mats as the mushrooms took effect. Wasson has left us a classic, beautiful description of his experience:

Your body lies in the darkness, heavy as lead, but your spirit seems to soar and leave the hut, and with the speed of thought to travel where it listeth, in time and space, accompanied by the shaman's singing and by the ejaculations of her percussive chant. What you are seeing and what you are hearing appear as one: the music assumes harmonious shapes, giving visual form to its harmonies, and what you are seeing takes on the modalities of music – the music of the spheres... All your senses are similarly affected... the bemushroomed person is poised in space, a disembodied eye, invisible, incorporeal, seeing but not seen. In truth, he is the five senses disembodied, all of them keyed to the height of sensitivity and awareness, all of them blending into one another most strangely, until the person, utterly passive, becomes a pure receptor, infinitely delicate, of sensations. (You, being a stranger, are perforce only a receptor. But the Mazatec communicants are also participants with the *curandera* in an extempore religious colloquy...) ... As your body lies there in its sleeping bag, your soul is free, loses all sense of time, alert as it never was before, living an eternity in a night, seeing infinity in a grain of sand... At last you know what the ineffable is, and what ecstasy means. Ecstasy! The mind harks back to the origins of that word. For the Greeks *ekstasis* meant the flight of the soul from the body. Can you find a better word than that to describe the bemushroomed state? In common parlance, among the many who have not experienced ecstasy, ecstasy is fun, and I am frequently asked why I do not reach for mushrooms every night. But ecstasy is not fun. Your very soul is seized and shaken until it tingles. After all, who will choose to feel undiluted awe, or to float through that door yonder into the Divine Presence?

Richardson, meanwhile, was having visions "of Chinese motifs, like Kubla Khan – palaces, oriental designs and so forth. After that, I saw the vision of a beautiful mantlepiece with the portrait of a Spanish caballero over it, which I happen to remember very well." This is because of what happened later that trip, when they got back to Mexico City: he and Wasson were invited to a hacienda where they had never been before. "When we walked into the drawing room, there was the portrait I had seen in my vision. I don't yet know what to make of that," Richardson puzzled, fully thirty-five years later.

A few days after this historic session, Wasson, with his wife and daughter, took mushrooms and became "so far as is known, the first white people to eat 'magic mushrooms' experimentally – removed from the native ceremonial setting." Wasson continued to make visits to Mexico, taking the mushrooms again on numerous occasions, and confirming that their use was widespread amongst certain groups of Mexican Indians, and wasn't confined solely to the Mazatecs. Among various specialists and experts who accompanied him on his expeditions was mycologist Roger Heim of Paris, who conducted botanical identification of the sacred mushrooms. He found that they were from the family *Strophariaceae*, roughly a dozen different species that had not previously been scientifically identified, most of them belonging to the genus *Psilocybe*. Heim had heard of Albert Hofmann's work with LSD at Sandoz. "Thus it was LSD that showed *teonanacatl* the way into our laboratory," Hofmann has remarked. Heim had cultivated a sample of *Psilocybe Mexicana* and it was this that Hofmann chemically analysed. To test if these samples were psychoactive, Hofman self-experimented with them. He took thirty-two mushrooms, and found the effects to be powerful:

> Thirty minutes after taking the mushrooms, the exterior world began to undergo a strange transformation. Everything assumed a Mexican character. As I was perfectly well aware that my knowledge of the Mexican origin of the mushroom would lead me to imagine only Mexican scenery, I tried deliberately to look on my environment as I knew it normally. But all voluntary efforts to look at things in their customary forms and colors proved ineffective. Whether my eyes were closed or open, I saw only Mexican motifs and colors.

When the doctor supervising the experiment bent over me to check my blood pressure, he was transformed into an Aztec priest and I would not have been astonished if he had drawn an obsidian knife. In spite of the seriousness of the situation, it amused me to see how the Germanic face of my colleague had acquired a purely Indian expression. At the peak of the intoxication…the rush of interior pictures, mostly abstract motifs rapidly changing in shape and color, reached such an alarming degree that I feared that I would be torn into this whirlpool of form and color and would dissolve… I felt my return to everyday reality to be a happy return from a strange, fantastic but quite real world to an old and familiar home.

Hofmann's analysis, published in 1958, revealed two new indole compounds, which he called psilocybin and psilocin, closely related in their structure as well as in their effects to LSD. They also possess a chemical structure very similar to the neurotransmitter serotonin in the human brain. Hofmann observed that it was possible to synthesise the new substances without the aid of mushrooms. (It was synthesised psilocybin tablets that powered Timothy Leary's first experiments at Harvard.) "Essentially, when all is said and done," Hofmann has noted with characteristic perceptivity, "we can only say that the mystery of the wondrous effects of *teonanacatl* was reduced to the mystery of the effects of two crystalline substances – since these effects canot be explained by science either, but can only be described."

Hofmann accompanied Wasson on one of his future forays into native Mexico looking for other ritual hallucinogens. But scientific colleagues weren't the only ones interested in joining Wasson on his expeditions. He had been approached by the CIA and asked if he would work with them. Wasson refused. Subsequently, James Moore, a chemist from the University of Delaware, made funding possible for Wasson's 1956 expedition on the proviso that he be allowed to take part in it personally. Unknown to Wasson, Moore was in fact a CIA operative. "At the time, all we knew was that we didn't like Jim.

Something was wrong with him," Allan Richardson dryly remarked many years later.

In 1957, Wasson reported his experiences at Huautla de Jiménez for *Life* magazine. The centuries-old secret of the Indian mushroom ritual was revealed, and over subsquent years a flood of thrill-seekers went to Oaxaca. They showed lack of respect for the Indian traditions and for the mushrooms, Maria Sabina's "saint children." The remote village was disrupted, and the saintly *curandera* felt the mushrooms were losing their power as a result of the influx of outsiders: "From the moment the foreigners arrived, the 'saint children' lost their purity. They lost their force; the foreigners spoiled them. From now on they won't be any good. There is no remedy for it."

Living traditions of sacred mushroom use have now been discovered amongst Mayan-speaking peoples in southern Mexico. Peter Furst has identified a number of mushroom ceramics representing the species *Psilocybe* in two-thousand-year-old tomb art in western Mexico. Native Americans' ritual use of hallucinogenic mushrooms outside of Mexico is indicated by the mushroom stones and by pre-Columbian gold pectorals from Colombia, which clearly display mushroom forms. Some of the Guatemalan mushroom stones seem to resemble that old mushroom of Eurasian shamanism, *Amanita muscaria*, the fly agaric. The red-capped variety of *Amanita muscaria* grows naturally in British Columbia, in the north-western United States, in southern upland areas of Mexico and in highland Guatemala, with a yellow-capped strain growing in more easterly areas of North America. Use of the mushroom has been discovered amongst the Dogrib Athabascan peoples in the Mackenzie mountains in north-western Canada, where it is used sacramentally in shamanism. One neophyte reported that in his initiatory seance he couldn't eat, sleep and didn't even think. "I wasn't in my body any longer." At a later session he recorded that he was "ripe for vision" and had "sung the note that shatters structure. And the note that shatters chaos…I have been with the dead and attempted the labyrinth."

Anthropologists have noted that the Coast Salish of the American Northwest, and also Alaskan Inuit (Eskimos), carefully preserved their urine which was thought to have magical and curative properties, and as late as 1886 were seen to offer urine for drinking. This strongly hints at a continuation of the Siberian tradition of using urine for recycled *Amanita muscaria* effects. Anthropologist Claude Lévi-Strauss noted that certain Inuit and Athabascan groups chew the ashes of a fungus that grows on birch trees (the host of *Amanita muscaria*), sometimes in conjunction with tobacco. It has also been discovered that the Ojibway of Michigan used *Amanita muscaria* as a sacred hallucinogen in an ancient annual ceremony. The mushroom in the Ojibway language is called *Wajashk-wedo,* "red-top mushroom." Moreover, red mushrooms figure in Ojibway legends. In Ohio, an intriguing find was made in a major necropolis of the powerful, shamanic Hopewell culture, which flourished around two thousand years ago. In what was clearly a shaman's mound in the necropolis ("Mound City," Chillicothe) the effigy of an apparently amanita-type mushroom was uncovered. About a foot long, it was fashioned from wood and had been covered with copper. Various other types of Hopewell shamanic artefacts have also

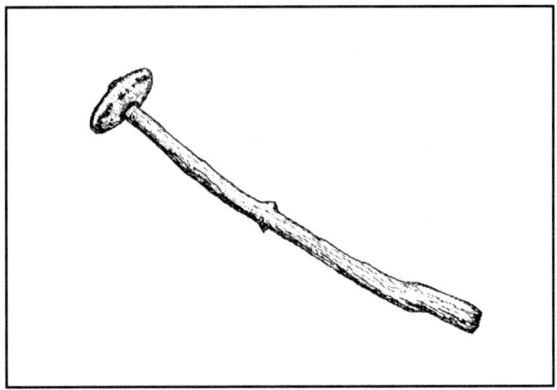

A drawing of the Hopewell Indian mushroom effigy found in a shaman's mound at Chillicothe, Ohio.

been found, including many clay pipes shaped as birds, ritual masks and deerantler headgear, clay figurines depicting men apparently in trance, and bird claws and swastika designs cut out of mica, designed for hanging on ceremonial costumes. Wasson felt that the swastika designs derived from geometric "entoptic" patterns seen in trance states, and especially hallucinogen-induced trance states.

In Mesoamerica, a miniature clay sculpture from Nyarit, thought to date to about A.D. 100, shows what clearly seems to be *Amanita muscaria* with a figure, apparently a shaman, sitting beneath it.

In Native American ritual use of *Amanita muscaria*, we may have the most profound New World vestige of Eurasian shamanism.

Datura

As discussed in my *Darklore* Volume 2 article "Witches' Brews", species of datura – belonging to the nightshade family – had a role to play in witchcraft and other magico-religious activities in the Old World. However, the genus has had an even wider ceremonial application in the Americas, where it has been used for prophecy, divination, diagnosing illness (by providing access to spirit knowledge), medicine (to relieve swellings and to ease the pains of childbirth and rheumatism), in puberty initiation rites and for the production of visionary states, as it characteristically tends to generate the classic shamanic experiences of spirit flight and transformation into animals.

In eastern North America, the Algonkian Indians issued a ritual drink, *wysoccan*, to youths undergoing rites of passage in the *Huskanawing* ceremony. The basis of this beverage was *Datura stramonium*, or jimson weed. Another known area of Native American datura usage was in the Southwest, notably southern California, Arizona, and New Mexico, where *Datura inoxia* was – and perhaps still is – used. The Chumash of coastal south California used the hallucinogen, and possibly *Datura stramonium* as well, for puberty rites and shamanic purposes, and its visionary effects are linked with the imagery in their rock art. Datura was ceremonially employed also by the Miwok, Mojave, Yokuts, Cahuilla, and numerous other Californian tribes. The Hopi and Navajo of Arizona are notable amongst the peoples there who used datura. The Navajo word for it is *ch'ohojilyh*. They used it for magic-oriented work, and visions seen under its influence were thought to show causes of disease. Ethnological references indicate that it was still being used for these kind of purposes up until recent decades, but the present status of *ch'ohojilyh* is not clear – it looks as if its use may have lapsed. The Zuni Indians of present-day New Mexico call *Datura inoxia a-neg-la-kya,* and use (or have used) it both ritually and medicinally. It figures in ancient Zuni legends, and could only be collected by Zuni rain priests or shamans, who applied the powdered root to their eyes to enable them to see at night, to see spirits, and to commune with birds. The antiquity of this ritual usage can be gauged from the fact that in the Zuni Kuaua kiva, near Albuquerque, there is a rare pre-Columbian mural depicting a shaman holding a species of datura.

The Mexican Indians call the hallucinogen *toloache*, from the Aztec *toaloatzin*. The Aztecs presumably used it in the same way that the modern Tarahumara do. A powerfully toxic and very distinct species of datura, *Datura ceratocaula*, known as "maddening plant," also grows in the marshes or shallow water of Mexico, and was used in ancient times there.

In South America, there are varieties of *Brugmansia*, so-called tree-daturas. These are now recognized as a separate genus, but they contain the same tropane alkaloids as datura, namely scopolamine, hyoscyamine and atropine. *Brugmansia* is biologically very complex, and it is thought that its species may all be cultigens – unknown in the wild. The leaves, flowers and seeds of all species of *Brugmansia* seem to have been used as hallucinogens for thousands of years, either alone or mixed with other plant substances, in the Andes from Colombia to Chile, and along the Pacific Coast. They were of extreme importance to ancient Indians such as the Inca and Chibcha, and are still used for divinatory rites by various remote Indian tribes in isolated areas of Colombia, Ecuador and Peru. Such Indians include the Shuar (Jívaro) of Ecuador, and the Kams and Ingano Indians (who Schultes considered possessed "the most intricate narcotic consciousness of any peoples in the New World") in the Valley of Sibundoy in Andean Colombia. For centuries these Indians have manipulated *Brugmansia aurea* so that numerous aberrant forms now exist in Sibundoy, each "owned" by a shaman and considered to have special virtues. The shamans or *payés* distinguish differing characteristics of the intoxication provided by the different strains, preferring the less powerful ones for use in divination and prophecy. This makes sense, as the effects of *Brugmansia* can be very disorienting: typically, a person who has just taken a substantial dose may become so violent and agitated that he has to be restrained, until he falls into a deep and disturbed sleep, in which visions appear.

In 1990, while in the Ecuadorian rainforest, psychologist Ralph Metzner had two experiences with *Brugmansia aurea*. In each case he took a small dose of the green juice prepared by squeezing the inner pulp or pith from the stem. Metzner lay down in bed, entering a "twilight sleep." His body felt very relaxed and he experienced floating sensations, with a feeling of expanding into the immediate environment and becoming keenly aware of people who were out of his sight and earshot. In his first session, he fell asleep for several hours, and in the morning had two dreams, one about a disagreement with his wife, the other about a dispute with someone with whom he planned a collaborative project. Later, he did indeed have a specifically similar conflict with his wife, and he found out information about his potential colleague which confirmed his decision not to proceed with the collaborative venture. His second session also yielded a dream, in which he saw a petite, dark-haired Spanish-speaking woman giving a lecture to the research group Metzner was part of. The next day, a woman fitting precisely this description and whom he had not seen previously, arrived to speak to the group. Metzner concluded from his limited experimentation that *Brugmansia* "does indeed have the potential for producing divinations, in this case verifiable precognitive dreams; possibly the precognitions are anticipatory warnings of personal conflicts."

Recently, an intriguing suggestion has been made, relating to a mysterious, prehistoric ground drawing (geoglyph) etched up to three feet deep into a sloping dune overlooking the Bay of Paracas on the Peruvian coast, about a hundred miles north of the equally mysterious desert lines at Nazca. The figure is so large – some six hundred feet long, and nearly two hundred feet across – that it can be seen from many miles out to sea. Pottery fragments found near it have been dated to around 200 B.C. Because of its symmetrical design, the three-pronged geoglyph is often referred to as "The Candelabra of the Andes" or "The Trident of Paracas." It is not a motif met with in studies of ancient South American art, and there are details in the design that argue against it depicting a trident (as unlikely as that would be in any case). It obviously acts as a landmark, but what is it? It may have been a religious symbol, but that still does not explain what it is supposed to depict. Researcher Frank Joseph has suggested that it is a stylised rendering of jimson weed. He has found a small version of the same design drawn on a rock in California's Cleveland National Park, and proposes that the ancient people of Paracas voyaged up the Pacific coast to California to collect this particular species of datura.

Vine of the Soul: "A drug for flying"

The most widely used Native American hallucinogens today are infusions and snuffs based on the vine or liana *Banisteriopsis caapi*, and other species of *Banisteriopsis*. The use of the vine is a South American phenomenon. Thousands of Indians use it in the western Amazon, the Orinoco, and on the slopes of the Pacific coast of Colombia and Ecuador. It is known by a variety of names in different places: *caapi, ayahuasca, yagé (yajé), natema, pinde, nape*, among others. *Banisteropsis* infusions – which we will refer to here as *ayahuasca*, the most commonly selected term among Western commentators today – typically promote a sensation of the spirit separating from the body, and though this is a common effect of many native hallucinogens (the very basis of ecstatic experience, in fact), *Banisteriopsis* concoctions seem particularly effective at producing this sensation. It is used in initiation ceremonies, for returning to the beginning of the universe to see the gods, and for prophetic and divinatory purposes, including travelling in spirit (usually in the form of a bird or animal, such as a jaguar) to distant places and seeing the things happening there. German scholar Hans Peter Duerr has written that *ayahuasca* "seems to be specifically a 'drug for flying'." (Interestingly, the Shua Indians use the term "trip" when referring to the ecstatic state, and, likewise, the Cashinahua Indians of Peru apply the word *bai*, meaning "trip," in the sense of a sightseeing excursion, just as did Western youth in the 1960s when referring to a psychedelic experience.)

In some regions the bark of *Banisteriopsis liana* is prepared in a cold-water infusion, but more commonly bark and stem, perhaps leaves too, are boiled in water for long periods. Sometimes, the fresh bark is chewed. Visions had under *Banisteriopsis* alone tend to be dull blue or grey unless certain additives are used, when more vivid colours are experienced and the hallucinogenic effect is altogether more potent. Most *ayahuasca* drinks do contain additives, but their full range and chemistry is largely unknown to Western science. Those that have been studied reveal sophisticated neurophysiological knowledge on the part of unknown generations of rainforest Indians. The active elements in *Banisteriopsis* are principally the alkaloids harmine and tetrahydroharmine, plus the less important harmaline. (It was first thought that new alkaloids had been found, and one was named telepathine on account of the divinatory and clairvoyant properties claimed for the hallucinogen, but it was later realised that all the alkaloids had already long been identified in Syrian Rue.) These are beta-carbolines which act as monoamine oxidase (MAO) inhibitors, which means that they prevent the degradation of certain neurotransmitters or amines administered from outside the body. It has been found that several of the traditional *ayahuasca* additives contain tryptamine alkaloids, specifically DMT (N, N-dimethyltryptamine, methoxy-N, N-dimethyltryptamine). This substance is not effective when taken by mouth, as it is broken down by the enzyme MAO before it can pass the blood-brain barrier. When it is combined with carbolines, however, as in *ayahuasca*, which inhibit the MAO, it becomes orally effective. In short, the *Banisteriopsis* base of *ayahuasca* acts as an enabler of the DMT hallucinogenic effects provided by the additives. Not only do the Indians display sophistication with this practical knowledge, but they also distinguish between different types of *ayahuasca*, all of which have their own names. The Turkano, for example, have six types, while the Harakmbet Indians have no less than twenty-two kinds, each noted for specific visionary effects and symbolism. At least one of these types of *ayahuasca* is said to confer permanent visionary effects.

The strong "flight" effects of *ayahuasca* were noted by outsiders from the beginning. In 1858, only seven years after its discovery by Richard Spruce, the Ecuadorian geographer Manuel Villavicencio made the first written report on the *ayahuasca* experience. "Its action appears to excite the nervous system; all the senses liven up and all faculties awaken…vertigo and spinning in the head, then a sensation of being lifted into the air…" the geographer wrote. "I can say for a fact that when I've taken *ayahuasca* I've experienced dizziness, then an aerial journey in which I recall perceiving the most gorgeous views, great cities, lofty towers, beautiful parks, and other extremely attractive objects; then I imagined myself to be alone in the forest and assaulted by a number of terrible beings from which I defended myself; thereafter I had the strong sensation of sleep…" Similar kinds of effects are reported today. An American informant told me that after she had taken *ayahuasca* in a rainforest setting, she suddenly found herself high up in the air above the tree canopy, with the stars overhead. The experience was completely "real" in both appearance and feeling. She spent most of the session in this apparently suspended state.

Some claim the ability to be able to see things at a distance while under the influence of *ayahuasca*. This is usually combined with the out-of-body or soul-flight experience. Peter Gorman, executive editor of *High Times* magazine, has described *ayahuasca* sessions he experienced in 1984 in Peru. During one session, he had a vision of a huge, brown bird with long, white-tipped wings, soaring over snowy mountain peaks. "I was looking at the bird from a great distance when I suddenly felt myself merging with it," Gorman recalled. "I saw from the bird's perspective, my sharp eyes picking out the most minute details of the landscape. I flew over a range of mountains, searching for something. While travelling at great speed, I looked down into a stream and saw fish moving slowly in shallow water. Although I was thousands of feet in the air, I could see sunlight glinting off individual scales on the blue and green fish. The colors were unimaginably rich." After diving down and catching and eating a fish, all in the richest and most realistic detail, Gorman returned to his body. But soon he drifted off again into more flying visions; he would sometimes fly with the bird, sometimes just below it. On two occasions he asked the bird to take him somewhere. First, he "went" to see his wife in California. He glimpsed her making love with someone, but as soon as he experienced a pang of jealousy, the image was snatched from him. The second was a visit to his apartment in New York, which he had sublet to two friends. There was nothing special about the scene, just two people sitting reading, talking occasionally. But they were wearing clothes he'd never seen on them before. Later, when Gorman returned to New York, he saw that these same friends had bought new shirts exactly like those he had seen in his vision.

A more dramatic instance of *ayahuasca*'s powers in promoting apparent remote viewing was brought home to anthropologist Kenneth Kensinger when he was with the Peruvian Cashinahua. He notes that the Cashinahua drink *ayahuasca* in order to learn about things, persons and events at a distance – geographically, in time, or both. He continues:

> Hallucinations generally involve scenes which are a part of the Cashinahua's daily experience. However, informants have described hallucinations about places far removed both geographically and from their own experience. Several informants who have never been to or seen pictures of Pucallpa, the large town at the Ucayali River terminus of the Central Highway, have described their visits under the influence of *ayahuasca* to the town with sufficient detail for me to be able to recognize specific shops and sights. On the day following one *ayahuasca* party six of nine men informed me of seeing the death of my chai, "my mother's father." This occurred two days before I was informed by radio of his death.

The Hunting of the Deer: Peyote

Peyote (*Lophophora williamsii*) is one of the best known of Native American hallucinogens, and the visionary experience and profound metaphysical and intellectual insight the small cactus vouchsafes has been relatively well documented. Its magic may have accompanied human beings for virtually the whole time they have inhabited the New World, for fossilised cactus buttons have been found that are several thousands of years old. The cactus has been recorded in stone as art in Mesoamerican tombs dating to 100 B.C., and is represented on a ceramic snuffing pipe from Monte Alban, Oaxaca, dating to 500 B.C. As a symbol employed in the Tarahumara Indian peyote ceremony, it is even depicted in prehistoric rock carvings.

The peyote cactus is small, somewhat turnip-like in shape and size, and has no spines, branches or leaves. Just its rounded crown peeps up above the ground, and it is this which becomes a "peyote button" when cut off and dried. The surface of the cactus is divided by a radial arrangement of ribs and segments which bear small tufts of grey-white hair, and it is this feature to which the botanical name *Lophophora* ("I bear crests") refers, and which inspired the Aztec name *peyotl*, which is a reference to cocoon-silk. The cactus is rich in phenylethylamine and tetrahydroisoquinoline types of alkaloids. The most active "visionary" alkaloid is trimethoxyphenylethylamine, called mescaline. However, due to complex and little-understood interactions between the various active constituents, traditional users of peyote feel that taken as an organic whole it provides a rather different experience to that of chemical mescaline taken on its own.

The cactus can be eaten raw or in dried form, or taken as a tea or mash. A "dose" would normally range between four to thirty buttons. The peyote experience is characterised by vividly-coloured hallucinations which often follow a sequence starting with geometric patterns and progressing to more complex representational scenes, both familiar and novel. Visual effects can be accompanied by tactile and auditory hallucinations, and with synesthesia, the mixing of sensory modalities, so one "hears" colours, and so forth. La Barre points out that auditory hallucinations had under peyote are known to have been the source of Indian songs and chants developed in fairly recent times – "Heyowiniho," for instance, came to the 1890s Ghost Dance leader John Wilson (Nishkúntu) from a peyote experience in which he heard the sound of the sun's rising. This inevitably raises an interesting question: how much Indian traditional ceremonial song, dance and costume had its source in hallucinatory states?

The first historical documentation of the use of peyote was, as might be expected, by the Spanish chroniclers of Aztec culture. Francisco Hernández wrote in 1651: "Ground up and applied to painful joints, it is said to give relief… This root…causes those devouring it to foresee and predict things…and other things of like nature… On which account, this root scarcely issues forth, as if it did not wish to harm those who discover it and eat it."

With their typical severity and assumed righteousness, the Spanish attempted to outlaw peyote use. Hence its medicinal and ceremonial use was kept secret by the Indians in the remote Mexican countryside, where it has survived among some Indian tribes up to the present day. Knowledge of peyote crossed what is now the Mexican-United States border a number of times in the unchronicled past, but the first documented reference to its use amongst North American Indians seems to have been in 1760 in Texas. Around 1880, the Kiowa and Comanche tribes developed a new kind of peyote ceremony which ultimately led to the establishment of the Native American Church. This is today a legal, highly-principled religious organisation which uses peyote as a sacrament. It claims around a quarter of a million Indian adherents amongst many tribes throughout North America, its influence stretching as far north as Saskatchewan, Canada. The big problem nowadays is the shortage of peyote, caused not only by the demands of the Native American Church, but by others seeking the cactus.

This is said to be the first published illustration of peyote, in *Curtis' Botanical Magazine,* 1847. It is usually just the grey-green crowns of peyote that are visible at or above ground level, with the rest of the cactus growing beneath the surface.

The best-preserved ancient peyote tradition is that of the Huichol Indians of the Sierra Madre Occidental of northern Mexico. They make an annual three-hundred-mile pilgrimage to Wirikúta, a high desert area of mythic, ancestral significance to them, situated in San Luis Potosí to the north-east of their present homeland. This area is traditionally rich in the peyote cactus, and the pilgrimage is a ritual "hunt" for peyote that lasts for several weeks. The sanctity of peyote is deeply rooted in Huichol culture, and La Barre has stated that "the unacculturated myths of the Huichol contain embedded in them elements of manifestly very great antiquity, some harking back to the mesolithic horizons of the Paleo-Siberian migrants who became the American Indians." Anthropologists were allowed to accompany and observe the Wirikúta pilgrimage for the first time in 1966, and Western outsiders have taken part in subsequent pilgrimages.

Until recent decades the trek was undertaken on foot, but now much of it is done by car, though holy places on the traditionally-defined route are still visited as much as possible, and veneration made at them appropriate to their mythic role. Many Huichol aspire to take this pilgrimage at least once in their lives, but it is not obligatory. It is led by a shaman or *mara'akame*. For the duration of the pilgrimage, he represents the Great Shaman, Tatewari ("Grandfather Fire"), who led the ancestral gods and goddesses on the first peyote hunt. Those going on the hunt, or who remain behind to maintain the sacred hearth fire in the temple, have to undergo a period of purification, abstaining from sex and, at the outset, naming in public every sexual partner they have had since puberty. This is done without recrimination or shame. For the period of the peyote hunt fasting is observed with only minimal food consumption during the journey and the stay at Wirikúta. Each pilgrim is "newborn," and for the purposes of the hunt represents one of the deities who took part in the original mythic, ancestral peyote quest.

The Huichols call the sacred cactus *hikuri*, and it is thought of as being a deer, or, more accurately, a manifestation of the supernatural Master of the Deer Species. To eat the fresh cactus is to eat the flesh of the sacred, primal deer itself. At Wirikúta, *hikuri* manifests as Elder Brother Deer who bestows the gift of transcendence upon the pilgrims. The Deer-Peyote concept is also associated with maize. Barbara Myerhoff, who took part in the 1966 pilgrimage, has written:

Together, deer, maize, and peyote account for the totality of Huichol life and history. The deer is associated with the Huichols' idealized historical past as nomadic hunters; the maize stands for the life of the present – mundane, sedentary, good and beautiful, utilitarian, difficult, and demanding; and peyote evokes the timeless, private, purposeless, aesthetic dimension of the spiritual life, mediating between former and present realities and providing a sense of being one people.

The *mara'akame* carries a hunting bow (also used as as a ritual musical instrument) and arrows in a deerskin quiver. When the region of Wirikúta is finally approached, the pilgrims are led by the *mara'akame* along a mythic route, retracing the ancestral steps, encountering, with much emotion, places that have mythic significance but which in physical appearance are unremarkable. A deer deity and culture hero called Elder Brother Kauyumarie is invoked as the *mara'akame's* spirit helper. Those making the trip for the first time are blindfolded on arriving at the boundary of Wirikúta "so as not to be blinded by the glory and brilliant light of the sacred land." When the feature known as "the water holes of Our Mothers" is reached, the blindfolds are ceremonially removed. At the appropriate place, the first camp fire is speedily "brought out" of a piece of wood, and all participants feed the sacred fire, the manifestation of Tatewari. A coal is taken from this and all fires lit during the hunt; each coal contains the *kupuri*, the essence or life force, of Tatewari.

Then the hunt for Deer-Peyote begins. Bows and arrows and offerings are readied . Beating the string of his bow, the *mara'akame* creeps forward until he sees the "tracks" of Deer-Peyote, and a cluster of *Lophophora williamsii*, are found. The cactus is "killed" by the *mara'akame* shooting or placing ceremonial arrows into it and in the Four Directions around it. The pilgrims ask Deer-Peyote to not punish them for killing him, for he will rise again. Offerings are made. The *mara'akame* sees the life essence coming out of the cactus like a rainbow of coloured rays of light, which are coaxed back into the cactus with a feathered prayer arrow. The cacti are then collected, but with enough root left in the ground so Elder Brother can regrow from his "bones." A piece of "Elder Brother's flesh" is ceremonially given to each participant with the admonition to "chew it well" so as to be able to "see your life." After some singing and dancing, and the consumption of more pieces of peyote, the harvest proper begins, with participants going off into the desert with baskets – "game bags" – looking carefully for the cacti. Ritual exchanges of peyote are made amongst participants as part of the traditional ethic of the hunt. Night-time is spent singing and dancing around the ceremonial fire consuming large quanties of the hallucinogenic cacti. The pilgrims go into trance, experiencing out-of-body flight, or falling into visionary reverie. It is thought by the Huichol that the visions of the *mara'akame*, as he stares into the fire, are different from those of the other participants.

Huichol Indians do not talk about their visions, but Prem Das, a yoga student and a writer who has researched altered states of consciousness, attended a Huichol pilgrimage at Wirikúta in the early 1970s and reported on his visionary experience. After receiving his peyote, he sat down to watch a spectacular sunset as the psychoactive plant took effect. When he next looked around him, he could see the sacred cacti, or "flowers" as the Huichol called them, apparently glowing with self-luminescence in many places in the desert. He was easily able to collect at least a hundred of the cacti in the bags he had with him. He ate some more. He felt peaceful and blessed in this Holy Land of the Huichol, but this ultimately caused him to weep as he thought of the harshness and lack of harmony of so many aspects of his own, Western society. He wondered why it was that we have become so estranged from the Earth.

> I heard an answer that seemed to come from all around me, and it rose in my mind's eye like a great time-lapse vision. I saw a human

being rise from the earth, stand for a moment, and then dissolve back into it. It was only a brief moment; and in that moment our whole lives passed. Then I saw a huge city rise out of the desert floor before me, exist for a second, and then vanish back into the vastness of the desert. The plants, rock, and earth under me were saying, Yes, this is how it really is, your life, the city you live in. It was as if in my peyotized state I was able to perceive and communicate with a resonance or vibration that surrounded me… An overwhelming realization poured through me – that the human race and all technology formed by it are nothing other than flowers of the earth. The painful problem which had confronted me disappeared entirely, to be replaced with a vision of people and their technology as temporary forms through which Mother Earth was expressing herself.

The pilgrims leave Wirikúta promptly when their activities there are finished (it is considered spiritually dangerous to linger too long), departing as they had entered, in single file, blowing horns. They implore the ancestral beings who inhabit Wirikúta not to leave, not to abandon their places, for they, the Huichol, will come again another year.

"Peyote may be viewed as the Huichol provision for that dimension of religious experience which can never be routinized and made altogether public – that sense of awe and wonder, the *mysterium tremendum et fascinans*, without which religion is mere ritual and form," Myerhoff has commented.

> It provides the ecstatic and enormous moment when the soul departs, flies upward, and loses itself in the other reality. The darkness explodes into dancing colors…Returning to ordinary reality, the pilgrims are left grief-stricken, exhausted, and exhilarated by the experience. An enormous undertaking has been accomplished. They have traveled to paradise, dwelled there as deities for a moment, and returned to mortal life.

The Psychedelic Temple

One of the hallucinogens to have had the longest use in the Americas is undoubtedly *Trichocereus pachanoi*, known in northern coastal Peru as San Pedro. As with peyote, the active principle of this cactus is mescaline. It is found in the general Andes region of South America. It is used today for curing sickness, divination and sorcery. Its use involves a moon-oriented ritual that has a Christian veneer, but which no doubt has a long history. This is indicated on an engraved stone panel in the wall of the circular sunken plaza of the Old Temple at Chavín de Huantar, which was built in the first millennium B.C. In this panel, a piece of the long, ribbed cactus is shown being grasped by a visionary human-animal being which has jaguar fangs – the jaguar is a motif strongly associated with South American shamanism. Rebecca Stone-Miller has suggested that this image actually depicts a costumed shaman holding the cactus as a staff of authority.

Chavín de Huantar is a large, profoundly mysterious ruined temple complex, located midway between coast and jungle in northern Peru. It stands at the confluence of two rivers at an altitude of over ten thousand feet. The entirely windowless building opens only to the east, and has processional routes carefully constructed to control the movement of people through the complex, and some of its architectural details subtly relate the whole structure to cosmological principles, such as the Four Directions. It has deeply enigmatic features, such as a labyrinth of internal, unlit passageways, rooms where the roaring sound of rushing water from the rivers is emphasised by architectural techniques, and others that are quite soundproof. The complex focuses on a fifteen-foot-high carved stone monument known as the Lanzón, situated within a cruciform gallery set deep in the centre of the temple structure.

Chavín de Huantar was an active centre from about 900 to 200 B.C., the heart of a shamanic cult that projected its influence for hundreds of miles around, and expressed it through an art style to which the complex gives its name. "Chavín is a very complex, 'baroque' and esoteric style, intentionally difficult to decipher, intended to disorient, and ultimately to transport the viewer into alternate realities," Stone-Miller informs. "Much of the cult's enormous success may be ascribed to the intense visual messages sent by the buildings, their decoration, and the portable ritual objects. Their strong perceptual effect, certainly calculated by Chavín artists, inspires confusion, surprise, fear, and awe through the use of dynamic, shifting images that contain varying readings depending on the direction in which they are approached. The terms 'hallucinatory' and 'transformational' aptly describe much Chavín subject matter and artistic effect."

A number of techniques were employed to produce the powerful psychedelic effects of Chavín art. One of these was to use lines that served double and triple duty, allowing images to form and dissolve in different parts of a visual display – much as the Necker-cube optical illusion allows the viewer to switch mentally from looking inside a transparent cube one moment, to staring at its exterior from another angle the next. Another trick was to use deeply-incised lines that used the high-contrast, inky-dark shadows cast by the crisp Andean sunlight to produce shifting outlines. Dozens of large sculpted heads studded the outside walls of the temple complex. "As if time-lapse photography, they document the dramatic process of shamanic transformation through hallucinogenics," Stone-Miller observes, for there are sequences of heads which show, stage by stage, human features transforming into exotic, hallucinatory creatures. Here, wrought in stone, is the hallucinogenic experience of the body-image changing into a were-animal.

Use of the San Pedro cactus is found throughout the record of Andean culture. Well-preserved textiles have been found at Karwa, a burial site three hundred miles from Chavín de Huantar, depicting images of San Pedro cacti, as do Chavín-style ceramic vessels. The much later Moche culture (c. A.D. 500) has yielded a stirrup-spout vessel depicting a female, owl-headed shaman (another image of

A drawing of the bas-relief at Chavin de Huantar depicting a supernatural being or priest in ritual garb holding a San Pedro cactus.

trance-transformation) with strings of mind-altering espingo seeds and the characteristic star-shape of the San Pedro that is vividly revealed in the cross-section of the cactus. Moche pottery designs also often depicted the tree *Anadenathera colubrina*, the seeds of which were used to produce the potently-hallucinogenic *wilka* snuff, and contain scenes that anthropologist Marlene Dobkin de Rios interprets as showing actual San Pedro sessions. Pottery of the Nasca culture (approximately 200 B.C. to A.D. 600) often show "flower" or "star" motifs which can readily be interpreted as San Pedro cross-sections. There are also various examples showing motifs alluding to ecstatic magical flight in ancient Andean art.

A Treasure Chest of Visions

While sacred mushrooms, *Banisteriopsis*, Red Bean or *Sophora secundiflora*, *ololiuqui* or morning glory seeds, datura, peyote and San Pedro cactus represent the most important of Native American hallucinogens, there are so many known in the New World (not to mention those that have not yet been identified), that there simply isn't space to describe all of them, but a few of the other, lesser-known ones can be briefly mentioned in order to give a sense of the sheer scale of the pharmacopoeia of visionary substances that the ancient Native Americans possessed.

American Indian usage of hallucinogens did not only involve drinking, chewing and smoking, but also snuffing: psychoactive snuffs have been employed from remotest antiquity (as have enemas, as well). There is ample evidence that the ancient use of psychedelic snuffs occurred over much of South America, in the Caribbean islands, and, at one time, in Mexico too. Snuff samples twelve hundred years old have been found in mummy bundles from northern Chile, while a bone snuffing tray and tubes (nose pipes) dating to 1600 B.C. has been excavated in Peru. "Archaeological remains in Argentina, Brazil, Chile, Colombia, Costa Rica, the Dominican Republic, Haiti, Peru and Puerto Rico testify to the broad range and antiquity of entheogenic [psychedelic] snuff use in the Caribbean and South America," notes Jonathan Ott. In Mexico, evidence of ancient snuffing goes back to "at least the second millenium B.C." People holding pipes to their nostrils are depicted in Colima tomb artefacts from Western Mexico dating to between 100 B.C. and A.D. 200; a double-stemmed bird-effigy nose pipe from a shaft-and-chamber tomb in Nyarit is of a similar age; nose pipes from Oaxaca are known which go back to 500 B.C., while at Xochipala, Guerrero, ceramic nose pipes dating to between 1300 and 1500 B.C. have been found. There are also Olmec jade "spoons," which were probably used for snuffing, that date to between 1200 and 900 B.C. For reasons unknown, snuffing seems to have ceased in Mexico at some point prior to A.D. 1000.

Psychoactive snuff was the first Native American hallucinogen to have been noted by Europeans. In a letter of 1496, Columbus himself commented on a strange Antillean "powder" which the Taino Indians would "snuff up" rendering them "like drunken men." This snuff was *cohoba*, which, centuries later, was identified as being prepared from the beans of a tree of the pea family, *Anadenanthera peregrina*. *Cohoba* has been found to be the same as the hallucinogenic snuff *yopo*, used by the Indians of the Orinoco Basin, and it was probably from that region that the use of the snuff spread to the West Indies. Indeed, the use of the drug seems to have diffused outward quite widely from the Orinoco. (The snuff is administered through a long, straight hollow cane pipe, one person to another, or hollow bone pipes arranged in a bifurcated Y-fashion for self-administration.) Another *Anadenanthera*-based snuff has traditionally been used in Peru, Bolivia and northern Argentina: it is known as *wilca* (*huilca* or *vilka*, and called *cébil* in Argentina) and derives from *Anadenanthera colubrina*.

The psychoactive elements in *Anadenanthera*-based snuffs are tryptamine derivatives including DMT and bufotenine (5-hydroxy-dimethyltryptamine). Trace amounts of monoamine oxidase-inhibiting beta-carbolines have, interestingly, also been found in the bark of *Anadenanthera peregrina*.

Another important range of hallucinogenic snuffs derive from the blood-red sap of *Virola* species trees, which are of the nutmeg family. Four or five species are selected by the Indians for these powerful snuffs. Tryptamine alkaloids are present in high concentrations in the scrapings of the inner bark of these trees. *Virola* snuffs are used by Indians of the Colombian Amazon, in the Orinoco Basin in Venezuela, and the Rio Negro Basin of Brazil. There are many names for Virola snuffs among the various Indian groups involved, including *yakee, yato, epena, parica* and *nyakwana*. DMT and 5-MeO-DMT has been found present in all *Virola* snuffs analysed.

Peter Furst has drawn attention to the iconography of ornamental snuffing paraphernalia found in the Americas. There is "an unmistakable symbol complex that ties shamanism and the ecstatic experience to the already familiar bird-feline-reptilian configuration we find so prominently in Mesoamerican and Andean cosmology and iconography," he states. Birds, serpents and, particularly, the jaguar – the dominant shamanic symbol of tropical American shamanism – are prominent representations in the imagery to be found on ancient snuffing equipment. Similar but more subtle associations are made by having snuffing pipes fashioned out of bird bones. "Where the bird motif is unspecific," Furst further comments, "it seems to stand for the power of flight that is the shaman's special gift and that is activated by the hallucinogen."

The most widespread substance snuffed by tribal Native Americans, however, is tobacco, and no review of New World hallucinogens would be acceptable without mention of the genus *Nicotiana*, which is a branch of the nightshade family. It is thought probable that about twelve species of *Nicotiana*, including *N. rustica* and *N. tabacum*, started to be cultivated in South America for religious and healing purposes perhaps as long ago as six or eight thousand years. Tobacco became a sacred plant, it is thought, because of its ability, like other members of the nightshade family, to grow spontaneously in disturbed soil, such as sprouting from graves like a gift from the ancestors.

Tobacco use was unknown in Europe prior to the colonisation of the Americas, and it was swiftly taken up as a hedonistic drug. In the Americas, its use had been restricted to shamanic practices, but after about 1700 a gradual shift towards generalised or profane use occurred. Westerners do not think of tobacco as being hallucinogenic, but it has to be remembered that the Native American shaman took extremely large doses, and in sufficiently large amounts tobacco certainly can cause altered states of consciousness. It was and is used in vision quests to induce trance states, and in curing procedures. Tobacco is taken in all manner of ways: chewing or sucking quids, snuffing, by the administration of suppositories and enemas, smoking, the drinking of tobacco juice and syrup, the licking of tobacco paste, eaten as a cake, and the application of tobacco preparations to the skin and eyes. When smoked, it is usually fashioned into large cigar-type rolls, sometimes with additives from other plants, or used in pipes.

When used for trance-induction purposes, in whatever manner, vast dosages are taken. In Guyana, for instance, shamans' apprentices are obliged to consume litres of tobacco juice, typically force-fed through a funnel, which brings them "to the brink of death," as anthropologist Johannes Wilbert puts it. Among the Tupinamba of Brazil, shamanic initiates are fed tobacco juice until they pass out and vomit blood. "South American shamans are known to ingest up to five three-foot-long cigars (while simultaneously chewing tobacco) in the course of a single séance," Wilbert informs. These kinds of massive doses cause convulsions, seizures, and transitory respiratory failure, causing the "temporary death" of the shaman. In this state he can have his out-of-body experience and visit the otherworlds of the spirits and ancestors. They also, of course, risk actual death – it is as dangerous a shamanic technique as it is an incredibly ancient one.

Noteworthy body changes occur in tobacco shamans. Their voices take on a gutteral, deeply hoarse quality, their eyesight under advanced nicotine intoxication becomes keenly effective in dim, twilight conditions because of neural changes in the retina, so they have night vision like the jaguar, and increased perspiration and the liberation of norepinephrine causes a drop in skin temperature, assisting them to demonstrate the shamanic mastery of fire by heat-defying feats.

Some of the other mind-altering substances that have been, or are believed to have been, used by Native Americans include other species of cacti and mushrooms. But there are also plants – also known of in the Old World – which possess perhaps unexpected psychoactive properties. For example, the white water lily (*Nymphaea ampla*) is pictured in ancient Mayan art, often in conjunction with animal transformations and other visionary subjects. It has been found to contain apomorphine, which is psychoactive. Mayan art also depicts frogs or toads, and Marlene Dobkin de Rios has argued that the Mayans may have used the psychoactive giant toad, *Bufo marinus*, which secretes bufotenine and buftalin. Other native hallucinogens are simply bizarre: *Heimia salicifolia*, for instance, a shrub the Mexicans call *sinicuichi*, is specifically an auditory hallucinogen – it does not produce visions. A person drinking an infusion made of its leaves will feel giddy, drowsy, and will visually experience a darkening of the surroundings, accompanied by alterations of time and space, and auditory hallucinations. Actual sounds will appear distorted and seem to come from very far away. Indians consider the plant to be sacred and to have supernatural powers. They claim that it helps them to recall long-ago events with great vividness, and even to remember prenatal events. Its ancient use is indicated by the fact that a *sinicuichi* bud appears with other plant hallucinogens on the Aztec statue of Xochipilli, the "Prince of Flowers," who is clearly depicted as being in an entranced state.

Other mind-altering plant substances seem to have only localised use, such as *Calea zacatechichi* ("bitter grass"), which appears to be used now only by the Chontal Indians of Oaxaca, who call it *thle-pelakano*, "leaf of god." This inconspicuous low, branching shrub is put to various purposes by the Indians, but its main use is in inducing dreams. A person taking an infusion of *Calea zacatechichi* falls into a drowsy sleep punctuated by very intense periods of dreaming, which are used by the Chontal for divination. Controlled scientific tests and anecdotal evidence from researchers have shown that *Calea zacatechichi* does indeed produce short episodes of "cat-naps" full of intense sequences of vivid dreams. And yet, no hallucinogenic constituent has so far been isolated from the plant. (My own experience with it included a rush of strongly-coloured dreams. In one brief but vividly "realistic" dream I saw a group of colourfully-dressed Indians looking down at me with a mix of amusement and gravity in their expressions.)

When contemplating the richness, depth and subtlety of the Native American knowledge of naturally-occurring visionary substances, our own naivety is apparent. Knowledge of some of the New World's ancient treasure chest of hallucinogens has already been lost to us, and much more will be if we fail to nurture and value those tenuously-surviving Native American tribal groups who have experience with these traditions.

Paul Devereux is an experienced and respected author and researcher primarily dealing with archaeological themes and ancient lifeways, unusual geophysical phenomena, and consciousness studies. His work spans the range from academic to popular. While making his subject matter attractive and accessible to a wide audience, his material is factually based. He has written or co-written 25 books since 1979, been involved in a number of television productions, and has also written a range of peer-reviewed academic papers. For more information, visit his official website (www.pauldevereux.co.uk).

This article is a modified excerpt from Paul Devereux's book *The Long Trip: A Prehistory of Psychedelia* (Daily Grail Publishing, 2008), reprinted with permission.

the NEW GODS

a short history of the fictional origins of modern paganism

by *Ian 'Cat' Vincent*

Many neo-pagans will tell you that their beliefs and practices have been celebrated consistently since before Christianity, although sometimes disguising their intent by adopting – or being co-opted by – the Church. It is a belief system which can offer great beauty and spiritual insight. What it *isn't* is ancient, historically accurate or, in most senses of the word, authentic.

The immediate ancestor of modern paganism – Druidry – was pretty much invented wholesale by Romantic poets and historians in the 17th to 19th centuries. Paganism as we know it today is partly a derivation of inaccurate Victorian and early 20th century historical and anthropological theories, mixed with a sizeable amount of plagiarism of the work of Aleister Crowley and then filled out with a variety of secondary sources.

In recent years, this point has been addressed by many, especially Professor Ronald Hutton. Hutton is a historian with great sympathy for the spirituality of pagan belief systems, but no truck with the often speculative, and occasionally downright shoddy, history taken as read by most of its adherents.

Hutton has said...

> The real danger is...the idea that all customs, indeed all superstitions, nursery rhymes, and anything that smacks of 'folkiness', are direct survivals of ancient pagan fertility rites, and are concerned with the appeasement of gods and spirits. Although the suggestion of an ancient origin for our folklore was the central tenet of the Victorian and Edwardian pioneers of folklore collection, this notion has only become generally known in the last forty years or so, and has taken hold with astonishing rapidity; the majority of the population now carry the virus in one form or another, while some are very badly infected. The problem here is not simply that these theories are unsupported by any evidence, but that their blanket similarity destroys any individuality. All customs will soon end up with the same story.

Fortunately for neo-paganism, it had a wider range of stories to draw upon in its recently evolved origins. Specifically, it drew greatly on the fictional genres of science fiction and fantasy.

This is a personal overview of their intertwining.

Worlds of Gods and Monsters

A book which is often taken as the starting point for science fiction (SF) is Mary Shelley's *Frankenstein, or The Modern Prometheus* (1818). Most people know the origin story of the book: Mary Shelley, her Romantic poet husband Percy Bysshe Shelley, Lord Byron, and

John Polidori gathered at the Villa Diodante in 1816, trying to out-do each other in creating horror stories on a dark and stormy night. As veteran British science fiction writer Brian Aldiss was first to note, this is a tale where the protagonist "makes a deliberate decision" and "turns to modern experiments in the laboratory" to achieve his aims...certainly within what we would now consider as SF. Nonetheless, *Frankenstein's* origins occupy the interface between nascent speculative fiction and Romanticism.

Other early SF works (then called Scientific Romances), such as those by Jules Verne, often involved that basic scheme of a creator going beyond the realms of then-known science, but only *slightly*...such as the ballistic spaceship launch system of *From The Earth To The Moon* (1865) or the weaponised submarine of *20,000 Leagues Under The Sea* (1870). Verne was far less concerned with the effects his creators had on their world, however, than he was with writing popular adventure stories – a trait that never really left the genre as a whole.

The same could not be said for H.G. Wells. All of Wells's science fiction works tend towards the didactic. *The Island of Doctor Moreau* (1896) and *The Invisible Man* (1897) are stern warnings about both hubris and the consequences of meddling with Nature, while *The Time Machine* (1895) and *The Shape Of Things To Come* (1933) are explicit warnings as to the possible future consequences of his society, expressed in fiction. It is interesting to note that, of his work, the two which take on SF's most-often-assumed base story of space travel – *The War of the Worlds* (1898) and *The First Men in the Moon* (1901), are his *least* didactic. Sometimes, less is more...and, always, science fiction is never as much about the worlds of Tomorrow as it is a method of using the fantastic as a tool to examine the world of Today.

Mention here should be also made of Lord Edward Bulwer-Lytton, the man who coined terms like "the great unwashed", "pursuit of the almighty dollar", "the pen is mightier than the sword", "dweller on the threshold" and "It was a dark and stormy night". His 1871 novel *The Coming Race* was of enormous yet rarely-spoken influence on the occult and spiritual currents that followed. In this book, he wrote of an anonymous explorer who discovers the Earth is hollow, its interior home to a race of superhumans who were adept in the manipulation of the life-force – which he called 'Vril'. This book was a huge influence on the thought of Helena Blavatsky, Rudolph Steiner and the proto-Nazi volkish occultists of the *Thule-Gesellschaft*. Variations on the concept of Vril appear in science fiction in many later forms... and it also gave its name to that ultimate expression of duality – the beef drink Bovril (advertised with the slogan "You either love it or you hate it").

Even this early on, the ideas of what would become SF were moving to other media: George Méliès' 1902 film *A Trip To The Moon* was, for its time in the very birth throes of cinema, a state-of-the-art special effects extravaganza. Thomas Edison himself would film the first of many movie versions of *Frankenstein* in 1910, and 1916 saw the first adaptation of Verne's *20,000 Leagues Under The Sea*. Audiences have certainly not lost their taste for such extravagant and flashy tales.

Print, however, is science fiction's real home – and, especially, cheap print. One of the reasons, I think, that many literary critics scorn SF is its origin as a populist medium. Nothing exemplifies this so much as the pulp magazines, especially *Amazing Stories*.

Founded by Hugo Gernsback in 1926, *Amazing Stories* was the first publication to focus on science fiction, and it was Gernsback who gave the genre its name...although he first called it 'Scientifiction'. The magazine, and competitors such as *Astounding Stories* and *Weird Tales* (the home of H.P. Lovecraft and the stories which would be later termed the Cthulhu Mythos) brought imaginative tales to anyone with a couple of nickels to buy them.

The year after *Amazing Stories* launched saw the premiere of Fritz Lang's *Metropolis* (1927), a savage social satire using what would later become common tropes of SF – a totalitarian dystopia, robots posing as humans – to comment on the political dangers of its time. And, though the trappings were technological, many scenes – such as the birth of the Maria-Robot – carried more than a hint of occult ritual.

Cinema, especially in serial form, found a rich seam to mine in SF, bringing weekly instalments of *Flash Gordon*, *Buck Rogers* and the technologically-enhanced detective *Dick Tracy* to eager audiences. Universal Pictures brought horror into the mix with its 1931 adaptation of *Frankenstein*: both it and *Bride Of Frankenstein* four years later did not lack for occult tropes. As Doctor Pratorius toasted in *Bride Of Frankenstein*...

'To a world of gods and monsters!'

The pulps and film – especially now that the talkies had arrived – continued to capture the popular imagination: by the 1930s, science fiction had acquired many avid fans – some of whom started to organise meetings. Britain's first science fiction convention took place in Leeds in 1938, and included such luminaries of future British SF as Arthur C. Clarke.

The Maria-Robot from Metropolis, with inverted pentagram in the background

Another enthusiastic British fan was Olaf Stapledon, who wrote a series of highly influential works in the 1930s which had more than their share of the mystical – the likes of *Last And First Men* (1930) and *Star Maker* (1937) influenced many of his contemporaries including C.S. Lewis, who was inspired to explore the combination of SF tropes and his own Christian apologia in *Out Of The Silent Planet* (1938) and its sequels. (This 'Space Trilogy' was inspired by conversations with his fellow Inkling J.R.R. Tolkien, of whom more later.)

The crossover between an interest in fantastic fiction and the Weird has dovetailed for a long time. Many attendees of that first SF convention were also connected to early Fortean groups – even H.G. Wells had read Charles Fort, though he hated his work. The rise in interest in spirituality after the Great War had also influenced the fans – as did the arrival in that same year of 1938 of a new phenomenon: the superhero comic book. (The first of which, let us not forget, portrayed a working class immigrant who used his

powers to aid the common folk – an idea that the vigorously socialist Wells and Stapledon would perhaps have admired.)

Needless to say, the Second World War changed everything. The multiple shocks to society worldwide of course had their echoes in pop culture – from the naked propaganda of Captain America punching out Hitler on the cover of his first ever comic (March 1941, before the U.S. entered the war), through newspaper and newsreel footage visions of a Total War startlingly similar to those shown in the 1936 movie version of Wells's *Shape Of Things To Come*, to legends of Hitler's interest in both the occult and 'high weird' technology – all of which was punctuated brutally by the nuclear destruction of Hiroshima and Nagasaki, which in turn would influence the next era of science fiction in both literature and cinema.

Despite rationing and the war, or perhaps because of them, the pulps were still going strong, and had been joined by the new publishing form of paperback books. Another important stage in the democratisation of the form, novels and anthologies – especially, later on, science fiction and fantasy books – became available to nearly everyone: the aim was, according to their inventor, an early SF fan named Ian Ballantine, to make novels available "for the price of a pack of cigarettes".

Amazing Stories, meanwhile, had acquired a level of High Weirdness under the editorship of Raymond Palmer, who in early 1945 began publishing a series of tales by a fan named Richard Shaver, purporting to be true stories of an evil race of 'Lemurians' who lived inside a Lyttonesque hollow Earth, who influenced human affairs via 'mind-rays' and communicated with equally evil aliens. Fans were bitterly divided about the so-called Shaver Mystery stories: fandom had already developed something of a split between the skeptical-engineer 'hard SF' fans and those who were more open to the spiritually and socially inquisitive stories. (This tale is covered extensively in Blair MacKenzie Blake's article in *Darklore* Volume 8.)

It must be said, however, that even the more skeptical and atheist fans and writers had their skirmishes with the Weird. Of these, few were as influential as Robert A. Heinlein.

Strangers in a Strange Land

Robert Heinlein got his start in *Astounding Science Fiction,* one of *Amazing Stories'* pulp rivals, in the 1930s along with Arthur C. Clarke and Isaac Asimov, who comprised the 'Big Three' of what became known as the Golden Age of SF.

A former U.S. Navy officer and naval engineer who had been discharged for health reasons before World War II, Heinlein's early works were exemplars of the hard SF form, in many cases helping define science fiction concepts such as time travel and the militarisation of space. As a result of his interests in both fandom and fringe politics, he did mix with some interesting people in the 1940s...including Jack Parsons and L. Ron Hubbard.

Parsons – a literal rocket scientist and convert to Aleister Crowley's Thelema in 1939 – knew Heinlein from the Mañana Literary Society. The group met in Laurel Canyon, California during the war and was primarily composed of science fiction fans and writers, including Leigh Brackett – who would later co-write *The Empire Strikes Back*. Through the Mañana Society, Parsons struck up a friendship with Hubbard, a prolific pulp writer at the time.

That was not a meeting that ended well for those concerned... except Hubbard. The roots of both Dianetics and Scientology in his pulp fiction – and his dalliance with Crowleyan occultism alongside Parsons – are a clear example that the interplay between fiction and religion is not necessarily a beneficial one.

Heinlein, meanwhile, was considered one of the leading lights of the genre though the Fifties in both the pulps and Ballantine's paperbacks, which supplied another vital ingredient to the mix with the paperback publication of Tolkien's *The Lord Of The Rings* in 1960.

Between this and popular editions of the works of Lovecraft, the Robert E. Howard *Conan The Barbarian* books, and the influential *Fafhrd and the Gray Mouser* series from Fritz Leiber, fantasy realms with strange gods and magicks were also becoming part of pop culture. Paperbacks also allowed for more poetical works which transcended the boundary of SF and fantasy to gain a readership, especially books from Ray Bradbury like *The Martian Chronicles* (1950), *Fahrenheit 451* (1953) and *Something Wicked This Way Comes* (1962).

There was also the rising media force of television: shows such as *The Twilight Zone* and *The Outer Limits* were bringing innovative SF ideas to an increasingly wide audience, with episodes often written by leading pulp authors such as Richard Matheson and Harlan Ellison.

By the late 1950s and early 1960s, SF and fantasy fandom – most especially Robert Heinlein's work – would influence a group whose beliefs and actions would make an indelible mark on paganism and other modern occult practices.

It began as a group of young high school and college students in Fulton, Missouri, including Lance Christie and Tim Zell, who later changed his name to Oberon Zell-Ravenheart. They and their friends shared an interest in SF, the self-actualisation philosophy of Abraham Maslow and the writings of right-wing firebrand Ayn Rand, author of *Atlas Shrugged*.

(I'm going to take a moment here and quote a popular comment from the modern TV and comics writer John Rogers: "There are two novels that can change a bookish fourteen-year old's life: *The Lord of the Rings* and *Atlas Shrugged*. One is a childish fantasy that often engenders a lifelong obsession with its unbelievable heroes, leading to an emotionally stunted, socially crippled adulthood, unable to deal with the real world. The other, of course, involves orcs.")

Christie and Zell and their friends were galvanised in 1961 by the publication of Heinlein's *Stranger In A Strange Land*. Christie described the experience as being "seized with an ecstatic sense of *recognition*. It was as if I had found in completed form the ideas which I was trying to gel into my own."

Stranger tells the story of Valentine Michael Smith: a human child abandoned on Mars and raised by the native Martians in their culture and beliefs. Key among these beliefs is a bonding ritual involving the sharing of water and the concept of 'grokking' – "to understand something so completely that you become part of it". On his rescue and return to Earth, Smith is first bewildered by human society, and then tries to integrate his Martian perspective with human beliefs and mores in a religion he called The Church of All Worlds, with far-reaching and, for Smith, tragic consequences.

The combination of this outsider perspective on human belief systems and Heinlein's espousal of many libertarian points-of-view, caught the group's imagination. They in turn took the fictitious religion Heinlein had created and combined it with their own political and psychological interests, and the burgeoning interest in pre-Christian beliefs…and formed their own version of The Church of All Worlds.

From Eris to Spock

When I first started doing the research for this piece, I was delighted to find a familiar name among those influential on the early development of the Church of All Worlds: Kerry Wendell Thornley.

Thornley – another member of the loose affiliation of rebellious libertarians in the late 1950s – was a former U.S. Marine and enthusiastic participant in the Californian drug and outsider cultures of the time. In 1958, in a bowling alley in Yorba Linda, California, the birthplace of Richard Nixon, he and a fellow contributor to the libertarian/atheist magazine *The Realist*, Greg Hill, had a shared vision (or, at least they *say* they had a shared vision) of the true nature of theological reality: in a world as beset with madness and chaos as ours, it made no sense to worship a male deity of rules and order…that the more useful deity would be Eris, the Greek goddess of chaos and discord. And so, the Discordian Society was born.

As part of the Discordian mind-altering pranks-as-propaganda project known as Operation Mindfuck, Thornley was a prolific writer under many pseudonyms. Writing as one of his Discordian personas, 'Young Omar', he contributed work to a newsletter of one of the Kerista communes of the time, in which he made the second of his notable contributions to modern mysticism: he popularised the use of the term 'paganism' in reference to modern nature religions.

In his piece, quoted in the pagan history *Drawing Down The Moon* (1979) by Margot Adler, he wrote…

> …let us look at the jobs of the far less intellectual, but far more constructively functional religions of old. These were the 'pagan' religions – the religions which survive to this day in England and the United States as 'witchcraft'…groups which both stabilised and overthrew the social structure.

Thornley also described paganism as "an institutionalised cultural countertrend" – concepts he cribbed from Margaret Murray, Robert Graves and others. Although some British witchcraft groups of the time were referring to pre-Christian worship in Europe as 'pagan', the modern usage of 'paganism' seems to have arisen solely from Thornley, and was popularised by the Church of All Worlds and associated groups.

After 1963, Thornley's life got even odder. The assassination of John F. Kennedy hit him particularly hard, as he had served in the Marines with Lee Harvey Oswald, and had been privy to discussions among right-wing extremists in New Orleans some years before regarding the feasibility of a presidential assassination. Further still, his girlfriend at the time was working as a secretary for New Orleans district attorney Jim Garrison – and it was on Garrison's copying machine that the first ever edition of the key Discordian text *Principia Discordia* was made in that same year. Garrison later went on to accuse Thornley of being the so-called 'Second Oswald' in his investigation into the JFK hit.

Meanwhile, the Church of All Worlds was evolving. Absorbing many influences, including some from the Discordian side of things, the Church was defining a set of beliefs which *required no dogma* – accepting various mythologies as having spiritual worth, including fictional ones – the Church once described science fiction as "the new mythology of our age". The Church itself had grown from its initial group or 'nest' of 100 members to a dozen or so other nests across America, all with deep connections to the SF fan world and its parallel Renaissance Fair gatherings, which strove to create an authentic-seeming simulation of an idealised historical life. These nests were also connected by the official Church magazine, *Green Egg*, whose influence on neo-paganism was considerable.

Another influence that was rapidly absorbed into the Church's combination of myths was a new TV show called *Star Trek*.

It's hard to appreciate nowadays just how unusual *Star Trek* was at the time. It not only showed a relatively mature human society with non-white and non-male figures of authority, but also used the format which creator Gene Roddenberry had originally pitched as 'Wagon Train to the stars' to tell a series of socially relevant metaphorical tales. It also introduced a philosophical concept that influenced both the Church and my young self strongly: IDIC.

IDIC stands for Infinite Diversity in Infinite Combination. The concept – and its triangle-within-a-circle symbol – first appeared in October 1968, in the episode "Is There In Truth No Beauty?". IDIC as a philosophy is easy to state – and like all such philosophical perspectives, far harder to practice than describe. This quote from the end of the episode sums it up:

> The glory of creation is in its infinite diversity.
> And the ways our differences combine to create meaning and beauty.

This idea – that there was everything to gain in the consideration and embrace of alternate meanings and perspectives, that difference is a *treasure* not a threat, became integral to the Church of All Worlds, who had been formally chartered as a religion in the United States – the first earth-based faith so recognised – on 4 March 1968, a few months before the episode aired.

There's a certain combination of both irony and aptness in this, as IDIC was created by Roddenberry and inserted into that episode for one reason: not to stimulate non-dualistic philosophies or to

IDIC Symbol

symbolically question the unstable status quo of the 1960s – but to try and sell a range of licensed IDIC merchandise.

HOLY BOOKS OF HYPER-REAL RELIGIONS

The Church of All Worlds, the IDIC philosophy and Discordianism are all good examples of a concept which, though not defined until the early 21st century, is worth noting here as it begins to become manifest: that of 'hyper-real religion'.

As I noted in my *Darklore* Volume 8 article "Believing In Fiction", the term hyper-real religion draws on the work of the sociologist Adam Possamai. Possamai considers that, in a postmodern, late-capitalist world, religious inspiration and even belief systems drawn from pop fiction can be as valid to its adherents as any orthodox faith.

As Possamai puts it...

> ...in this consuming world, the individual becomes his or her own authority; the postmodern person in the West no longer tolerates

being told what to believe and what to do...he or she is faced with a proliferation of 'spiritual/religious/philosophical knowledges', which he or she researches and experiences.

This personal seeking for truth has manifested in a variety of ways. For some, it allows them to find new and vivid metaphors for their existing beliefs. A fine example can be seen in the murals of the Buddhist White Temple of Chiang Rai in Thailand: they combine renditions of traditional Buddhist and folk deities with many pop culture images, including the starship Enterprise, Spider-Man and Neo from *The Matrix*.

For others, it can give them the chance to move beyond the beliefs of their kin and tribe to find other beliefs (or, of course, to reject belief as a concept entirely). It can also bring some people to find or even create a whole new range of faiths, based on the stories they find within pop culture.

From the 1960s, with its rise in paperback books of both fiction and non-Western belief systems, a resurgence of the comic book industry and the rise of popular cinema and television, there were so very many stories to choose from.

Science fiction at the end of the Sixties and start of the Seventies was in a very different place than at the start of the Fifties. Key works exploring beliefs and social structures had risen to popularity: a major example being the celebrated Frank Herbert novel *Dune* (1964) and its sequels. This vast tale of a religious power struggle between a galactic empire and the decidedly Islamic-influenced desert dwellers of the eponymous planet Dune, which was the sole source of the mind-altering 'Spice' which allowed both interstellar travel and precognition, found a home on the shelves of many of those who were also reading Heinlein's *Stranger in a Strange Land*, Tolkien's *Lord of the Rings* and the mystical non-fiction books of the time.

It also, quite by accident, gave modern occultism one of its most powerful spell-mantras: 'The Litany Against Fear' (I've lost count of how many times I have used this mantra, and it works *every damn time*):

> I must not fear.
> Fear is the Mind-Killer.
> Fear is the little-death that brings total obliteration.
> I will face my fear.
> I will permit it to pass over me and through me.
> And when it has gone past I will turn the inner eye to see its path.
> Where the fear has gone there will be nothing.
> Only I will remain.

The Sixties had also seen a rise of newer voices in SF, talking about aspects the heavily hard science and engineering-oriented fans and writers had often neglected. Authors such as Ursula Le Guin and Samuel Delaney were producing works that critically examined their culture, as well as exploring gender, sexual and racial identities, in a science fiction context. Le Guin also wrote the *Earthsea* fantasy series, which won the hearts of many people who would later find a connection to paganism. Philip K. Dick and William S. Burroughs were exploring SF themes in combination with harsh perspectives informed both by the counterculture drug scene and mysticism, and the New Wave in SF, led by the prolific author Michael Moorcock in his British magazine *New Worlds*, was bringing in both new perspectives and new fans – many of them with roots deep in the counterculture.

Comic books in the Sixties – especially at Marvel Comics under the watch of creators such as Stan Lee, Jack Kirby and Steve Ditko – were pushing the boundaries of what the four-colour funnybooks could do. They introduced characters such as Spider-Man, the Fantastic Four and the X-Men, using them to tell metaphorical stories about the boundaries of science and the struggles of being considered different in a society which mostly treasures conformity. And, with books like

Doctor Strange and *The Mighty Thor*, magic and pagan gods also found their place on the newsstands.

Science fiction cinema was also changing: inventive SF films such as *Planet of the Apes* (1968) and the French New Wave entries *Alphaville* (1965) by Jean-Luc Goddard and the Francois Truffaut-helmed adaptation of Bradbury's *Fahrenheit 451* in 1966 were far from the B-movies of the previous decade. 1968 saw the release of *2001: A Space Odyssey*, where Stanley Kubrick took Arthur C. Clarke's original tale of a humanity manipulated since prehistoric times by advanced aliens and produced a solemn and beautiful masterpiece of the imagination – one which the counterculture took to its heart after it was cleverly marketed under the slogan 'The Ultimate Trip'.

It also produced one of the oddest film-to-comic-book adaptations of all time, when Jack Kirby took the story and ran with it to the psychedelic realms familiar to readers of *Doctor Strange* and other Marvel books. It is perhaps a sign of the times that Kirby, a gruff ex-marine and hard drinker, was known to never use either cannabis or entheogens, but could still create comic pages such as those shown on the facing page.

And, of course, British homes had been invaded on a weekly basis since the day of the Kennedy assassination with the tales of that shape-shifting trickster god known simply as 'The Doctor'. *Doctor Who* still endures after thirteen-ish incarnations, and his influence on modern mysticism, especially in the U.K., is considered in depth by John Higgs in *Darklore* Volume 7 and elsewhere.

The Next Generation

Science fiction fandom was also developing by leaps and bounds. In both the U.S. and the U.K., fan conventions and small-circulation amateur magazines known as Fanzines were drawing in people from all walks of life – and the mix of counterculture interests which

Panel from *Doctor Strange*

Panel from Jack Kirby's *2001* adaptation

marked groups such as the Church of All Worlds made for a place where different types of people could mix freely.

Star Trek fandom, for example, was strongly inclusive; embracing the IDIC philosophy, it was often a place where people with many different outsider spiritual, sexual and other interests could meet and share perspectives. It was Trek fandom which first produced the heavily sexualised romantic fan stories which became known as Slash Fiction – where fans would set their imaginations to consider romantic encounters between the characters they enjoyed. The first of these were a series of vigorously described sexual scenes between Captain Kirk and Mr. Spock, which became known as K/S. As other pairings were explored, the slash between the initials became the term for the subgenre.

The early Seventies, in many ways a retreat from the giddy optimism and cultural meshing of the 60s, continued a lot of the themes of the SF and fantasy outpourings of the time, though often with a bitter, cynical twist. British TV writers who had cut their teeth on *Doctor Who* produced shows such as *Doomwatch*, an explicitly ecologically-minded show which tackled themes of pollution and uncontrolled scientific experimentation, and the vicious post-plague-apocalyptic dystopia, *Survivors*.

Seventies British TV, especially children's programming, had some remarkable SF and fantasy ideas, ranging from the teenage wish-fulfilment of *The Tomorrow People* and *Sky*, to pagan and occult-tinged works such as *Ace of Wands*, *The Changes* and *Children of the Stones,* all of which drew many viewers into their first encounters with pagan ideas.

In 1975, the SF book world received the latest and most explicit manifestation of Kerry Thornley's association with the Heinlein-influenced American libertarian and pagan movements. Back in '68, Thornley had met a young *Playboy* letters page editor who was becoming increasingly involved with the counterculture scene and, especially, conspiracy theory. He was such an enormous Heinlein fan that he had changed his middle name from George to one which was a single letter away from Heinlein's middle name of Anson – becoming known as Robert Anton Wilson.

With fellow *Playboy* editor Robert Shea, Wilson set out to produce a massive satirical SF novel of both modern America and, especially, its post-Kennedy obsession with conspiracies. Thornley's friendship brought Discordianism into the mix – the dogma-rejecting influence of the Church of All Worlds (of which he was a member) fascinated Wilson especially, and he set about not only co-writing the novel, but deliberately changing his own consciousness in regards to both belief and consensus reality, using a combination of techniques derived from his friendship with counterculture figures such as Bill Burroughs, Alan Watts and Timothy Leary. All of this became part of the story.

That novel, delayed for some years in publication, was called *Illuminatus!* and its impact was strongly felt in the counterculture. Wilson's autobiographical follow-up to *Illuminatus!* three years later, *Cosmic Trigger: Final Secret of the Illuminati* – telling of his personal experiments in multi-model perspectives on belief and occultism – appeared, in a striking example of Charles Fort's 'Steam Engine Time', at the same historical moment as a group of experimental occultists working in London and Leeds were developing a multi-model approach to magic which would come to be known as 'chaos magic'.

1975 also saw the publication of a collection of short stories by Harlan Ellison, called *Deathbird Stories*. Subtitled *A Pantheon of Modern Gods,* this collection was grouped around the idea that the old gods were being replaced by newer gods: deities born from electricity and city, the machinery of slot machines and the horrors of drug abuse and social isolation. Although Ellison is a staunch atheist, his poetic visions planted the seed in many readers of the possibility that the modern age was evolving modern gods to fit it.

The science fiction cinema of the Seventies produced a lot of strong works, often with paranoid or dystopian themes, such as 1973's *Westworld* and *Soylent Green* and the ecologically-minded *Silent Running* (1972), directed by *2001*'s special effects designer Douglas Trumbull – but these were only modest box office successes. It wasn't until 1977 that SF and fantasy combined in a truly game-changing cinematic form, and one which lead to a vast shift in the hyper-real belief stakes.

The runaway success of *Star Wars,* with its stunning special effects and revival of the spirit of the 1930s serials – an ironic side-effect of George Lucas being unable to secure the rights to a *Flash Gordon* reboot – not only gave viewers a hell of a good time at the pictures, it also provided a new spiritual metaphor: a Joseph Campbell-influenced syncretic mix of the 1960s' Westernised versions of Eastern beliefs *and* a revival of Bulwer-Lytton's Vril – 'The Force'.

Star Wars led to many imitators, most of which were not as successful – although one of these, the TV show *Battlestar Galactica,* would later be rebooted into a show which would examine the nature of the soul in artificial intelligences in a striking manner. *Star Wars'* success did, however, open the doors for other SF films to be made which went beyond its space-opera form. The early Eighties brought two superb examples: the Philip K. Dick adaptation *Blade Runner* (1982), and *Altered States* (1980) – a science fiction exploration of the burgeoning interest in psychedelic mysticism. Both these films explored complex questions of the soul in a visually striking and serious manner.

Paganism was developing greatly, also. 1979 saw the publication of two massively influential books: *The Spiral Path* by Starhawk and Margot Adler's *Drawing Down The Moon* – the latter including a detailed history of the Church of All Worlds, which was continuing to thrive. Both of these emphasised the importance of feminist influences on paganism, and were in turn influential on a book which was the introduction to pagan concepts for a whole generation – Marion Zimmer Bradley's 1983 novel, *The Mists Of Avalon*.

Bradley, a practicing Wiccan, brought her beliefs – especially their feminist aspects – to this retelling of the Arthurian mythos, and it also led to a resurgence of interest in fantasy fiction.

Parallel with this rise in paganism was the appearance of chaos magic, which drew partly on the Discordian influences in Robert Anton Wilson's work and elements of Michael Moorcock's fantasy fiction. This decidedly post-modern approach to magic, with its rejection of dogma and even the very idea of *belief itself* as being anything more than a tool in the sorcerer's hands, would in turn find an enthusiastic audience and go on to influence later fantasy fiction, especially in the subgenre of 'Urban Fantasy'.

RISE OF THE NEUROMANCERS

Although well accounted-for in popular visual media, SF literature by the eighties was starting to feel a little stale, possibly as a result of TV and film plundering the genre's back catalogue for ideas. Partly following on from the punk rock rebellion against the old guard of rock music, but mostly inspired by the rise of the pervasive new communications technology called the Internet, a group of young writers broke the mould with a movement called Cyberpunk.

The breakthrough works of cyberpunk – William Gibson's *Neuromancer* trilogy and Neal Stephenson's *Snow Crash* – were both concerned, as SF always is, with reflecting the concerns of their time. The rise of corporate power, ecological damage and the role of the individual in an increasingly connected world were examined through a glass very darkly. Both took on elements of pagan and other non-Christian belief: Gibson's trilogy involved the rise of artificial intelligences which took on the persona of the Voodoo Loa, and *Snow Crash* is, among other things, a retelling of the Babylonian Inanna myth beloved of many feminist pagans. In turn, these books were to directly influence the people who built the World Wide Web as we know it.

Science fiction fans have always had a tendency towards *neophilia* – Robert Anton Wilson's term for those who enjoy and pursue novelty – and as a result, tend to be early adopters of new technology. A majority of the communications engineers who built the internet were avid fans – and, because of the overlapping interests we've seen earlier, they had a tendency to be interested in alternative political and religious systems. Subsequently, the early bulletin boards skewed heavily towards the interests of fans and pagans alike.

Cyberpunk and the rise of the internet was also a major influence on a new movement known as technopaganism. Taking elements from both neo-pagan and modern occult beliefs and combining them with the network-oriented models that are the basis of the internet – as well as a healthy dollop of Wilson's multi-model approach – technopaganism was a modern, hyper-real angle on belief, magical praxis and how those can integrate with technology as readily as with the biological world.

Although fantastic fiction has always had its fans, most people don't pursue that interest deeply and it's previously been a minority interest, even in times where the genre has done well financially. This is partly because of their outsider status – the perennial war between 'jocks' and 'nerds' – but another factor was the difficulty of participation. Hand-made fanzines and traveling to rare conventions required connections, time and money. With the rise of the internet and personal computing, entry costs plummeted. As a result, fans began to more easily find their tribes: these became less geographically located and more international in scope, allowing the West to discover the delights of Japanese anime and manga. Major works such as *Akira* (1988) and *Ghost In The Shell* (1995) found enthusiastic audiences, and in turn came to influence cyberpunk and other SF.

Falling for Fantasy

Another fiction which inspired many people into their first discovery of the possibilities of paganism was the 1984 arrival of the British show *Robin of Sherwood,* created by Richard Carpenter, who had previously explored the crossover of SF and fantasy with the children's series *Catweazle*, the tale of an 11th century hedge-witch transported to the 1970s. Carpenter's retelling of the Robin Hood myth was unafraid to embrace a darker version of the tale – for example its Will Scarlet, played by a young Ray Winstone, was a traumatised sociopath – but it was especially innovative in its consideration of Robin Hood as a pagan figure. Key to this was Herne the Hunter: a combination of the Cernunnos myth with the legend of its namesake, Herne was shown to be an English version of a shaman, possessed by the Horned God and sent to guide Robin to serve the common folk of Albion. Despite vicious retaliation by the likes of Mary Whitehouse and other Christian fuddy-duddies who were aghast at this heathen display on children's programming, the show ran for three seasons.

Other popular British fantasy works which were especially inspiring to many young proto-pagans and magicians were the novels of two sadly now-deceased British writers: Terry Pratchett and Diana Wynne Jones.

Although Jones's work is less well-known, she is a beloved influence among many fantasy writers – including Pratchett, whose popular *Discworld* books were once the most shop-lifted books in Britain, and Neil Gaiman, with whom Pratchett would collaborate on the apocalyptic comedy novel *Good Omens* (1990). Their works led to many readers feeling their first stirrings of an interest in paganism, and even hyper-real religious manifestations. (Gaiman once told me of an attempt by an American pagan group to replicate the spell to capture the incarnation of Death shown in *Sandman's* first issue.) While Jones, Pratchett and Gaiman were not necessarily pagans or occultists themselves, they certainly had many friends and acquaintances in British fandom who were. The deep mythology of Pratchett's Discworld, with its Eight Colours of Magic and no-nonsense approach to both magic and the gods, was also readily absorbed into chaos magic's toolbox.

Gaiman was heavily involved in a decidedly more adult shift in comic books, coming to fame as part of the DC Comics British Wave of the late 80s and early 90s, which brought writers such as Alan Moore and Grant Morrison to a huge readership. Works such as *Sandman, Hellblazer, Doom Patrol* and *From Hell* did not shy away from pagan and magical concepts, expressed in far more explicit terms than the medium had previously seen. These books were reaching a wider audience thanks to the publishing phenomenon of repackaging monthly issues of comics into omnibus editions called 'graphic novels', which were more easily sold in regular bookshops.

Media, Magic and the Millennium

The 1990s provided strong showings for SF and fantasy television, which would be influential not only within the genre but in television production generally. The rise of internet fandom and the availability of first VHS, and then DVD versions of shows, gave fans a chance not only to discuss their favourite series but watch them again at

'Dream', from Neil Gaiman's acclaimed *Sandman* comic book series

any time, and thus examine them in more detail, allowing fandoms to explore shows in a new, deeper way. Many significant series were aired: ranging from the occult surrealism of *Twin Peaks,* the *Star Trek* revivals of *The Next Generation* and *Deep Space Nine, The X Files* – with its innovative serialisation, deep internal mythology and drawing on the UFO and Fortean fringes which have always interested fandom – and a heavily serialised space series with a complex spiritual perspective, one of the first true Novels For Television, whose creator was an early internet adopter: *Babylon 5.*

All these series explored familiar SF themes of societal change due to technological and extra-terrestrial influence, and the possibility of human transcendence to higher states of being – these in turn influenced the rising technological secular belief in Transhumanism and the Singularity – the so-called 'Rapture of the Nerds'. Although a majority of transhumanists tend to be atheists, there are also the Grinders – DIY transhumanism enthusiasts and theorists who not only often borrow freely from technopagan concepts, but took their name from a comic book: Warren Ellis and Ivan Rodriguez's *Doktor Sleepless.*

Another show of the time which gained a great deal of love from the pagan and magical subcultures was *Buffy The Vampire Slayer,* whose lesbian witch Willow Rosenberg became an inspiration to many viewers who were questioning both their parents' belief systems and their own sexuality.

A new and influential literary subgenre arising at the time was that of Urban Fantasy: stories which take magical elements and place them in recognisable modern environments, often with elements of romance. Ranging from one end with the monster-hunting post-Buffy warrior women typified in Laurel K. Hamilton's 'Anita Blake' series, to noirish, less sexy works such as former *Hellblazer* scribe Mike Carey's 'Felix Castor' books, magic and its application in the modern world gained a whole new range of metaphors to inspire mystically-minded fans. Many of their authors are openly pagans or magicians.

As the end of the twentieth century loomed, many works were caught up in its implications: Grant Morrison, already a practicing magician, deliberately set in motion an act of post-modern magic by encoding both chaos techniques and autobiographical elements in his apocalyptic comic series *The Invisibles*, which in turn (alongside anime such as *Akira*) would strongly influence a film which was the most successful and influential of 1999's many Gnostically-tinged movies: *The Matrix*.

Indeed, 1998 and 1999 saw several films with an almost Phil-Dickian theme of Your Reality Isn't Real. Although *The Matrix* was the most popular, there were many others such as *Pleasantville, Being John Malkovich, eXistenZ, The Thirteenth Floor* and my own favourite, *Dark City* (which includes one of the best magical combat scenes in cinema). These films offered receptive viewers a strong hint that their consensus reality was not *that* much of a consensus and not necessarily all that *real* either.

And, of course, there was *Harry Potter*.

J.K. Rowling's runaway success set publishing and the associated media ablaze: like *Star Wars* before it, it inspired a lot of imitators and also opened the way for movies to invest more heavily in fantasy works. Between the rise of what's become known as Young Adult fiction and expensive adaptations such as *The Lord of the Rings* and its like, we're still feeling the effects of that.

Post-Millennial Gods

The awaited apocalypse at the end of 1999 didn't come, of course – and 2001 was hardly a space odyssey. Instead, we got 9/11, and a resurgence in the Clash of Civilisations us-or-them narratives between monotheist extremists. But 2001 also saw a decidedly hyper-real religious development.

In that year, the U.K., Australia, New Zealand and Canada undertook a national census, the first in which those surveyed were asked to state their religion. In the U.K. and Australia in particular, there was an enthusiastic internet-based campaign to encourage people to claim Jedi Knight as their religion of choice.

This was a remarkable success: 390,000 U.K. citizens and over 70,000 Australians were now, officially, members of the Jedi faith. These figures made Jedi Knight the fourth largest religion in the United Kingdom – far ahead of Judaism and all of the non-Mosaic Eastern faiths and considerably higher than the number of either Pagan or Scientology adherents. Of course, many of those claiming Jedi as their faith probably did so ironically, but many meant it – as many have since they first learned of The Force. And, after receiving a substantial amount of publicity as a result, the wider public awareness of what was now becoming known as Jediism grew. It wasn't alone.

Online fandom's crossover with pagan beliefs exploded with the rise of social media, especially on Tumblr. Pop culture magic was starting to be discussed openly, and many young fans not only found apt metaphors in their favourite shows, stories and comics, but developed belief systems directly based on them. Hyper-real paganism was growing in the realisation that for a great many people, to use the title of Christopher Knowles' 2007 consideration of comic books as modern mythology, 'our gods wear spandex'.

The immense popularity of superhero-based films, especially the Marvel Comics movie series, has only expanded this tendency. We can now see Lee and Kirby's half-century-old inspirational characters on the big screen, with state-of-the-art special effects and leading actors in the roles. The new pagan fans of these incarnations of the gods (especially, for some reason, Tom Hiddleston's Loki) are enthusiastic and innovative. Others take inspiration from TV shows such as the long-running series *Supernatural*, with its drastically reimagined mythological deities.

Further still, some fans take their fictional or personal mythos so deeply to heart that they believe their souls are *not human*, but creatures of myth. These 'Otherkin', as they are known, have developed a robust hyper-real belief set of their own – ironically, one divided bitterly between those who hold that their soul is a generic entity (elf, wolf etc.), and those who believe they are a direct reincarnation of a fictional character, such as Neo from *The Matrix* or a wide variety of anime characters.

Among the highly profitable blockbusters, there has also been room for smaller movies which used modern effects combined with deeply mythic storytelling to give us profoundly moving spiritual works. Of those in recent years, ones I found especially affecting was the 2006 Darren Aronofsky film *The Fountain,* and the ultra-low-budget tale of clashing afterlife spirits influencing the mortal world, *Ink* (2009).

Magic and Myth in the Modern World

It's an odd time for science fiction/fantasy literature in the midst of all these successful movies, however. SF/F is now a multi-billion dollar industry, with fandom as much a part of the media's business plan as any other branch of advertising: remember that *50 Shades of Grey* started life as a *Twilight* slash fiction. But, science fiction literature outside of young adult dystopian tales is struggling.

One reason for this is how very fast technological change is these days. We are living in what Warren Ellis has called 'The Science Fiction Condition': our world is now one where the technologies which would have been dreams of the future a mere decade or two ago are the actual concerns of our modern society. This makes writing SF, especially near-future stories, increasingly difficult, as a writer's inventions can often be overtaken by reality between the writing and publishing of their book.

But the metaphors remain. Some are being revised and rebooted, such as the spandex gods of the comics. Others find new forms of expression which still say something about our times. Post 9/11 surveillance society, and strides in artificial intelligence research, for example, have led to the brilliant U.S. television series *Person Of Interest,* which combines those themes with an exciting action format to consider the role of humans in a world of warring A.I. gods – not bad for prime time American TV.

Science fiction and fantasy's influence upon paganism and magic have always been a matter of symbiosis. Paganism as we know it sprang from a combination of influences, both historical and fictional – and has, in return, influenced those fictions. Much of modern paganism has a tendency to look to the past – the trend towards reconstruction of older belief systems has grown over the years; its adherents have a somewhat hardline attitude to systems that partake of popular culture. There are many pagan writers who passionately espouse the idea that the modern technological world is somehow not part of nature and must be rejected or 'rewilded' in part or whole – a romanticised bucolic perspective which, frankly, seems to me more like a Renaissance Fair than a true picture of our rural past.

This is more than ironic – it's a rejection of the very origin of neo-paganism, born as it was from fans recontextualising the concepts portrayed in Heinlein's books, *Star Trek* and other SF works. It also defies much of that which makes us human...always the perennial subject of science fiction. Although one can't deny that many aspects of our late-capitalist world are perilous and harmful, to retreat from it completely denies us our most powerful tools – and our species' use of tools, especially language, symbols and stories, are the core aspect of our development.

And, if anyone doubts that hyper-real religion is becoming increasingly accepted, I would note this 2014 news item. A Cardiff man died of cancer, and his funeral involved a rather special honour guard... of Imperial Stormtroopers.

Fan-based weddings are also increasingly common. If a fiction can play a role in our most important rituals of life and death, can it be truly said to be less than any other belief?

I feel the new, pop-culture-informed hyper-real beliefs have an important role to play in not only approaching the powers and gods of this world, but in demonstrating that human imagination itself is the most basic, powerful form of magic there is. We have a whole generation of smart, passionate and engaged young people who grew up with the internet and mass media, and have found myths that closely matched their truths, that – like for Lance Christie and *Stranger in a Strange Land* – bring that 'ecstatic sense of recognition'. The old gods simply do not speak to them as clearly as Harry Potter and Katniss Everdeen, Sam and Dean Winchester and Tiffany Aching.

As one anonymous pop culture pagan put it, speaking to those old gods and their worshippers:

> You say they're only characters.
> You say they're not real.
> But where were you when I needed to grow?
> Where were you when I needed to believe?
> Where were you when I was dying?
> Who saved my life?
> Because it wasn't you.
>
> They're more than fiction.
> They were there for me even if they weren't *real*.
> They were there when you weren't.
> They're more than you think they are.

I can only hope that all believers – in gods old, new and both – can find a way in these turbulent and uncertain times to learn from each other, to treasure each other's differences, to find Infinite

Diversity in Infinite Combination...and that we may all Live Long and Prosper.

Ian 'Cat' Vincent was born on Imbolc-Groundhog Day in 1964. He is a lifelong student of the occult, and a former professional combat magician and curse-breaker. His writing and talks on Forteana and magic can be seen at catvincent.com, tinyurl.com/catvtalks, and occasionally in *Fortean Times*. He lives in Yorkshire, England with his wife, the artist Kirsty Hall. He is often found on Twitter as @catvincent.

His favourite deities are Babalon, Eris, Ganesha and Valen from *Babylon 5*.

'Fossil Angel', by Chris Butler

FOSSIL ANGELS

RE-INVENTING THE ARTE OF MAGICK AS THE MAGIC OF ART

by *Alan Moore*

Regard the world of magic. A scattering of occult orders which, when not attempting to disprove each other's provenance, are either cryogenically suspended in their ritual rut, their game of Aiwaz Says, or else seem lost in some Dungeons & Dragons sprawl of channelled spam, off mapping some unfalsifiable and thus completely valueless new universe before they've demonstrated that they have so much as a black-lacquered fingernail's grip on the old one. Self-consciously weird transmissions from Tourette's-afflicted entities, from glossolalic Hammer horrors. Fritzed-out scrying bowls somehow receiving trailers from the Sci-Fi channel. Far too many secret chiefs, and, for that matter, far too many secret indians.

Beyond this, past the creaking gates of the illustrious societies, dilapidated fifty-year-old follies where they start out with the plans for a celestial palace but inevitably end up with the Bates Motel, outside this there extends the mob. The psyche pikeys. Incoherent roar of our hermetic home-crowd, the Akashic anoraks, the would-be wiccans and Temple uv Psychic Forty-Somethings queuing up with pre-teens for the latest franchised fairyland, realm of the irretrievably hobbituated. Pottersville.

Exactly how does this confirm an aeon of Horus, aeon of anything except more Skinner-box consumerism, gangster statecraft, mind-to-the-grindstone materialism? Is what seems almost universal knee-jerk acquiescence to conservative ideals truly a sign of rampant Theleme? Is Cthulhu coming back, like, anytime soon, or are the barbarous curses from the outer dark those of Illuminists trying to find their arses with a flashlight? Has contemporary western occultism accomplished anything that is measurable outside the séance parlour? Is magic of any definable use to the human race other than offering an opportunity for dressing up? Tantric tarts and vicars at Thelemic theme nights. *Pentagrams In Their Eyes*. "Tonight, Matthew, I will be the Logos of the Aeon." Has magic demonstrated a purpose, justified its existence in the way that art or science or agriculture justify their own? In short, does anyone have the first clue what we are doing, or precisely why we're doing it?

Two Separate Ways of Seeing

Certainly, magic has not always been so seemingly divorced from all immediate human function. Its Palaeolithic origins in shamanism surely represented, at that time, the only human means of mediation with a largely hostile universe upon which we as yet exerted very little understanding or control. Within such circumstances it is easy to conceive of magic as originally representing a one-stop reality, a worldview in which all the other strands of our existence…hunting, procreation, dealing with the elements or cave-wall painting…

were subsumed. A science of everything, its relevance to ordinary mammalian concerns both obvious and undeniable.

This role, that of an all-inclusive "natural philosophy", obtained throughout the rise of classical civilization and could still be seen, albeit in more furtive fashion, as late as the 16th century, when the occult and mundane sciences were not yet so distinguishable as they are today. It would be surprising, for example, if John Dee did not allow his knowledge of astrology to colour his invaluable contributions to the art of navigation, or vice-versa. Not until the Age of Reason gradually prevented our belief in and thus contact with the gods that had sustained our predecessors did our fledgling sense of rationality identify the supernatural as a mere vestigial organ in the human corpus, obsolete and possibly diseased, best excised quickly.

Science, grown out of magic, magic's gifted, pushy offspring, its most practical and thus materially profitable application, very soon decided that the ritual and symbolic lumber of its alchemic parent-culture was redundant, an encumbrance and an embarrassment. Puffed up in its new white lab coat, ballpoints worn like medals at the breast, science came to be ashamed in case its mates (history, geography, P.E) caught it out shopping with its mum, with all her mumbling and chanting. Her third nipple. Best that she be nutted off to some secure facility, some Fraggle Rock for elderly and distressed paradigms.

The rift this caused within the human family of ideas seemed irrevocable, with two parts of what had once been one organism sundered by reductionism, one inclusive "science of everything" become two separate ways of seeing, each apparently in bitter, vicious opposition to the other. Science, in the process of this acrimonious divorce, might possibly be said to have lost contact with its ethical component, with the moral basis necessary to prevent it breeding monsters. Magic, on the other hand, lost all demonstrable utility and purpose, as with many parents once the kid's grown up and gone. How do you fill the void? The answer, whether we are talking about magic or of mundane, moping mums and dads with empty nests, is, in all likelihood, "with ritual and nostalgia".

The magical resurgence of the nineteenth century, with its retrospective and essentially romantic nature, would seem to have been blessed with both these factors in abundance. Whilst it's difficult to overstate the contributions made to magic as a field by, say, Eliphas Levi or the various magicians of the Golden Dawn, it's just as hard to argue that these contributions were not overwhelmingly synthetic, in that they aspired to craft a synthesis of previously existing lore, to formalise the variegated wisdoms of the ancients.

It does not belittle this considerable accomplishment if we observe that magic, during those decades, was lacking in the purposeful immediacy, the pioneering rush characterising, for example, Dee and Kelly's work. In their development of the Enochian system, late Renaissance magic would seem typified as urgently creative and experimental, forward-looking. In comparison, the nineteenth century occultists seem almost to have shifted magic into a revered past tense, made it a rope-railed museum exhibit, an archive, with themselves as sole curators.

All the robes and the regalia, with their whiff of the historical re-enactment crowd, a seraphic Sealed Knot Society, only with fractionally less silly-looking gear. The worryingly right-wing consensus values and the number of concussed and stumbling casualties, upon the other hand, would probably have been identical. The rites of the exalted magic orders and the homicidal beered-up maulings of the Cromwell tribute-bands are also similar in that both gain in poignancy by being juxtaposed against the grim, relentless forward trundle of industrial reality. Beautifully painted wands, obsessively authentic pikes, held up against the bleak advance of chimney-stacks. How much of this might be most accurately described as compensatory fantasies of the machine age? Role-playing games which only serve to underline the brutal fact that these activities no longer have contemporary human relevance. A wistful recreation of long-gone erotic moments by the impotent.

Lip-synching Dead Men's Rituals

Another clear distinction between the magicians of the sixteenth and the nineteenth centuries lies in their relation to the fiction of their day. The brethren of the early Golden Dawn would seem to be inspired more by the sheer romance of magic than by any other aspect, with S.L MacGregor Mathers lured into the craft by his desire to live out Bulwer-Lytton's fantasy *Zanoni*. Encouraged Moina to refer to him as "Zan", allegedly. Woodford and Westcott, on the other hand, anxious to be within an order that had even more paraphernalia than Rosicrucian Masonry, somehow acquire a contact in the fabled (literally) ranks of the *Geltische Dämmerung*, which means something like "golden tea-time". They are handed their diplomas from Narnia, straight out the back of the wardrobe. Or there's Alex Crowley, tiresomely attempting to persuade his school-chums to refer to him as Shelley's Alastor, like some self-conscious Goth from Nottingham called Dave insisting that his vampire name is Armand. Or, a short while later, there's all of the ancient witch-cults, all the blood-line covens springing up like children of the dragon's teeth wherever Gerald Gardner's writings were available. The occultists of the nineteenth and early twentieth centuries all seemed to want to be Aladdin's uncle in some never-ending pantomime. To live the dream.

John Dee, conversely, was perhaps more wilfully awake than any other person of his day. More focussed and more purposeful. He did not need to search for antecedents in the fictions and mythologies available to him, because John Dee was in no sense pretending, was not playing games. He inspired, rather than was inspired by, the great magic fictions of his times. Shakespeare's Prospero. Marlow's *Faust*. Ben Johnson's piss-taking *The Alchemist*. Dee's magic was a living and progressive force, entirely of its moment, rather than some stuffed and extinct specimen, no longer extant save in histories or fairytales. His was a fresh, rip-roaring chapter, written entirely in the present tense, of the ongoing magical adventure. By comparison, the occultists that followed some three centuries down the line were an elaborate appendix, or perhaps a bibliography, after the fact. A preservation league, lip-synching dead men's rituals. Cover versions. Sorcerous karaoke. Magic, having given up or had usurped its social function, having lost its *raison d'être,* its crowd-pulling star turn, found itself with just the empty theatre, the mysterious curtains. Dusty hampers of forgotten frocks, unfathomable props from cancelled dramas. Lacking a defined role, grown uncertain of its motivations, magic seems to have had no recourse save sticking doggedly to the established script, enshrining each last cough and gesture, the by-now hollow performance freeze-dried, shrink-wrapped; artfully repackaging itself for English Heritage.

How unfortunate, then, that it was this moment in the history of magic, with content and function lost beneath an over-detailed ritual veneer, all mouth and trousers, which the later orders chose to crystallize about. Without a readily apparent aim or mission, no marketable commodity, the nineteenth century occultist would seem instead to lavish an inordinate amount of his attention on the fancy wrapping paper. Possibly unable to conceive of any group not structured in the hierarchical manner of the lodges that they were accustomed to, Mathers and Westcott dutifully imported all the old Masonic heirlooms when it came to furnishing their fledgling order. All the outfits, grades and implements. The mindset of a secret and elite society. Crowley, of course, took all this heavy and expensive-looking luggage with him when he jumped ship to create his O.T.O, and all orders since then, even purportedly iconoclastic enterprises such as, say, the I.O.T, would seem to have eventually adopted the same High Victorian template. Trappings of sufficient drama, theories intricate enough to draw attention from what the uncharitable might perceive as lack of any practical result, any effect upon the human situation.

Aleister Crowley in magical garb

Fossil Angels

The fourteenth (and perhaps final?) issue of the estimable Joel Biroco's *KAOS* magazine featured a reproduction of a painting, a surprisingly affecting and hauntingly beautiful work from the brush of Marjorie Cameron, scary redhead, Dennis Hopper and Dean Stockwell's housemate, putative Scarlet Woman, top Thelemic totty. Almost as intriguing as the work itself, however, is the title: *Fossil Angel,* with its contradictory conjurings of something marvellous, ineffable and transitory combined with that which is by definition dead, inert and petrified. Is there a metaphor available to us in this, both sobering and instructive? Could not all magical orders, with their doctrines and their dogmas, be interpreted as the unmoving calcified remains of something once intangible and full of grace, alive and mutable? As energies, as inspirations and ideas that danced from mind to mind, evolving as they went until at last the limestone drip of ritual and repetition froze them in their tracks, stopped them forever halfway through some reaching, uncompleted gesture? Trilobite illuminations. Fossil angels.

Something inchoate and ethereal once alighted briefly, skipping like a stone across the surface of our culture, leaving its faint, tenuous impression in the human clay, a footprint that we cast in concrete and apparently remain content to genuflect before for decades, centuries, millennia. Recite the soothing and familiar lullabies or incantations word for word, then carefully restage the old, beloved dramas, and perhaps something will happen, like it did before. Stick cotton-reels and tinfoil on that cardboard box, make it look vaguely like a radio and then maybe John Frumm, he come, bring helicopters back? The occult order, having made a fetish out of pageants that passed by or were rained off some half-a-century ago, sits like Miss Haversham and wonders if the beetles in the wedding cake in any way confirm *Liber Al vel Legis*.

Once again, none of this is intended to deny the contribution that the various orders and their works have made to magic as a field, but merely to observe that this admittedly considerable contribution is of, largely, a custodial nature in its preservation of past lore and ritual, or else that its elegant synthesis of disparate teachings is its principal (perhaps only) achievement. Beyond such accomplishments, however, the abiding legacy of nineteenth century occult culture would seem mostly antithetical to the continued health, proliferation and ongoing viability of magic, which, as a technology, has surely long outgrown its ornate late-Victorian vase and is in dire need of transplanting. All of the faux-Masonic furniture and scaffolding imported by Westcott and Mathers, basically for want of being able to imagine any other valid structure, is, by our own period, become a limitation and impediment to magic's furtherance. Leftover hoodwinks, too-tight ceremonial sashes that constrain all growth, restrict all thought, limit the ways in which we conceive of or can conceive of magic. Mimicking the constructs of the past, thinking in terms that are today not necessarily applicable – perhaps they never really were – seems to have rendered modern occultism utterly incapable of visualizing any different method by which it might organise itself; unable to imagine any progress, any evolution, any *future,* which is probably a sure-fire means of guaranteeing that it doesn't have one.

If the Golden Dawn is often held up as a paragon, a radiant exemplar of the perfect and successful order, this is almost certainly because its ranks included many well-known writers of proven ability and worth whose membership loaned the society more credibility than it would ever, by return, afford to them. The luminous John Coulthart has suggested that the Golden Dawn might be most charitably regarded as a literary society, where slumming scribes searched for a magic that they might have found demonstrable and evident, already there alive and functioning in their own work, were they not blinded by the glare of all that ceremony, all of that fantastic kit. One author who quite clearly contributed more that was of real magical value to the world through his own fiction than through any operations at the lodge was Arthur Machen. While admitting to his great delight at all the mystery and marvel of the order's secret ceremonies, Machen felt compelled to add when writing of the Golden Dawn in his autobiography, *Things Near and Far,* that "as for anything vital in the secret order, for anything that mattered two straws to any reasonable being, there was nothing in it, and less than nothing...the society as a society was pure foolishness concerned with impotent and imbecile Abracadabras. It knew nothing whatever about anything and concealed the fact under an impressive ritual and a sonorous phraseology." Astutely, Machen notes the seemingly inverse relationship between genuine content and baroque, elaborate form characterizing orders of this nature, a critique as relevant today as it was then, in 1923.

The territory of magic, largely abandoned as too hazardous since Dee and Kelly's period, was staked out and reclaimed (when that was safe to do) by nineteenth century occult enthusiasts, by middle-class suburbanites who turned the sere, neglected turf into a series of exquisitely appointed ornamental gardens. Decorative features, statues and pagodas of great intricacy, were contrived in imitation of some over-actively imagined priesthood past. Terminal gods among the neat beds of azaleas.

The problem is that gardeners sometimes quarrel. Boundary disputes. Tenant vendettas and evictions, moonlight flits. Once-enviable properties are boarded up, are often squatted by new problem families, new cabals. Hang on to the old nameplate, keep the same address but let the place go, and allow its grounds to fall into a state of disrepair. Slugs in the moly, bindweed spreading out amongst twenty-two-petal roses. By the nineteen-nineties, magic's landscape garden was a poorly maintained sprawl of tired, low-yield allotments with bad drainage, paintwork peeling on the cod-Egyptian summer houses, now become mere sheds where paranoid Home Counties vigilantes sat awake all night, nursing their shotguns and expecting teenage vandals. There's no produce that's worth mentioning. The flowers are without perfume and no longer manage to enchant. Y'know, it were all fancy lamens and Enochian chess round here once, and now look at it. The straggly hedgerows with their Goetic topiary as parched as tinder, dry rot in that Rosicrucian-look gazebo's listing timbers. What this place could do with is a good insurance fire.

No, seriously. Scorched earth. It has a lot to recommend it. Think how it would look when all the robes and banners caught. Might even take out that whole *Mind, Body, and Spirit* eyesore if the wind were in the right direction. Loss of life and livelihood would of course be inevitable, some collateral damage in the business sector, but it sure would be real pretty. Temple beams collapsing in a gout of sparks. "Forget me! Save the cipher manuscripts!" Amongst the countless Gnostic Masses, oaths and calls and banishings, whatever caused them to forget one lousy fire drill? Nobody's quite certain how they should evacuate the inner plane, don't even know how many might still be in there. Finally there emerge heart-wrenching tales of individual bravery. "H-He went back in to rescue the LAM drawing, and we couldn't stop him." Afterwards, a time for tears, for counselling. Bury the dead, appoint successors. Crack open the seal on Hymenaeus Gamma. Cast a rueful eye across our blackened acres. Take it one day at a time, sweet Jesus. Blow our noses, pull ourselves together. Somehow we'll get through.

Supernatural Selection

What then? Scorched earth, of course, is rich in nitrates and provides a basis for slash-and-burn agriculture. In charred dirt, the green shoots of recovery. Life boils up indiscriminately, churning from black soil. We could give all of these once-stately lawns and terraces back to the wilderness. Why not? Think of it as astral environmentalism, the reclaiming of a psychic greenbelt from beneath the cracked Victorian occult paving-slabs, as an encouragement to increased metaphysical biodiversity. Considered as an organizing principle for magic work, the complex and self-generating fractal structure of a jungle would seem every bit as viable as all the spurious imposed chessboard order of a tiled lodge floor; would seem, in fact, considerably more natural and vital. After all, the traffic of ideas that is the essence and lifeblood of magic is more usually transacted these days by bush telegraph of one kind or another, rather than as ritual secrets solemnly attained after long years of cramming, Hogwarts' CSEs. Hasn't this rainforest mode of interacting been, in fact, the default setting of practical western occultism for some time now? Why not come out and admit it, bulldoze all these lean-to clubhouses that are no longer any use nor ornament, embrace the logic of lianas? Dynamite the dams, ride out the flood, allow new life to flourish in the previously moribund endangered habitats.

In occult culture's terms, new life equates to new ideas. Fresh-hatched and wriggling, possibly poisonous conceptual pollywogs, these brightly-coloured pests must be coaxed into our new immaterial eco-system if it is to flourish and remain in health. Let us attract the small ideas that flutter, neon-bright but frail, and the much tougher, more resilient big ideas that eat them. If we're fortunate, the feeding frenzy might draw the attention of huge raptor paradigms that trample everything and shake the earth. Ferocious notions, from the most bacterially tiny to the staggeringly big and ugly, all locked into an unsupervised glorious and bloody struggle for survival, a spectacular Darwinian clusterfuck.

Lame doctrines find themselves unable to outrun the sleek and toothy killer argument. Mastodon dogmas, elderly and slipping down the food-chain, buckling and collapsing under their own weight to make a meal for carrion memorabilia salesmen, somewhere for that droning buzz of chat-room flies to lay their eggs. Memetic truffles grown up from a mulch of decomposing Aeons. Vivid revelations sprung like London Rocket from the wild, untended bombsite sprawl. Panic Arcadia, horny, murderous and teeming. Supernatural selection. The strongest, best-adapted theorems are allowed to thrive and propagate, the weak are sushi. Surely this is hardcore Theleme in action, as well as representing a productive and authentic old-skool Chaos that should warm the heart of any Thanateroid. From such vigorous application of the evolutionary process, it is difficult to see how magic as a field of knowledge could do otherwise than benefit.

For one thing, by accepting a less cultivated, less refined milieu where competition might be fierce and noisy, magic would be doing no more than exposing itself to the same conditions that pertain to its more socially-accepted kinfolk, science and art. Put forward a new theory to explain the universe's missing mass, submit some difficult conceptual installation for the Turner Prize and be in no doubt that your offering will be subjected to the most intensive scrutiny, much of it hostile and originating from some rival camp. Each particle of thought that played a role in the construction of your statement will be disassembled and examined. Only if no flaw is found will your work be received into the cultural canon. In all likelihood, sooner or later your pet project, your pet theory will end up as scattered down and claret decorating the stained walls of these old, merciless public arenas. This is how it should be. Your ideas are possibly turned into road-kill but the field itself is strengthened and improved by this incessant testing. It progresses and mutates. If our objective truly is advancement of the magic worldview (rather than advancement of ourselves as its instructors), how could anyone object to such a process?

Unless, of course, advancement of this nature is not truly our objective, which returns us to our opening questions: what exactly are we doing and why are we doing it? No doubt some of us are engaged in the legitimate pursuit of understanding, but this begs the question as to why. Do we intend to use this information in some manner, or was it accumulated solely for its own sake, for our private satisfaction? Did we wish, perhaps, to be thought wise, or to enhance lacklustre personalities with hints of secret knowledge? Was it rank we sought, some standing that might be achieved more readily by a pursuit like occultism where there are, conveniently, no measurable standards that we might be judged by? Or did we align ourselves with Crowley's definition of the magic arts as bringing about change according to one's will, which is to say achieving some measure of power over reality?

This last would, at a guess, provide the motive that is currently most popular. The rise of Chaos magic in the 1980s centred on a raft of campaign promises, most notable amongst these the delivery of a results-based magic system that was practical and user-friendly. Austin Spare's unique and highly personal development of sigil magic, we were told, could be adapted to near-universal application, would provide a simple, sure-fire means by which the heart's desire of anyone could be both easily and instantly accomplished. Putting to one side the question "Is this true?" (and the attendant query "If it is, then why are all its advocates still holding down a day-job, in a world grown surely further from the heart's desire of *anyone* with every passing week?"), we should perhaps ask whether the pursuit of this pragmatic, causal attitude to occult work is actually a worthy use of magic.

If we're honest, most of causal sorcery as it is practiced probably is done so in the hope of realizing some desired change in our gross, material circumstances. In real terms, this probably involves requests for money (even Dee and Kelly weren't above tapping the angels for a fiver every now and then), requests for some form of emotional or sexual gratification, or perhaps on some occasions a request that those we feel have slighted or offended us be punished. In these instances, even in a less cynical scenario where the purpose of the magic is to, say, assist a friend in their recovery from illness, might we not accomplish our objectives far more certainly and honestly by simply taking care of these things on a non-divine material plane?

If, for instance, it is money we require then why not emulate the true example set by Austin Spare (almost unique amongst magicians

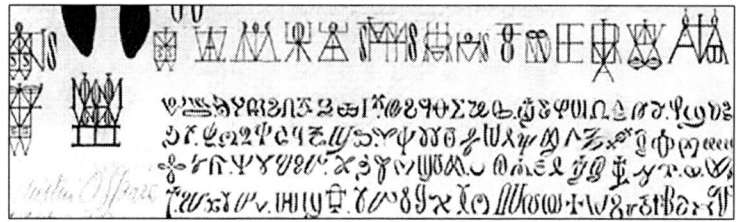
Sigils of Austin Osman Spare

in that he apparently saw using magic to attract mere wealth as an anathema) regarding such concerns? If we want money, then why don't we magically get off of our fat arses, magically perform some work for once in our sedentary magic lives, and see if the requested coins don't magically turn up some time thereafter in our bank accounts? If it's the affections of some unrequited love-object that we are seeking, the solution is more simple still: slip roofies in her Babycham, then rape her. After all, the moral wretchedness of what you've done will be no worse, and at the very least you won't have dragged the transcendental into things by asking that the spirits hold her down for you. Or if there's someone whom you genuinely feel to be deserving of some awful retribution then put down that lesser clavicle of Solomon and get straight on the dog and bone to Frankie Razors or Big Stan. The hired goon represents the ethical decision of choice when compared with using fallen angels for one's dirty work (this is assuming that just going round to the guy's house oneself, or maybe even, you know, getting over it and moving on, are not viable options). Even the sick friend example cited earlier: just go and visit them. Support them with your time, your love, your money or your conversation. Christ, send them a card with a sad-looking cartoon bunny on the front. You'll both feel better for it. Purposive and causal magic would too often seem to be about achieving some quite ordinary end without doing the ordinary work associated with it. We might well do better to affirm, with Crowley, that our best and purest actions are those carried out "without lust of result".

Neither Science Nor Religion

Perhaps his other famous maxim, where he advocates that we seek "the aim of religion" utilising "the method of science", however well intentioned, might have led the magical community (such as it is) into these fundamental errors. After all, religion's aim, if we examine the word's Latin origins in *religare* (a root shared with other words like 'ligament' and 'ligature'), would seem to imply that it's best if everyone is "bound in one belief". This impulse to evangelism and conversion must, in any real-world application, reach a point where those bound by one ligament come up against those tied together by another. At this point, inevitably and historically, both factions will pursue their programmed urge to bind the other in their one and only true belief. So then we massacre the taigs, the prods, the goys, the yids, the kuffirs and the ragheads. And when this historically and inevitably doesn't work, we sit and think about things for a century or two, we leave a decent interval, and then we do it all again, same as before. The aim of religion, while clearly benign, would seem to be off by a mile or two, thrown by the recoil. The target, the thing they were aiming for, stands there unscathed, and the only things hit are Omagh or Kabul, Hebron, Gaza, Manhattan, Baghdad, Kashmir, Deansgate, and so on, and so on, and so on, forever.

The notion of binding together that lies at the etymological root of religion is also, revealingly, found in the symbolic cluster of bound sticks, the fasces, that gives us the later term fascism. Fascism, based upon mystical concepts such as blood and 'volk', is more properly seen as religion than as a political stance, politics being based upon some form of reason, however misguided and brutal. The shared idea of being bound in one faith, one belief; that in unity (thus, unavoidably, in uniformity) there lies strength, would seem antithetical to magic, which, if anything, is surely personal, subjective and pertaining to the individual, to the responsibility for every sentient creature to reach its own understanding of and thus make its own peace with

God, the universe and everything. So, if religion can be said to find a close political equivalent in fascism, might magic not be said to have more natural sympathy with anarchy, fascism's opposite (deriving from *an-archon* or "no leader")? Which of course returns us to the burned-down temples, dispossessed and homeless order heads, the scorched earth and the naturally anarchic wilderness approach to magic, as suggested earlier.

The other half of Crowley's maxim, wherein he promotes the methodology of science would also seem to have its flaws, again, however well intentioned. Being based upon material results, science is perhaps the model that has led the magic arts into their causal cul-de-sac, described above. Further to this, if we accept the ways of science as a procedural ideal to which our magic workings might aspire, aren't we in danger of also adopting a materialist and scientific mindset with regard to the quite different forces that preoccupy the occultist? A scientist who works with electricity, as an example, will quite justifiably regard the energy as value-neutral, mindless power that can as easily be used to run a hospital, or warm a lava-lamp, or fry a black guy with a mental age of nine in Texas. Magic on the other hand, from personal experience, does not seem to be neutral in its moral nature, nor does it seem mindless. On the contrary, it would seem, as a medium, to be aware and actively intelligent, alive rather than live in the third rail sense. Unlike electricity, there is the intimation of a complex personality with almost-human traits, such as, for instance, an apparent sense of humour. Just as well, perhaps, when one considers the parade of prancing ninnies that the field has entertained and tolerated down the centuries. Magic, in short, does not seem to be there merely to power up sigils that are astral versions of the labour saving gadget or appliance. Unlike electricity, it might be thought to have its own agenda.

Quite apart from all this, there are other sound, compelling reasons why it limits us to think of magic as a science. Firstly and most glaringly, it isn't. Magic, after it relinquished any and all practical or worldly application following the twilight of the alchemists, can no more be considered as a true science than can, say, psychoanalysis. However much Freud might have wished it otherwise, however he deplored Jung dragging his purported scientific method down into the black and squirming mud of occultism, magic and psychoanalysis cannot, by definition, ever be allowed a place amongst the sciences. Both deal almost entirely with phenomena of consciousness, phenomena that cannot be repeated in laboratory conditions and which thus exist outside the reach of science, concerned only with things that may be measured and observed, proven empirically. Since consciousness itself cannot be shown to provably exist in scientific terms, then our assertions that said consciousness is plagued either by penis envy or by demons of the Qlippoth must remain forever past the boundary limits of what may be ascertained by rational scrutiny. Frankly, it must be said that magic, when considered as a science, rates somewhere just above that of selecting numbers for the lottery by using loved ones' birthdays.

This would seem to be the crux: magic, if it is a science, clearly isn't a particularly well-developed one. Where, for example, are the magical equivalents of Einstein's General or even Special theories of Relativity, let alone that of Bohr's Copenhagen Interpretation? Come to that, where are our analogues for laws of gravity, thermodynamics and the rest? Eratosthenes once measured the circumference of the Earth using geometry and shadows. When did we last manage anything as useful or as neat as that? Has there been anything even resembling a general theory since the Emerald Tablet? Once again, perhaps magic's preoccupation with cause and effect has played a part in this. Our axioms seem mostly on the level of "if we do A then B will happen". If we say these words or call these names then certain visions will appear to us. As to *how* they do so, well, who cares? As long as we get a result, the thinking seems to run, why does it matter how this outcome was obtained? If we bang these two flints together for a while they'll make a spark and set all that dry grass on fire. And have you ever noticed how if you make sure to sacrifice a pig during eclipses, then the sun always returns? Magic is, at best, Palaeolithic science. It really had best put aside that Nobel Prize acceptance speech until it's shaved its forehead.

The Art of Magic

Where exactly, one might reasonably enquire, does all this leave us? Having recklessly discarded our time-honoured orders or traditions and torn up our statement of intent; having said that magic *should* not be Religion and *can* not be Science, have we taken this Year-Zero Khmer Rouge approach too far, cut our own jugulars with Occam's razor? Now we've pulled down the landmarks and reduced our territory to an undifferentiated wilderness, was this the best time to suggest we also throw away our compass? Now, as night falls on the jungle, we've decided we are neither missionaries nor botanists, but what, then, are we? Prey? Brief squeals in pitch dark? If the aims and methods of science or religion are inevitably futile, ultimately mere dead ends, what other role for magic could conceivably exist? And please don't say it's anything too difficult, because for all the black robes and the spooky oaths, we tend to frighten easily.

If what we do cannot be properly considered as science or religion, would it be provocative to tender the suggestion that we think of magic as an art? Or even The Art, if you like? It's not as if the notion were entirely without precedent. It might even be seen as a return to our shamanic origins, when magic was expressed in masques and mimes and marks on walls, the pictograms that gave us written language so that language could in turn allow us consciousness. Music, performance, painting, song, dance, poetry and pantomime could all be easily imagined as having originated in the shaman's repertoire of mind-transforming magic tricks. Sculpture evolving out of fetish dolls, Willendorf Venus morphing into Henry Moore.

Costume design and catwalk fashion, Erte and Yves St. Laurent, arising out of firelit stomps in furs and beads and antlers, throwing shapes designed to startle and arouse. Baroness Thatcher, in her baby-eating prime, suggested that society once more embrace "Victorian values", an idea that certainly would seem to have caught on within the magical fraternity. This clearly goes nowhere near far enough, however. Let us call instead for a return towards Cro-Magnon values: more creative and robust, with better hair.

Of course, we need not journey so far back into admittedly speculative antiquity for evidence of the uniquely close relationship enjoyed by art and magic. From the cave-wall paintings at Lascaux, on through Greek statuary and friezes to the Flemish masters, on to William Blake, to the Pre-Raphaelites, the Symbolists and the Surrealists, it is only with increasing rarity that we encounter artists of real stature, be they painter, writer or musician, who have not at some point had recourse to occult thinking, whether that be through the agency of their alleged involvement with some occult or Masonic order, as with Mozart, or through some personally cultivated vision, as with Elgar. Opera has its origins, apparently, in alchemy, originated by its early pioneers like Monteverdi as an art-form that included all the other arts within it (music, words, performance, costumes, painted sets) with the intent of passing on alchemical ideas in their most comprehensively artistic and thus most celestial form. Likewise, with the visual arts we need not invoke obvious examples of an occult influence such as Duchamp, Max Ernst or Dali, when there are more surprising names such as Picasso (with his youth spent saturated in hashish and mysticism, with his later work preoccupied with then-occult ideas pertaining to the fourth dimension), or the measured squares and rectangles of Mondrian, created to express the notions woken in him by his study of Theosophy. In fact, the greater part of abstract painting can be traced to famed Blavatsky-booster Annie Besant, and the publication of her theory that the rarefied essential energies of Theosophy's rays and currents and vibrations could be

William Blake, *The Great Red Dragon and the Woman Clothed in Sun*.

represented by intuited and formless swirls of colour, an idea that many artists of a fashionably mystic inclination seized on eagerly.

Literature, meanwhile, is so intrinsically involved with magic's very substance that the two may be effectively considered as the same thing. Spells and spelling, Bardic incantations, grimoires, grammars, magic a "disease of language" as Aleister Crowley so insightfully described it. Odin, Thoth and Hermes, magic-gods and scribe-gods. Magic's terminology, its symbolism, conjuring and evocation, near-identical to that of poetry. In the beginning was the Word. With magic almost wholly a linguistic construct, it would seem unnecessary to recite a roll-call of the occult's many literary practitioners. In writing, as in painting or in music, an intense and intimate connection to the world of magic is both evident and obvious, appears entirely natural. Certainly, the arts have always treated magic with more sympathy and more respect than science (which, historically, has always sought to prove that occultists are fraudulent or else deluded) and religion (which, historically, has always sought to prove that occultists are flammable). While it shares the social standing and widespread respect afforded to the church or the laboratory, art as a field does not seek to exclude, nor is it governed by a doctrine that's inimical to magic, such as might be said of its two fellow indicators of humanity's cultural progress. After all, while magic has, in relatively recent times, produced few mighty theologians of much note and even fewer scientists, it has produced a wealth of inspired and inspiring painters, poets and musicians. Maybe we should stick with what we know we're good at?

The advantages of treating magic as an art seem at first glance to be considerable. For one thing, there are no entrenched and vested interests capable of mounting an objection to magic's inclusion in the canon, even if they entertained objections in the first place, which is hardly likely. This is patently far from the case with either science or religion, which are by their very natures almost honour-bound to see that magic is reviled and ridiculed, marginalized and left to rust there on history's scrap-heap with the Flat Earth, water-memory and phlogiston. Art, as a category, represents a fertile and hospitable environment where magic's energy could be directed to its growth and progress as a field, rather than channelled into futile struggles for acceptance, or burned uselessly away by marking time to the repeated rituals of a previous century. Another benefit, of course, lies in art's numinosity, its very lack of hard-edged definition and therefore its flexibility. The questions "what exactly are we doing and why are doing it", questions of 'method' and of 'aim', take on a different light when asked in terms of art. Art's only aim can be to lucidly express the human mind and heart and soul in all their countless variations, thus to further human culture's artful understanding of the universe and of itself, its growth towards the light. Art's method is whatever can be even distantly imagined. These parameters of purpose and procedure are sufficiently elastic, surely, to allow inclusion of magic's most radical or most conservative agendas? Vital and progressive occultism, beautifully expressed, that has no obligation to explain or justify itself. Each thought, each line, each image made exquisite for no other purpose than that they be offerings worthy of the gods, of art, of magic itself. The Art for The Art's sake.

Paradoxically, even those occultists enamoured of a scientific view of magic would have cause for celebration at this shift in emphasis. As argued above, magic can never be a science as science is currently defined, which is to say as being wholly based upon repeatable results within the measurable and material world. However, by confining its pursuits entirely to the world of the material, science automatically disqualifies itself from speaking of the inner, immaterial world that is in fact the greater part of our human experience. Science is perhaps the most effective tool that human consciousness has yet developed with which to explore the outer universe, and yet this polished and sophisticated instrument of scrutiny is hindered by one glaring blind-spot in that it cannot examine consciousness itself. Since the late 1990s the most rapidly expanding field of scientific interest is

Adam Scott Miller, *The Witness*

apparently consciousness studies, with two major schools of thought-on-thought thus far emerging, each contending with the other. One maintains that consciousness is an illusion of biology, mere automatic and behaviourist cerebral processes that are dependent on the squirt of glands, the seep of enzymes. While this does not seem an adequate description of the many wonders to be found within the human mind, its advocates are almost certainly backing a winner, having realised that their blunt, materialistic theory is the only one that stands a chance of proving itself in the terms of blunt material science. In the other camp, described as more transpersonal in their approach, the current reigning theorem is that consciousness is some peculiar 'stuff' pervading the known universe, of which each sentient being is a tiny, temporary reservoir. This viewpoint, while it probably elicits greater sympathy from those of occult inclinations, is quite clearly doomed in terms of garnering eventual scientific credibility. Science cannot even properly discuss the personal, so the transpersonal has no chance. These are matters of the inner world, and science cannot go there. This is why it wisely leaves the exploration of mankind's interior to a sophisticated tool that is specifically developed for that usage, namely art.

If magic were regarded as an art it would have culturally valid access to the infrascape, the endless immaterial territories that are ignored by and invisible to Science, that are to scientific reason inaccessible, and thus comprise magic's most natural terrain. Turning its efforts to creative exploration of humanity's interior space might also be of massive human use, might possibly restore to magic all the relevance and purpose, the demonstrable utility that it has lacked so woefully, and for so long. Seen as an art, the field could still produce the reams of speculative theory that it is so fond of (after all, philosophy and rhetoric may be as easily considered arts as sciences), just so long as it were written beautifully or interestingly. While, for example, *The Book of the Law* may be debatable in value when considered purely as prophetic text describing actual occurrences or states of mind to come, it cannot be denied that it's a shit-hot piece of writing, which deserves to be revered as such. The point is that if magic were to drop its unfulfillable pretensions as a science and come out of the closet as an art, it would ironically enough obtain the freedom to pursue its scientific aspirations, maybe even sneak up on some unified field theorem of the supernatural, all in terms acceptable to modern culture. Marcel Duchamp's magnum opus, *The Bride Stripped Bare by Her Bachelors,* is more likely to be thought of seriously as genuine alchemy than is the work of whichever poor bastard last suggested that there might be something to cold fusion. Art is clearly a more comfortable environment for magic thinking than is science, with a more relaxing decor, and much better-looking furniture.

Even those damaged souls so institutionalised by membership of magic orders that they can't imagine any kind of lifestyle that does not involve belonging to some secretive, elite cabal need not despair at finding themselves homeless and alone in our proposed new wilderness. Art has no orders, but it does have movements, schools and cliques with all the furtiveness, the snottyness and the elitism that anyone could wish for. Better yet, since differing schools of art are not so energetically competing with each other for the same ground as are magic orders (how can William Holman Hunt, for instance, be said to compete with Miro, or Vermeer?), this should obviate the need for differing schools of occult thought to feud, or snipe, or generally go on like a bunch of sorry Criswell-out-of-*Plan 9*-looking bitches.

Just as there is no need to entirely do without fraternities, then similarly there is no necessity for those who've grown attached to such things to discard their ritual trappings or, indeed, their rituals. The sole requirement is that they approach these matters with a greater creativity, and with a more discerning eye and ear for that which is profound; that which is beautiful, original or powerful. Make wands and seals and lamens fit to stand in exhibitions of outsider art (How hard can that be? Even mental patients qualify), make every ritual a piece of stunning and intense theatre. Whether one considers magic to be art or not, these things should surely scarcely need be said. Who are our private rituals and adornments meant to please, if not the gods? When did they ever give us the impression they'd be pleased by that which was not suitably exquisite or original? Gods, if they're anything at all, are known to be notoriously partial to creation, and may therefore be presumed to be appreciative of human creativity, the closest thing that we've developed to a god-game and our most sublime achievement. To be once more thought of as an art would allow magic to retain all that is best about the field it was, while at the same time offering the opportunity for it to flourish and progress into a future where it might accomplish so much more.

A Jungle or a Circus

How would this mooted change of premise impact, then, upon our methodology? What shifts of emphasis might be entailed, and could such changes be to the advantage of both magic as a field and us as individuals? If we seriously mean to reinvent the occult as The Art, one basic alteration to our working methods that might yield considerable benefit would be if we resolved to crystallise whatever insights, truths or visions our magical sorties had afforded us into some artefact, something that everybody else could see as well, just for a change. The nature of the artefact, be it a film, a haiku, an expressive pencil-drawing or a lush theatrical extravaganza, is completely unimportant. All that matters is that it be art, and that it remain true to its inspiration. Were it adopted, at a stroke, a relatively minor tweak of process such as this might utterly transform the world of magic. Rather than be personally-motivated, crudely causal workings of both dubious intent and doubtful outcome, hand-job magic ended usually in scant gratification, our transactions with the hidden world would be made procreative, generating issue in the form of tangible results that everyone might judge the worth of for themselves. In purely evangelic terms, as propaganda for a more enlightened magic worldview, art must surely represent our most compelling 'evidence' of other states and planes of being. While the thoughts of Austin Spare are undeniably of interest when expressed in written form as theory, it is without doubt his talents as an artist that provide the sense of entities and other worlds actually witnessed and recorded, the immediate authenticity which has bestowed on Spare much of his reputation as a great magician. More importantly, work such as Spare's provides a window on the occult world, allowing those outside a clearer and perhaps more eloquent expression of what magic is about than any arcane tract, offering them a worthwhile reason to approach the occult in the first place.

In our wilderness scenario for magic, with the fierce and fair Darwinian competition between ideas that's implied, treating the occult as an art would also lend a means of dealing with (or carrying out) any disputes that might arise. Art has a way of sorting out such squabbles for itself, inarguably, without resorting to lame processes like, for example, violent conflict resolution, litigation, or, much worse, girly democracy. With art, the strongest vision will prevail, even if it takes decades, centuries to do so, as with William Blake. There is no need to even take a vote upon which is the strongest vision: that would be the one just sitting quietly in its undisputed corner of our culture, nonchalantly picking its teeth with the sternums of its rivals. Mozart brings down Salieri, sleeps for two days after feasting, during which time the savannah can relax. Lunging out suddenly from tower-block shadows, J.G. Ballard takes out Kingsley Amis, while Jean Cocteau be all over D.W. Griffiths' scrawny Imperial Cyclops ass like a motherfucker. An artistic natural selection, bloody-minded but balanced, seems a far more even-handed way of settling affairs than arbitrary and unanswerable rulings handed down by heads of orders, such as Moina Mathers telling Violet Firth her aura lacked the proper symbols.

Also, if the vicious struggle for survival is enacted purely in the terms of whose idea is the most potent and most beautiful in its expression, then bystanders at the cockfight are more likely to end up spattered with gorgeous metaphors than with dripping, still-warm innards. Even our most pointless and incestuous feuds might thereby have a product that enriched the world in some small measure, rather than no outcome save that magic seem still more a bickering and inane children's playground than everyone thought it was already. Judged on its merits, such a jungle-logic attitude to magic, with its predatory aesthetics and ideas competing in a wilderness that's fertilised by their exquisite cultural droppings, would appear to offer the occult a win-win situation. How could anyone object, except for those whose ideas might be seen as plump, slow-moving, flightless and a handy source of protein; those well-qualified as primary prey who are perhaps beginning to suspect that this is all a tiger's argument for open-plan safari parks?

Upon consideration, these last-mentioned doubts and fears, while surely trivial within a context of magic's well-being as a field, are likely to be the most serious obstacles to any wide acceptance of a primal swampland ethic such as is proposed. However, if we accept that the sole alternatives to jungle are a circus or a zoo, the notion is perhaps more thinkable. And if our precious ideas should be clawed to pieces when they're scarcely out the nest, then while this is of course distressing, it's no more of an ordeal than that endured by any spotty schoolboy poet or Sunday painter who exposes their perhaps ungainly effort to another's scrutiny. Why should fear of ridicule or criticism, fear that the most lowly karaoke drunk is seemingly quite capable of overcoming, trouble occultists who've vowed to stand unflinching at the gates of Hell itself? In fact, shouldn't the overcoming of such simple phobias be a prerequisite for anyone who wants to style his or her self as a magician? If we regarded magic as an art and art as magic, if like ancient shamans we perceived a gift for poetry as magic power, magically bestowed, wouldn't we finally have some comeback when the ordinary person in the street asked us, quite reasonably, to demonstrate some magic, then, if we think we're so thaumaturgical?

Bringing Whisk-Brooms to Life

How empowering it would be for occultists to steadily accumulate, through sheer hard work, genuine magical abilities that can be provably displayed. Talents the ordinarily intelligent and rational person can quite readily accept as being truly magical in origin; readily engage with in a way that current occultism, with its often wilful and unnecessary obscurantism, cannot manage. Urgently expressed and heartfelt though most modern grimoires most assuredly may be, a skim through Borges' *Fictions* or a glimpse of Escher or a side or two of Captain Beefheart would be much more likely to persuade the ordinary reader to a magically receptive point of view. If consciousness itself, with its existence in the natural world being beyond the power of science to confirm, is therefore super-natural and occult, surely art is one of the most obvious and spectacular means by which that supernatural realm of mind and soul reveals itself, makes itself manifest upon a gross material plane.

Art's power is immediate and irrefutable, immense. It shifts the consciousness, noticeably, of both the artist and her audience. It can change men's lives and thence change history, society itself. It can inspire us unto wonders or else horrors. It can offer supple, young, expanding minds new spaces to inhabit or can offer comfort to the dying. It can make you fall in love, or cut some idol's reputation into ribbons at a glance and leave them maimed before their worshippers, dead to posterity. It conjures Goya devils and Rosetti angels into visible appearance. It is both the bane and most beloved tool of

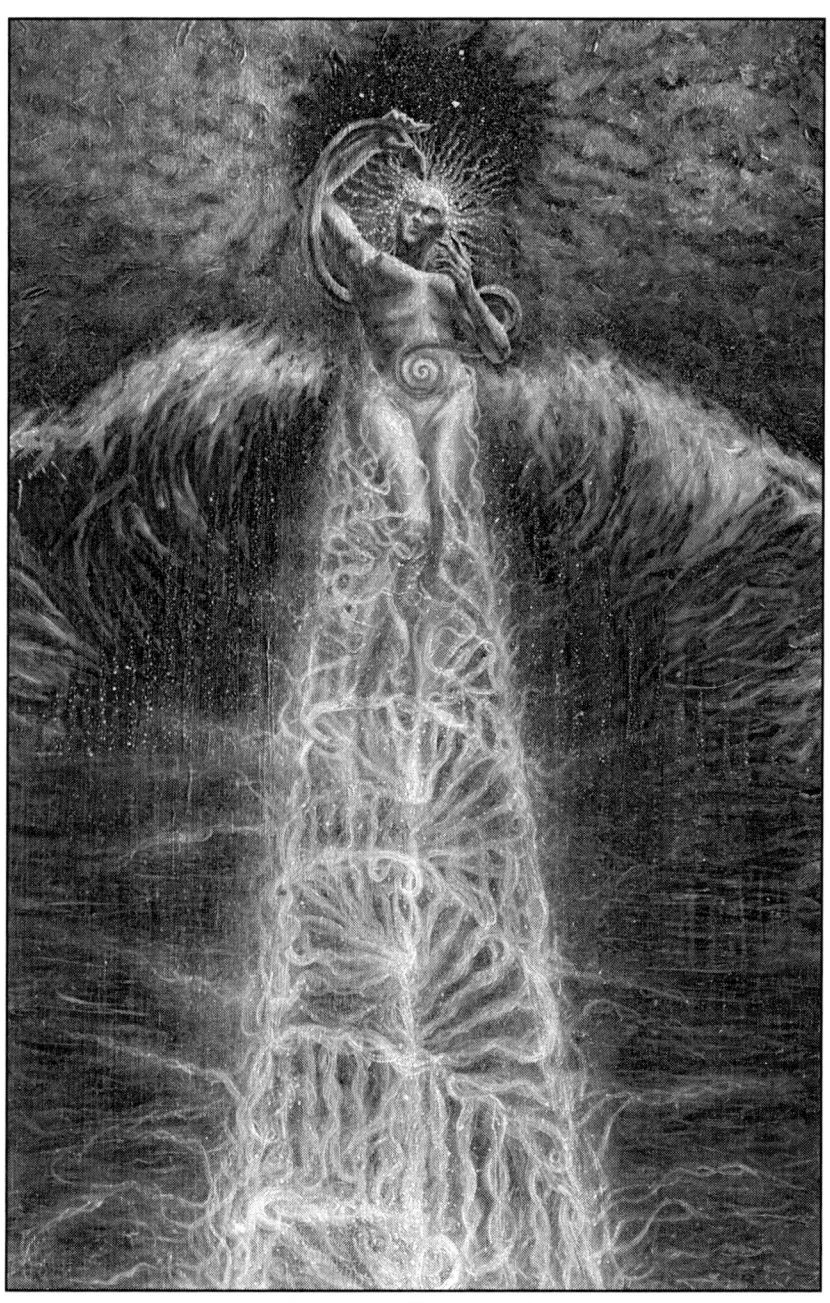

Adam Scott Miller, *Immaculata*

tyrants. It transforms the world which we inhabit, changes how we see the universe, or those about us, or ourselves. What has been claimed of sorcery that art has not already undeniably achieved? It's led a billion into light and slain a billion more. If the accretion of occult ability and power is our objective, we could have no more productive, potent means or medium than art whereby this is to be accomplished. Art may not make that whisk-broom come to life and multiply and strut round cleaning up your crib…but nor does magic, for that matter…yet simply dreaming up the image must have surely earned Walt Disney enough money so he could pay somebody to come by and take care of that stuff *for* him. And still have enough change to get his head put in this massive hieroglyphic-chiselled ice cube somewhere underneath the Magic Kingdom. There, surely to God, is all of the implacable Satanic influence that anybody, sane or otherwise, could ever ask for.

In reclaiming magic as The Art, amok and naked in a Rousseau wilderness devoid of lodges, it is probable that those made most uneasy by the proposition would be those who felt themselves unprivileged by such a move, those who suspected that they had no art to offer which might be sufficient to its task. Such trepidations, while they may be understandable, surely cannot sit well with the heroic, fearless image one imagines many occultists to have confected for themselves; seem somehow craven. Is there truly nothing, neither craft nor art, which they can fashion to an implement of magic? Do they have no talent that may be employed creatively and magically, be it for mathematics, dancing, dreaming, drumming, stand-up comedy, striptease, graffiti, handling snakes, scientific demonstration, cutting perfectly good cows in half or sculpting scarily realistic busts of European monarchy from their own faeces? Or, like, anything? Even if such abilities are not at present plentiful or evident, cannot these timorous souls imagine that by application and some honest labour talents may be first acquired then honed down to a useful edge? Hard work should not be a completely foreign concept to the Magus. This is not even The Great Work that we're necessarily discussing here, it's just the Good-But-Not-Great Work. Much more achievable. If that still sounds too difficult and time-consuming, you could always make the acquisition of profound artistic talent and success your heart's desire and simply spadge over a sigil. Never fails, apparently. So what excuse could anybody have for not embracing art as magic, magic as The Art? If you are truly, for whatever reason, now and for all time incapable of any creativity, then are you sure that magic is the field to which you are most eminently suited? After all, the fast-food chains are always hiring. Ten years and you could be a branch manager.

A Product and a Purpose

By understanding art as magic, by conceiving pen or brush as wand, we thus return to the magician his or her original shamanic powers and social import, give back to the occult both a product and a purpose. Who knows? It might turn out that by implementing such a shift we have removed the need for all our personally-motivated causal charms and curses, our hedge-magic. If we were accomplished and prolific in our art, perhaps the gods might be prepared to send substantial weekly postal orders, all without us even asking. In the sex and romance stakes, as artists we'd all make out like Picasso. Women, men and animals would offer themselves naked at our feet, even in Woolworth's. As for the destruction of our enemies, we simply wouldn't bother to invite them to our launch-parties and openings, and they'd just *die*.

This re-imagining of magic as The Art could clearly benefit the occult world in general and the individual magician in particular, but let's not overlook the fact that it might also benefit the arts. It must be said that modern mainstream culture, for the greater part and from most civilised perspectives, is a Tupperware container full of sick. The artists of the age (admittedly, with a few notable exceptions) seem intent upon reflecting the balloon-like hollowness and consequent obsession with mere surface that we find amongst our era's governments and leaders. Just a year or two ago, the old Tate Gallery's Blake retrospective drew from critics sharp comparisons with the Brit-artists currently inhabiting Blake's Soho stamping ground, observing that the modern crop of tunnel-visionaries pale when held up to Blake's Lambeth light. The studied and self-conscious 'craziness' of Tracey Emin is made tame beside his holy tyger madness, all accomplished within howling-range of Bedlam. Damien Hirst is shocking in a superficial manner, but not shocking to the point where he has loyalty oaths, vigilante lynch-mobs and sedition trials to deal with. Jake and Dinos Chapman's contributions to *Apocalypse* (the exhibition, not the situation with Iraq) are not in any sense a revelation. William Blake could pull a far superior apocalypse from *The Red Dragon*'s sculpted crimson butt without a second thought. The modern art world deals now in high-concept items, much like the related (through Charles Saatchi) field of advertising. It appears to be bereft of vision, or indeed of the capacity for such, and offers little in the way of nourishment to its surrounding culture, which could use a decent and sustaining meal right about now. Couldn't a reaffirmation of the magical as art provide the inspiration, lend the vision and the substance that are all so manifestly lacking in the world of art today? Wouldn't such a soul-infusion allow art to live up to its purpose, to its mission, to insist that the interior and subjective human voice be heard in culture, heard in government, heard on the stained Grand Guignol stages of the world? Or should we just sit back and wait for praeter-human intellects from Sirius or Disney's walking whisk-brooms or the Aeon of Horus to arrive and sort this mess out for us?

A productive union, a synthesis of art and magic propagated in a culture, an environment, a magic landscape lacking temple walls and heirloom furnishings that everyone tripped over anyway. Staged amidst the gemming ferns and purpled steam-heat of a re-established occult biosphere, this passionate conjunction of two human faculties would surely constitute a Chemic Wedding which, if we were lucky and things got completely out of hand at the Chemic Reception, might precipitate a Chemic Orgy, an indecent, riotous explosion of suppressed creative urges, astral couplings of ideas resulting in multiple births of chimerae and radiant monsters. Fierce conceptual centaurs with their legs of perfume and their heads of music. Mermaid notions, flickering silent movies that are architecture from the waist down. Genre sphinxes and style manticores. Unheard of and undreamed mutations, novel art-forms breeding and adapting fast enough to keep up with the world and its momentum, acting more like life-forms, more like fauna, more like flora to proliferate in our projected magic wilderness. The possible release of fusion energy made suddenly available when these two heavy cultural elements, magic and art, are brought into dynamic close proximity might fairy-light our jungle, might even help to illuminate the mainstream social mulch that it, and we, are rooted in.

Crying Out for the Numinous

Nothing prevents us throwing off the callipers and the restraints, the training wheels that have retarded magic's forward progress for so long that moss obliterates its railway tracks and branch-line sidings both. Nothing can stop us, if we have the will, from redefining magic as an art, as something vital and progressive. Something which in its ability to deal with the interior human world has a demonstrable utility, can be of actual use to ordinary people, with their inner worlds increasingly encroached upon by a tyrannical, colonialist exterior that's intent on strip-mining them of any dreams or joy or self-determination. If we so resolved we could restore to magic a potential and a potency, a purpose it has barely caught a glimpse of in the last four hundred years. Were we prepared to take on the responsibility for this endeavour then the world might see again the grand and terrible magicians that, outside of bland and inoffensive children's books or big-screen and obscenely-budgeted extravagances, it has all but managed to forget. It might be argued that at this nerve-wracking juncture of our human situation, magical perspectives are not merely relevant but are an indispensable necessity if we are to survive with minds and personalities intact. By redefining the term magic we could once again confront the world's iniquities and murk in our preferred, time-honoured method: with a word.

Make the word magic mean something again, something worthy of the name, something which, as a definition of the magical, would have delighted you when you were six; when you were seventy. If we accomplish this, if we can reinvent our scary, wild and fabulous art for these scary, wild and fabulous new times that we are moving through, then we could offer the occult a future far more glorious and brimming with adventure than we ever thought or wished its fabled past had been. Humanity, locked in this penitentiary of a material world that we have been constructing for ourselves for centuries now, has perhaps never needed more the key, the cake-with-file-in, the last-minute pardon from the governor that magic represents. With its nonce-case religions and their jaw-droppingly demented fundamentalists, with its bedroom-farce royalties, and with its demagogues more casually shameless in their vile ambitions than they've been in living memory, society at present, whether in the east or west, would seem to lack a spiritual and moral centre, would indeed appear to lack even the flimsiest pretence at such a thing. The science which sustains society, increasingly, at its most far-flung quantum edges finds it must resort to terminology from the kabbala or from Sufi literature to adequately state what it now knows about our cosmic origins. In all its many areas and compartments, all its scattered fields, the world would seem to be practically crying out for the numinous to come and rescue it from this berserk material culture that has all but eaten it entire and shat it through a colander. And where is magic, while all this is going on?

It's trying to force our boyfriend to come back to us. It's scraping cash together to fend off the black hole in our plastic, trying to give that prick that our ex-wife ran off with something terminal. It's making sure that Teen Witch slumber parties go successfully. It's putting wispy New Age people into contact with their wispy New Age angels, and they're all, like, "No way", and the angels are all, like, "Whatever". It's attending all of our repeated rituals with the enthusiasm of a patron come to see *The Mouse Trap* for the seven hundredth time. It spends its weekends trying to read our crappy sigils under their obscuring glaze of jiz, and in retaliation only puts us into contact with outpatient entities, community-care Elohim that rant like wino scientologists and never make a lick of sense. It's at the trademarks office, registering magic seals. It's handling an introductions agency that represents our only chance of ever meeting any strange Goth pussy. It's off getting us a better deal on that new Renault, helping to prolong the wretched life of our incontinent and blind pet spaniel Gandalf, networking like crazy to secure those Harry Potter Hogwart's Tarot rights. It's still attempting to sort out the traffic jam resulting from the Aeon of Horus having jack-knifed through the central reservation and into the southbound carriageway, hit head-on by the Aeon of Maat, which spilled its cargo of black feathers onto the hard shoulder. It's not sure the ketamine was such a good idea. It's sitting looking nervous on a thousand bookshelves between lifestyle interviews with necrophiles and fashion retrospectives on the Manson family. It's hanging out at neo-Nazi jamborees near Dusseldorf. It's wondering if it should introduce a "Don't Ask, Don't Tell" policy regarding the 11th Degree. It's advising Cherie Blair on acupuncture studs, the whole of Islington upon Feng Shui. It's pierced its cock in an attempt to shock its middle-class Home Counties parents, who've been dead for ten years, anyway. It wishes it were David Blaine. It wishes it were Buffy. Or, quite frankly, anyone.

We could, if we desired it, have things otherwise. Rather than magic that's in thrall to a fondly imagined golden past, or else to some luridly-fantasized Elder God theme-park affair of a future, we could try instead a magic adequate and relevant to its own extraordinary times. We could, were we to so decide, ensure that current occultism be remembered in the history of magic as a fanfare peak rather than as a fading sigh; as an embarrassed, dying mumble; not even a whimper. We could make this parched terrain a teeming paradise, a tropic where each thought might blossom into art. Under the altar lies the studio, the beach. We could insist upon it, were we truly what we say we are. We could achieve it not by scrawling sigils but by crafting stories, paintings, symphonies. We could allow our art to spread its holy psychedelic scarab wings across society once more, perhaps in doing so allow some light or grace to fall upon that pained, benighted organism. We could be made afresh in our fresh undergrowth, stand reinvented at a true dawn of our Craft within a morning world, our paint still wet, just-hatched and gummy-eyed in Eden. Newborn in Creation.

Alan Moore is one of the most highly-regarded and influential comics writers in the history of the medium, authoring such classics as *Watchmen, V for Vendetta, From Hell* and *The League of Extraordinary Gentlemen*. His latest novel is the epic *Jerusalem*, released in September 2016. Alan lives in Northampton in England.

"Fossil Angels" was written in December 2002, and was to appear in *KAOS* #15, which unfortunately was never published. Alan gave permission for it to be published online at Glycon (http://glycon.livejournal.com/13888.html) in 2010, and for its appearance in print here in *Darklore* in 2016.

Endnotes

Mike Jay - Secrets of the Club des Hachischins (p. 9)

Versions of this article have appeared previously in Mike's *Emperors of Dreams: Drugs in the nineteenth century* (2000, revised ed. 2011) and in *Literature and Intoxication: Writing, politics and the experience of excess* (ed. Eugene Brennan and Russell Williams, 2015).

Adam Gorightly - The Most Important Man on the Planet (p. 23)

Notes:

1. "The Curse of Greyface" is explained on page 00042 of *Principia Discordia or How I Found Goddess and What I did To Her When I Found Her,* Rip Off Press, San Francisco, 1970.
2. Canfield, Michael and Weberman, Alan J., *Coup d'etat In America: The CIA and the Assassination of John F. Kennedy,* The Third Press, New York, 1975. (p. 22-23)
3. Keith, Jim, *Mind Control, World Control,* Adventures Unlimited Press, 1998. (Chapter 18)
4. Thornley, Kerry, *The Dreadlock Recollections,* Kindle Edition, ovo127.com
5. 1997 interview with Kerry Thornley, courtesy of Rosemary Tantra Bensko.
6. Unpublished Kerry Thornley essay, *Star Witness Story* (Greg Hill's Discordian Archives.)
7. Canfield, Michael and Weberman, Alan J., *Coup d'etat In America: The CIA and the Assassination of John F. Kennedy,* The Third Press, New York, 1975. (Chapter 11)
8. Kerry Thornley, September 19th, 1975 letter. (Greg Hill's Discordian Archives.)
9. Email correspondence with R.N. Taylor.

10. Jones, J. Harry, Jr., *The Minutemen*, Doubleday 1968, New York. (p. 10)
11. Author's interview with Grace Zabriskie, 2002.
12. Vankin, Jonathan, *Conspiracies, Coverups and Crimes*, IllumiNet Press, 1996. (pp. 5-6)

Greg Taylor - Rocks in Your Head (p. 73)

Notes:

1. https://www.monticello.org/site/blog-and-community/posts/who-liar-now
2. Thanks to Martin Kottmeyer for bringing some of these to my attention.
3. Maria Golia, *Meteorite: Nature and Culture*.
4. Ibid.
5. Ibid.
6. William Whiston, M.A , *An account of a surprizing meteor seen in the air March 19. 1718/19 at night. Containing a description of this meteor, from the original letters of those who saw it in different places.*
7. Much of the history of electrophonic meteor research over the next few pages is taken from Colin S.L. Keay, "Progress in Explaining the Mysterious Sounds Produced by Very Large Meteor Fireballs".
8. Colin S.L. Keay, "Progress in Explaining the Mysterious Sounds Produced by Very Large Meteor Fireballs".
9. Ibid.
10. https://www.newscientist.com/article/dn25667-fireball-meteors-emit-unique-radio-wave-signals/
11. Goran Zgrablic´ et al, "Instrumental recording of electrophonic sounds from Leonid fireballs".
12. '365 Days of Astronomy' podcast, http://www.podcasts.astrospacenow.com/episode.php?view=2475
13. http://www.science-frontiers.com/sf038/sf038p17.htm
14. http://www.abovetopsecret.com/forum/thread681024/pg1
15. https://groups.yahoo.com/neo/groups/meteorobs/conversations/topics/39599, cited at http://www.abovetopsecret.com/forum/thread681024/pg1
16. Note too, though, there is some skepticism about these reports, see for example this: http://magoniamagazine.blogspot.com.au/2014/01/engine-stoppers.html. There is also the problem of diesel engine interference when they don't use electrical sparking

for internal combustion. This possibility has even manifested in UFO reports - see for example this incident in the link referenced: "Rodeghier reported that for a long time that it was only the gasoline engines that stalled but diesel engines seemed to be immune. Rodeghier wrote, 'For example, a UFO passed over two tractors in Forli, Italy, on November 14, 1954, one tractor with a diesel engine the other with an internal combustion engine. The engine of the diesel tractor continued to operate, but the other tractor's engine stopped and could not be started until the UFO had vanished.'"

17. Dr. J. Allen Hynek, *The UFO Experience*
18. http://www.auforn.com/Keith_Basterfield_14.htm
19. Though does the diesel factor suggest it was a coincidence, rather than electrical burnout?
20. http://home.pacific.net.au/~ddcsk1/solutio1.htm
21. D. Vinkovic et al., "Global Electrophonic Fireball Survey: a review of witness reports".
22. https://sacredneurology.com/2015/05/31/the-tectonic-strain-theory-and-the-haunted-room-a-blog-by-dr-michael-persinger/

John Reppion - The History and Practice of English Magic (p. 97)

References:

Susanna Clarke (2005), *Jonathan Strange & Mr. Norrell*
http://hurtfew.wikispaces.com

Notes:

1. http://tinyurl.com/guhoy38
2. http://tinyurl.com/j48djkg
3. Heinrich Cornelius Agrippa von Nettesheim (1533) *De Occulta Philosophia libri III* (http://tinyurl.com/z4x775q)
4. William Godwin (1834) *Lives of the Necromancers: or, An account of the most eminent persons in successive ages, who have claimed for themselves, or to whom has been imputed by others, the exercise of magical power* (http://tinyurl.com/hfetceu)
5. http://tinyurl.com/zvnuy7l
6. http://tinyurl.com/jhs78b9
7. Isack, H., & Reyer, H. (1989). *Honeyguides and Honey Gatherers: Interspecific Communication in a Symbiotic Relationship Science*, 243 (4896), 1343-1346 DOI: 10.1126/science.243.4896.1343.

8. http://time.com/3847987/researchers-bird-ancestor-discovery/
9. http://www.bbc.co.uk/news/science-environment-31718336
10. http://tinyurl.com/h9j8bq9
11. http://www.sacred-texts.com/neu/celt/tfm/
12. Sir Augustus Henry, James Murray (1875) *The romance and prophecies of Thomas of Erceldoune, printed from five manuscripts* (https://archive.org/details/romanceandproph00murrgoog)
13. W. B. Yeats (1888) *Fairy and Folk Tales of the Irish Peasantry* http://www.sacred-texts.com/neu/yeats/fip/fip23.htm
14. Joseph Jacobs (1890) *English Fairy Tales* (http://www.sacred-texts.com/neu/eng/eft/)
15. Robert Kirk and Andrew Lang (1893) *The Secret Commonwealth of Elves, Fauns and Fairies* (http://www.sacred-texts.com/neu/celt/sce/sce02.htm)
16. Marc Alexander (2002) *A Companion to the Folklore Myths and Customs of Britain*
17. Robert Kirk and Andrew Lang (1893) *The Secret Commonwealth of Elves, Fauns and Fairies*
18. Jennifer Westwood and Jacqueline Simpson (2006) *The Lore of the Land*
19. Laura Dabundo (2009) *Encyclopedia of romanticism: culture in Britain, 1780s-1830s*
20. http://www.rcpsych.ac.uk/healthadvice/bookreviews/books/johnclare/review1.aspx
21. Allan Beveridge (2001) "A disquieting feeling of strangeness?: the art of the mentally ill" (http://www.ncbi.nlm.nih.gov/pmc/articles/PMC1282252/)
22. http://www.popsubculture.com/pop/bio_project/richard_dadd.html
23. Allan Beveridge (2001) "A disquieting feeling of strangeness?: the art of the mentally ill" (http://www.ncbi.nlm.nih.gov/pmc/articles/PMC1282252/)
24. http://www.tate.org.uk/art/artworks/dadd-the-fairy-fellers-master-stroke-t00598
25. Sigmar Polke (2004) "Private View" (http://www.tate.org.uk/context-comment/articles/tate-etc-issue-1)
26. http://www.bbc.co.uk/nottingham/content/articles/2004/09/15/entertainment_books_susanna_clarke_feature.shtml
27. Gillian Edwards (1974) *Hobgoblin and sweet Puck : fairy names and natures*
28. http://boldoutlaw.com/puckrobin/puckages.html
29. Ibid.
30. Margaret Murray (1933) *The God of Witches*
31. Ibid.
32. Charles P. G. Scott (1895) *The Devil and His Imps: An Etymological Inquisition* (http://www.jstor.org/stable/pdf/2935696.pdf?acceptTC=true)
33. Marc Alexander (2002) *A Companion to the Folklore Myths and Customs of Britain*
34. https://en.wikipedia.org/wiki/Robert_Fitzooth
35. http://www.votenationalbird.com/

Robert M. Schoch, Ph.D. - The Lycanthropes (p. 141)

Notes:

1. Daniel 4:28-37. In a footnote to verses 32-33 in *The New Oxford Annotated Bible*, third edition, New Revised Standard Version (2001. Michael D. Coogan, editor. Oxford and New York: Oxford University Press) it is related that another, later, Babylonian king, Nabonidus (reigned circa 556–539 BCE; the last king of the Neo-Babylonian Empire), left Babylon to spend several years in northern Arabia, and Nabonidus suffered for seven years from some sort of illness that was ultimately cured by a Jewish exorcist.
2. As suggested by: Younis, A. A., and H. F. Moselhy. 2009. "Lycanthropy alive in Babylon: the existence of archetype." *Acta Psychiatrica Scandinavica*, vol. 119, pp. 161-164.
3. Younis and Moselhy [note 2]; Garlipp, P., T. Gödecke-Koch, D. E. Dietrich, and H. Haltenhof. 2004. "Lycanthropy – psychopathological and psychodynamical aspects." *Acta Psychiatrica Scandinavica*, vol. 109, pp. 19-22.
4. For overviews, see: Rawcliffe, D. H. 1959. *Illusions and Delusions of the Supernatural and Occult*. New York: Dover Publications [see particularly Chapter 15, "Lycanthropy", pp. 261-271]; de Vesme, Caesar. 1931. *A History of Experimental Spiritualism*. Vol. I, *Primitive Man*. Translated from the French by Stanley de Brath. London: Rider and Company [see particularly the sections on "Lycanthropy" in Africa, pp. 118-128, and "Lycanthropy and Witchcraft" in Latin America, pp. 188-190].
5. See, for instance: Anonymous ("The Lycanthropologist"). 2012. "Myths & Legends: Zeus and Lycaon." Available at http://werewolftheory.blogspot.com/2012/03/myths-legends-zeus-and-lycaon.html Dated 19 March 2012; Accessed 12 November 2015; Poulakou-Rebelakou, E., C. Tsiamis, G. Panteleakos, and D. Ploumpidis. 2009. "Lycanthropy in Byzantine times (AD 330 – 1453)." *History of Psychiatry*, vol. 20, no. 4, pp. 468-479.
6. Bagot, Richard. 1918. "The Hyenas of Pirra." *Cornhill Magazine*, October 1918; quoted by de Vesme [note 4], p. 123 "; bracketed material in quotations by R. Schoch.
7. de Vesme [note 4], p. 124.
8. Rawcliffe [note 4], p. 263.
9. See, for instance: Wagner, Stephen. Undated. "The Werewolf of Bedburg." Available at http://paranormal.about.com/od/werewolves/a/The-Werewolf-Of-Bedburg.htm Accessed 10 November 2015.
10. Blom, Jan Dirk. 2014. "When doctors cry wolf: a systematic review of the literature on clinical lycanthropy." *History of Psychiatry*, vol. 25, no. 1, pp. 87-102; Garlipp et al. [note 3].

11. Garlipp et al. [note 3], p. 20, their reference citations removed.
12. Blom [note 10].
13. Hutton, J. H. 1941. "Presidential Address." *Folklore*, vol. 52, no. 2, pp. 83-100; see p. 88.
14. Blom [note 10], p. 94.
15. de Vesme [note 4], p. 183.
16. Quoted by de Vesme [note 4], p. 188.
17. Nasirian, Mansourch, Nabi Banazadeh, and Ali Kheradmand. 2009. "Rare Variant of Lycanthropy and Ecstasy." *Addiction and Health*, vol. 1, no. 1, pp. 53-57.
18. Blom [note 10]; Garlipp et al. [note 3].
19. Hutton [note 13].
20. Riggs, Ransom. 2010. "Miryachit, The Mysterious Siberian Mental Disorder." Available at http://mentalfloss.com/article/23934/miryachit-mysterious-siberian-mental-disorder Dated 11 February 2010; Accessed 24 Jan 2015.
21. Shirokogoroff, Sergei Mikhailovich. 1935. *Psychomental Complex of the Tungus*. London: Kegan Paul, Trench, Trubner. Reprint, Berlin: Reinhold Schletzer Verlag, 1999, pp. 248-252.
22. Hutton [note 13], pp. 86-87; Hutton cites Oesterreich, T. K. 1921. *Possession, Demoniacal and Other*.
23. See for instance: Pednaud, J. Tithonus. Undated. "PETRUS GONZALES – Wolf Boy of the Canary Islands." Available at: http://www.thehumanmarvels.com/petrus-gonzales-wolf-boy-of-the-canary-islands/ Accessed 10 November 2015.
24. See for instance: Pednaud, J. Tithonus. Undated. "FEDOR JEFTICHEIVE – Jo-Jo The Dog-Faced Boy." Available at: http://www.thehumanmarvels.com/fedor-jefticheive-jo-jo-the-dog-faced-boy/ Accessed 10 November 2015. The surname has been spelled various ways, such as Jefticheive or Jefticheiv.
25. Illis, L. 1964. "On Porphyria and the Ætiology of Werwolves." *Proceedings of the Royal Society of Medicine, Section of the History of Medicine*, vol. 57, pp. 23-26. [Illis uses the spelling "werwolf".]
26. Mayo Clinic Staff. 2014. "Porphyria." Available at: http://www.mayoclinic.org/diseases-conditions/porphyria/basics/definition/con-20028849 Dated 20 May 2014; Accessed 12 November 2015.
27. Mayo ClinicStaff [note 26].
28. Illis [note 25] and Blom [note 10].
29. Translation by F. Adams (1844, *The Seven Books of Paulus Aegineta*. London: Sydenham Society.) as quoted by Poulakou-Rebelakou et al. [note 5], p. 472.
30. Illis [note 25], p. 26.

31. Schoch, Robert M., and Logan Yonavjak, compilation and commentary. 2008. *The Parapsychology Revolution: A Concise Anthology of Paranormal and Psychical Research*. New York: Jeremy P. Tarcher/Penguin.
32. Hutton [note 13].
33. For a discussion of "warg" and "warging" in "The Game of Thrones", see: "Warg – Game of Thrones Wiki." Available at http://gameofthrones.wikia.com/wiki/Warg Accessed 9 November 2015.
34. de Vesme [note 4], pp. 118-119.
35. de Vesme [note 4], pp. 119-120.
36. Quoted by de Vesme [note 4], p. 185.
37. Quoted by de Vesme [note 4], p. 185.
38. See discussion in: Schoch, Robert M. 2012. *Forgotten Civilization: The Role of Solar Outbursts in Our Past and Future*. Rochester, Vermont: Inner Traditions, pp. 245-249.
39. Rawcliffe [note 4], p. 269.
40. Hutton [note 13], p. 97.

Ian 'Cat' Vincent - *The New Gods (p. 201)*

This article is based upon the talk "Science Fiction's Gifts To Paganism", given at Treadwells Bookshop, London on 12 February 2015ce.

Footnotes and other information can be found at http://tinyurl.com/darkloreSF

Lightning Source UK Ltd.
Milton Keynes UK
UKOW02f0805281116
288701UK00001B/193/P